CHINA'S SCIENCE AND TECHNOLOGY SECTOR AND THE FORCES OF GLOBALISATION

Series on Contemporary China   (ISSN: 1793-0847)

Series Editors: Joseph Fewsmith *(Boston University)*
Zheng Yongnian *(University of Nottingham)*

Published

Series on Contemporary China – Vol. 13

CHINA'S SCIENCE AND TECHNOLOGY SECTOR AND THE FORCES OF GLOBALISATION

Editors

Elspeth Thomson
Energy Studies Institute,
National University of Singapore, Singapore

Jon Sigurdson
Stockholm School of Economics, Sweden

World Scientific

NEW JERSEY · LONDON · SINGAPORE · BEIJING · SHANGHAI · HONG KONG · TAIPEI · CHENNAI

Published by

World Scientific Publishing Co. Pte. Ltd.

5 Toh Tuck Link, Singapore 596224

USA office: 27 Warren Street, Suite 401-402, Hackensack, NJ 07601

UK office: 57 Shelton Street, Covent Garden, London WC2H 9HE

Library of Congress Cataloging-in-Publication Data
China's science and technology sector and the forces of globalisation / editors Elspeth Thomson
   and Jon Sigurdson.
     p. cm. -- (Series on contemporary China ; v. 13)
     ISBN-13: 978-981-277-100-1
     ISBN-10: 981-277-100-X
     1. Technological innovations--Economic aspects--China. 2. Research, Industrial--China.
   3. Technology and state--China. 4. Science and state--China. I. Thomson, Elspeth, 1960–
II. Sigurdson, Jon.

   HC430.T4C464 2008
   303.48'30951--dc22

                        2007047524

British Library Cataloguing-in-Publication Data
A catalogue record for this book is available from the British Library.

Typeset by Stallion Press
Email: enquiries@stallionpress.com

Printed in Singapore.

Contents

Acknowledgements

This volume is based partially on papers presented at the conference, "Globalisation and China's Development in Science and Technology", organised by the East Asian Institute of the National University of Singapore in November 2004.

We would like to thank the former Director, Professor Wang Gungwu, and the Research Director, Professor John Wong, for their patience in awaiting this volume. Special thanks also go to the EAI administrative staff, Ms. Lian Wee Li and James Tan who play vital roles at EAI and whose attentiveness and efficiency are exceptional.

Elspeth Thomson and Jon Sigurdson
November 2007

Introduction

Elspeth Thomson

The role of science and technology is pivotal in any country's economic development. Many forces shape a country's national agenda for science and technology research initiatives. The obvious ones are the political system, planning and funding allocation mechanisms, number of government levels and research institutes involved, availability of capital, availability of labour with the required specialised scientific skills, physical scientific infrastructure, etc.

Equally important, but less quantifiable are competitive economic and political pressures from other countries, as well as the presence or lack thereof, of an entrepreneurial culture, informal networks among all participants, synergy between the academic research community and the industrial sector, agglomeration forces, etc.

It is imperative for governments to continuously review the administrative structures in the science and technology sector in order that the society's changing needs can be met over time and that research overlap and redundancy can be avoided. Decisions pertaining to a country's development of its science and technology sector require expertise in economics, finance, management as well as the many branches of science.

The Chinese leadership is now devoting considerable attention to the development of technologies which will make the country globally competitive. As the "factory of the world", China already wields formidable economic influence. However, this success has been largely based on the use of foreign technologies to make manufactured goods.

The Government is keenly aware that global economic leadership and power will be increasingly driven by intellectual property, not the export of manufactured goods. Thus, to become globally competitive, China confronts two challenges: not only to greatly develop its indigenous technological abilities, but to make rapid, substantial progress in indigenous high technologies.

This book is devoted to examining China's development of its science and technology sector in the context of globalisation. China is still affected by its being a developing economy and one that is in transition from central planning to market socialism. There are enormous physical as well as bureaucratic problems to overcome. However, modernising much later than the western world, China is in the fortunate position of being able to "leapfrog" some development processes. Tremendous progress can be expected to occur over the next few decades as Chinese researchers become increasingly integrated with global companies, research institutes and centres. In today's interconnected world, the decisions that the Chinese Government makes now with respect to science and technology will potentially not only affect the Chinese population for many generations, but also the world as a whole.

In the first chapter, Cao provides an overview of the technological development challenges faced by Chinese industry. The fundamental question he asks is whether or not China has the technological wherewithal to maintain its momentum in terms of economic growth and modernisation, and at the same time integrate into the world economy.

Cao is generally pessimistic. He argues there is no endogenous and indigenous technological capability because (a) many industrial firms have little in the way of financial resources to do innovative

R&D work; (b) there is a serious lack of trained people due to the brain drain of talent to other countries and foreign-invested enterprises located in China; (c) most of the spending on technology imports has been devoted to hardware instead of technology licences, i.e., it has been easier for domestic companies to import technology than to take the risk of doing their own R&D; (d) enterprises lack interest in engaging domestic learning institutions with respect to R&D. Many flatly do not wish to acquire technology from domestic sources; and (e) few Chinese enterprises own independent intellectual property rights (IPR) in core technologies. They have been more interested in utility model and design patents.

It is acknowledged that China's economic and industrial development has progressed at a high speed and that the country has become a globalised economy, able to manufacture and export good-quality, low-priced products to expanding consumer markets. However, Cao contends that any stature that China's high-tech sector has gained to date has been through the huge influx of foreign capital and components, and through FDI-embodied technology. He worries that using FDI as a means of tech-transfer may reinforce dependency, and he also raises the concern that some enterprises may become so large and bureaucratic that they may lose both their ability to innovate and their entrepreneurial spirit.

The next two chapters are concerned with patenting activity in China. Governments grant patents to inventors in order to prevent others from making, using or selling the invention without the permission of the inventor. They are granted for new industrial processes or for significant improvements to existing ones for a fixed period of time and become the property of the inventor.

Lu and Hu examine the regional variation in patenting in the light of local economic institutions such as business participation and technology market development. The geographical distribution of innovation is important in a country as large and diverse as China. The Government cannot be seen to be ignoring the research efforts of the more remote areas. The analysis reveals large differences in science and technology capability and activity among China's regions. These are a function of variations in human capital, pre-reform conditions, inherent development potentials, location with respect to international markets, government policies, speed of economic reforms, etc. Another factor is researchers' varying propensities to patent, which in turn may be related to enforcement of proprietary rights, technology market conditions and degree of international transactions.

A patents production function is estimated to test the main hypothesis that the re-orientation of China's national innovation system from a centrally planned system towards a market-driven one is critical in explaining the variation of patent output across China's regions. The key findings are that (a) higher participation of enterprises has facilitated research on proprietary technologies; (b) a more developed technology market has had similar effects; (c) better patent protection for proprietary technology accelerated reforms of state-owned enterprises in the late 1990s and China's joining of the WTO have all positively affected such research.

Lin and Zhang reveal that individuals, as opposed to industrial enterprises and research institutes, have accounted for over 70 percent of all patent applications filed domestically; that innovators in China, including the industrial enterprises, have been devoting their R&D resources disproportionately to small innovations (utility models and external designs), rather than to major ones (inventions); and that there is no evidence that the large- and medium-sized enterprises are the main force for innovation in China.

The authors believe that a major factor hampering innovation activity in China may be the low degree of industrial concentration. They attribute it primarily to regional competition and regional protectionism in China. They also contend that China must replace its industrial-oriented innovation policy — one where the Government has tightly controlled which resources, especially foreign direct investment, are allocated to which selected industries and projects — with one that is market-failure-based, i.e., one in which market forces guide resources towards industries requiring R&D investment the most.

The fourth chapter is devoted to reviewing some of the key standard-setting cases in China and the world. A company or country that develops a technical standard first can dominate that industry for years or even decades afterward. Standards have sometimes been used as weapons by multi-national companies to protect themselves.

The patent portfolio of Chinese companies in the United States is small and the majority of patents granted by the Chinese Patent Office are still held by foreign-based companies. Suttmeier and Yao note that Chinese companies have suffered complaints from IPR holders in Japan and the United States, and that the lack of patent and technical standards has seriously affected the competitiveness of Chinese companies. Thus, the Chinese Government is today strongly supporting the development of various industrial technology standards in a number of areas.

Standardisation has in recent years become a very important element of China's technology strategy. On the one hand, China would like to harmonise interests and development among China, Japan and Korea. On the other, it would like to establish its own technological platform in as many areas as possible to gain independence from foreign high-tech companies and drastically reduce the level of licence fees. Being able to establish, or at least influence global standards has become vital in national technological efforts. Defining and owning new international standards is a matter of pride and prestige for China's high-technology industry.

Although China is adapting to the realities of techno-globalism, a "neo-techno-nationalism" characterises China's technology policy and standards strategy. It is expected that China's standards strategy, as outlined in the *Medium and Long-term Plan for Scientific Development,* will see many adjustments over the next 15 years. It will necessarily be a gradual process because the industrial, government and research sectors all have varying preferences.

The next chapter examines some of the financial aspects of China's R&D. With the largest foreign exchange reserves in the world and an enormous trade surplus, the Chinese Government would seem to be in an enviable position with respect to nurturing domestic research and importing foreign technologies.

While a considerable amount has been written on how to encourage high-tech industrial development, little has been written on the consequences of high-tech industry on the economy, particularly the financial consequences. Ma employs a three-sector overlapping generations model to assess the impact of the development of high-tech industry on the traditional industries (low- and medium-low-tech industries with mature, traditional technology) and the impact of financing the high-tech industry on the deposit and lending rates of bank loans, the total amount of loans borrowed by the traditional and high-tech sectors and the implications for household savings (the primary source for bank loans). While the household sector maximises its inter-temporary utility by allocating income into saving and consumption, the banking sector maximises its profits by offering banking services to their clients (depositors and borrowers).

The results reveal substitution and expansion effects on the bank loans. The substitution effect tends to substitute the loans borrowed by traditional industry by that of the high-tech industry while the expansion effect tends to increase the total bank loans due to the new activities in the high-tech industry. It supersedes the substitution effect rendering an increase in total bank loans. The implication is that deposit rates must rise to attract more savings from the household sector, meaning that the banks must charge a higher lending rate to the traditional industrial sector to cover the increased finance costs. Thus, the government ought to subsidise high-tech firms to give them greater incentive to innovate, and also ought to subsidise the traditional firms during the transition process. Alternatively, Ma suggests the provision of open-bid grants to both high-tech and traditional industries.

The sixth chapter spotlights two key regions where the Government in recent years has boldly encouraged R&D in the high-tech sectors. When making plans for the development of China's remote western provinces and autonomous regions, the hope was expressed that "footloose" high-tech industries would be suitable because the physical inputs required are often minimal compared to most other industrial pursuits. The main requirement is highly trained labour. As the coastal region becomes more crowded and the costs of living there rise, perhaps more high-tech industries will indeed locate in some of China's more remote areas. However, in the meantime, most of the highest-level R&D is occurring in areas in the east and south where agglomeration forces have been at work for several decades.

Sigurdson focuses on Ningbo and Dalian, where there have been long traditions of industrial activity. In recent years, the Government has established zones specifically designed for high-tech industrial development. The various projects launched to promote high-tech industries are described in detail. Ningbo, near Shanghai, is well known for its entrepreneurship. Several new universities and colleges have been established there to generate large numbers of graduates trained in cutting-edge research. Ningbo will continue to produce a wide range of manufactured goods, ranging from motorcycles to mobile phones but in the coming years will also incubate a number of high-tech industries in biotechnology and Internet-related products.

Dalian's economic history has also involved multiple industries, ranging from machinery manufacturing, shipbuilding and fisheries to chemical engineering and electronics. The city is now also famous for its software industry which began in the 1980s. Software contracting for export began in the early 1990s and Dalian has achieved notable international stature in this area. Today, there are over 450 software companies in the vicinity. The Government has actively nurtured this industry, designating large parcels of land and investment packages for incubators, labs, high-tech parks and zones. Sigurdson describes the history and current research thrusts of some of the key domestic and foreign companies in Dalian. Although numerous institutions of higher learning have been built in Dalian, there are still critical shortages of labour trained in software development.

Over the past 30 years, the country has faced a severe brain drain. Many of the brightest minds left China to work abroad or went to study abroad and never returned. In recent years, however, many of these people have returned. At the same time, fewer students are choosing to remain abroad. Another factor contributing to the shortages of skilled labour are vestiges of central planning which delay a fully efficient use of R&D manpower.

The penultimate chapter charts the progress and challenges faced in one particular sector, the "chips" industry. Semiconductor devices, or "chips" are found in almost all electronic products nowadays. More and more products, ranging from home and office appliances to weapons, use them. The production of chips in China lags far behind demand. Heng notes that it is presently mainly foreign companies operating in China, including Taiwan, Hong Kong and Macau companies which require the chips for their manufacturing enterprises, and that most of the demand is for low-end chips, i.e., specific-application chips (personalised digital products) and commodity memory chips. At the end of 2005, China had 479 chip design houses. About 380 were domestic firms and the others were design units of international MNCs operating in China. The Government is anxious to upgrade the chip industry from "made in China" to "innovated in China."

The book ends with a discussion of some of the political/social issues surrounding the rapidly expanding use of the latest communications technologies in China. While the Chinese Government acknowledges that the Internet creates tremendous opportunities for the global sharing of information of all kinds, it regards it as a potential threat to domestic political stability.

Due to the country's enormous size geographically and demographically, the Chinese Government is constantly worried that localised grievances could expand, gain momentum and wash across the country in an uncontrollable wave. With the introduction of the Internet as well as mobile phones, the Government has little ability to prevent instantaneous communications across the country. Since the quiet, seemingly imperceptible organisation of a massive Falun Gong demonstration in 1999, the Government has taken many steps to try to monitor Internet use.

Lagerkvist considers how the managers (entrepreneurs) of news, i.e., people operating news portals and networks satisfy the often opposite demands of the state (propaganda departments) and the citizenry. The main subject areas which seem to give the Chinese Government the greatest cause for concern are pornography, online gaming, religious superstition, negative discussions about the Chinese Communist Party and its leaders, succession from the state and some foreign policy issues. Non-Chinese online media companies, such as Yahoo, Google and Microsoft are also very aware of potential state action should they encourage any "unhealthy" activities.

In recent years, instead of using harsh, abrupt language when trying to dissuade "unhealthy discussions" and resist cultural globalism, the state has made allusions to "traditional" Chinese values, or "new Confucianism". Blurring the lines between culture and politics, the masses are implored to cultivate and uphold high morals, and be loyal towards the current political system.

Throughout history, advances in science and technology have typically occurred in waves. Flurries of activity and astonishing results have sometimes been followed by longish periods of seemingly low productivity. In the case of China, the national system of innovation is being transformed, i.e., the responsibility and process of carrying out technological learning is being shifted from the central research and design institutes to enterprises, and enterprises are learning to play the supply–demand market game. There are bound to be delays as the leadership determines what course of action best corresponds to its conception of market socialism. The Chinese Government is beginning to recognise that projects which apparently have no commercial success can nonetheless generate economic, societal and/or environmental benefits.

China, as a whole, is rapidly gaining an entrepreneurial culture. In any country, and particularly in one such as China with its extraordinary size and diversity, technological innovation will take place in a number of its regions. Huge numbers of innovations — of a gradual and incremental nature — are already taking place in manufacturing firms all over China, though primarily in the dynamically evolving coastal areas. As industrial experience and technological capacity accumulate at the enterprise level, the Chinese rate of innovation will rise sharply, and though it may seem a long way off now, China may one day be setting the standards for most products and technologies simply by virtue of the size of the Chinese market and the rapid growth rate of the economy.

Technological Development Challenges in Chinese Industry

Cong Cao

Since the late 1970s, especially in the 1990s, massive foreign direct investment (FDI), accompanied by the importation of foreign technology, have to a large extent recast China's industrial base and upgraded its industrial technology.[1] In 2001, China became the world's leader in terms of its mobile phone subscriber base with 461 million users by the end of 2006. Its 368 million fixed phone lines represented the largest number in the world.[2] Overtaking Japan in 2002, China is expected to surpass the United States as the world's largest PC market by 2010, if not earlier.[3] Barely known in China until the mid-1990s, the Internet now attracts almost 172 million Chinese

---

[1] Yasheng Huang argues that the inflow of FDI into China has in fact denied growth opportunities for China's most efficient firms, namely, non-government enterprises (*minying qiye*). See his *Selling China: Foreign Direct Investment during the Reform Era* (Cambridge: Cambridge University Press, 2003).

[2] See http://mii.gov.cn/art/2007/02/09/art_169_28756.html (October 19, 2007).

[3] See http://msn-cnet.com.com/2100-1006_3-5091384.html (March 4, 2004).

users.[4] Merchandise labelled "Made in China" has gone beyond toys, garments and sneakers to consumer electronics products and high-tech gadgets. China was the 10th largest high-tech exporting country in the world in 1998–1999.[5] In 2006, China's high-tech exports hit US$281 billion, representing a more than 100-fold increase over those in 1991.[6] Most recently, China has started to use technology standards — notably the third-generation wireless standard TD-SCDMA (Time Division-Synchronous Code Division Multiple Access) and wireless encryption standard WAPI (Wired Authentication and Privacy Infrastructure) — as a technology policy instrument.[7] In some 20 years, China has gradually evolved from a closed and planned economy dominated by agriculture and heavy industry, to an economy dynamised by information, knowledge, skills and competence.

Yet, whether the Chinese industrial and high-tech sector can actually sustain growth remains an empirical question. Domestic politics and the macroeconomic situation aside, the ability to maintain the momentum will ostensibly be determined by endogenous and indigenous technology. In fact, the technological reality behind the economic growth has not been fully revealed, and may consequently have been somewhat distorted and misunderstood. With its further integration into the world economic system in the post-WTO era, China has been facing fiercer international competition. How well might China survive in this global technological competition? Is China capable of developing an indigenous technological capability to support its global economic competition in the short and medium

---

[4] See http://tech.sina.com.cn/i/2007-10-13/08281790659.shtml (October 19, 2007).

[5] United Nations Development Programme, *Human Development Reports 2001: Making New Technologies Work for Human Development* (New York: Oxford University Press, 2001), 42.

[6] See http://www.sts.org.cn/tjbg/gjscy/documents/2007/070618.htm (October 19, 2007).

[7] For a discussion of this see Richard P. Suttmeier and Yao Xianggui, "China's Post-WTO Technology Policy: Standards, Software, and the Changing Nature of Techno-Nationalism," *NBR Special Report*, No. 7 (Seattle, WA: National Bureau of Asian Research, May 2004).

term? This chapter addresses these issues by examining the technological challenges that China's industrial development has been encountering. The author tries to pinpoint the reasons why the challenges will become more serious, and how the Chinese Government is responding to them.

GOVERNMENT'S TECHNOLOGY POLICY

China's technology policy in recent years has aimed to stimulate growth in indigenous industrial technological capability. The 1997 National Conference on Technological Innovation promoted the role of enterprises in the nation's R&D activities. Immediately following the Conference, the then State Economic and Trade Commission selected Baoshan Iron and Steel, Changhong, Jiangnan Shipbuilding, Northern China Pharmaceutical (all SOEs), Haier (a collective), and Founder (a university spin-off) to experiment on technological innovation.[8] At the 1999 National Conference on Technological Innovation, the Government further demanded that high-tech enterprises spend at least five percent of their annual sales on R&D.[9] The most recent policy measures include allowing R&D expenditure to be counted as cost, implementing a technology-standard and patent-focused strategy in enterprise innovation endeavours, and supporting software products "Made in China" in government procurements.[10]

In the information and communications technology (ICT) area, emphasis has been placed on developing China's semiconductor industry. Firms have been encouraged to develop central processing units (CPUs) used in certain consumer electronics products and

---

[8] Yang Shenghua, *Zhongguo: Chuangxin shengchun (China: Survival Through Innovation)* (Guangzhou: Huacheng Press, 2000), 50.

[9] Ministry of Science and Technology (comp.), *Zhongguo jishu chuangxin zhengce (Policies on Technological Innovation in China)* (Beijing: Kexue jishu wenxian chubanshe, 2000), 1–9.

[10] *Kexue shibao (Science Times)*, March 13, 2002; *Zhongguo jingji shibao (China Economic Times)* May 27, 2002; http://tech.sina.com.cn/it (May 28, 2002); *Keji ribao (Science and Technology Daily)*, July 4, 2002.

mobile phone handsets. Attention has also been paid to design application-specific integrated circuits (ASICs) used in ICT, an area with advanced technological sophistication, wider usability as well as higher added value. China's computer industry has campaigned for the introduction and use of the open-source Linux operating system and related application software packages. Due to the government mandate, the Linux-based operating system and office applications developed by Chinese software companies have eroded Microsoft's dominance in software procurement, which signals not only the sensitivity given the size of the procurement and strategic importance, but also the viability for these companies.[11] Under these circumstances, the normally aggressive Microsoft had to be defensive by agreeing to invest RMB6.2 billion to help develop China's software industry and win over China's e-government initiative.[12]

One of the high-profile technology policy measures is the so-called "technology-standard" strategy by which China intends to formulate its own standards to leverage its large market in international competition.[13] China's participation in the worldwide third-generation (3G) wireless communications standard setting is one such example.

China's telecom equipment manufacturing sector was among the first to open to global competition. It is also a sector in which domestic players have attained critical mass. When China started its massive telecom equipment manufacturing in the early 1980s, technology transfer through direct imports and Sino-foreign joint ventures played an important role. Through absorbing and assimilating foreign technology and most importantly indigenous R&D efforts, some of the Chinese firms, represented by Great Dragon, Datang,

---

[11] There is suspicion that these Linux software users would eventually switch back to the Microsoft products given their familiarity with, or addiction to them, the greater number of Microsoft applications, and possible incompatibility between Linux-based packages and Microsoft products which are much more widely used. See *Beijing qingnian bao (Beijing Youth Daily)*, March 12, 2002, 36.

[12] *Ershiyi shiji jingji daobao (21st Century Economic News)*, July 12, 2002; *Zhongguo jingji shibao (China Economic Times)*, August 4, 2002.

[13] Suttmeier and Yao, "China's Post-WTO Technology Policy".

Zhongxing and Huawei (JuDaZhongHua according to the first characters of the firms' Chinese names), gradually acquired advanced technology and accumulated technology capability to develop their own products. These firms employ a higher percentage of scientists and engineers with master's and doctorate degrees, and invest 10 percent or more of their sales revenue on R&D.[14] They may still lack some critical technology such as ASICs, and could acquire them through participating in the international division of labour — outsourcing those to foreign firms.[15] They are not in the same league as the world's big players either in size, technology, quality or performance of the equipment because most of the manufacturers are technology followers rather than innovators, and by the time they reverse-engineer the imported products and develop the manufacturing capability to imitate them, their international competitors would have introduced a successive generation. Nevertheless, because of their presence, foreign firms have to give up the low-end product market or reduce price for similar products sold in China. Domestic suppliers accounted for 43 percent of the stored programme-controlled central office switches in 2000 from none in 1982 (from another angle, the statistics show why China's international competitiveness in communication exports increased).[16]

Therefore, as China, along with other countries is moving towards 3G mobile communications, it offers a domestically-proposed and International Telecommunications Union approved

---

[14] Xiongjian Liang and Kaisheng Ding, "Manufacturing Industry," in *Telecommunications in China: Development and Prospects,* ed. Jintong Lin, Xiongjian Liang and Yan Wan (Huntington, NY: Nova Science Publishers, 2001), 75–98; Xiaobai Shen, *The Chinese Road to High Technology: A Study of Telecommunications Switching Technology in the Economic Transition* (New York: St Martin, 1999); Zixiang Alex Tan, "Product Cycle Theory and Telecommunications Industry: Foreign Direct Investment, Government Policy, and Indigenous Manufacturing in China," *Telecommunications Policy* 26, no. 1 (2002): 17–30.

[15] Zixiang Alex Tan, "Product Cycle, Wintelism, and Cross-National Production Network (CPN) for Developing Countries: China's Telecom Manufacturing Industry as a Case," *INFO: The Journal of Policy, Regulation and Strategy for Telecommunications* 4, no. 3 (2002): 57–65.

[16] Tan, "Product Cycle Theory and Telecommunications Industry."

standard — TD-SCDMA, jointly developed by China's Datang and Germany's Siemens — to compete with the cdma2000 standard by the US mobile network developer Qualcomm, the owner of key patents behind the code division multiple access (CDMA) standard, and the wideband CDMA (WCDMA) standard, also known as universal mobile telecommunications service (UMTS), from Europe. The Chinese Government has also allocated more radio spectrum to the home-grown TD-SCDMA standard than to its competitors — WCDMA and cdma2000, which gives greater likelihood that China will request that one of its telecom operators adopt this 3G mobile telecommunications standard and in turn boost the R&D activities among China's leading high-tech firms. Although the Chinese standard may not be as advanced as the other two standards, and it is premature to suggest that one of China's mobile operators would adopt the standard, the case itself — some may label it techno-nationalist — at least suggests that China's technical community has realised the importance of independent intellectual property rights and devoted its innovative capability to developing the most advanced technology. It remains to be seen whether the government initiative will lead to indigenous innovation at the firm level.

RECENT MOVES IN CHINA'S INDUSTRIAL TECHNOLOGICAL DEVELOPMENT

Facing more challenges and fiercer competition in the post-WTO environment, Chinese firms are feeling fearful because without access to updated technology and managerial know-how, they may lose their battle with their foreign competitors. For example, FDI agreements may not mandate the technology transfer requirement; the phasing out of many tariffs means a gradually eroded price advantage for domestic products; the domination of technology, quality and cost, rather than price in competition; and restrictions on subsidising industrial R&D.

In the meantime, multinational corporations (MNCs) have expanded their R&D presence in China through opening independent R&D centres and collaborating with Chinese researchers. This is part of the global development strategy of the parent companies, i.e., being close to their Chinese operations and localising technology developed in the "home base," so that their contribution to China's R&D should not be exaggerated. But it is possible for MNCs to tap the high-quality researchers, even from domestic enterprises, so as to go beyond the use of cheap labour in their creation of systems of production in China.[17] Under these circumstances, it is a matter of ultimate responsibility and survival, not choice, for China's domestic enterprises to upgrade their technologies and products on their own. In this regard, the Chinese Government has also tried its best to stimulate innovation and provide policy guidance.

INCREASED R&D ACTIVITIES IN ENTERPRISES

In 2000, China's R&D spending by Chinese enterprises exceeded 60 percent for the first time, implying that enterprises had become a more important player in research and innovation. A study of all high-tech firms in the Haidian District of Beijing where the Zhongguancun Science Park is located finds that current sales revenue of the firm provides an important driving force for private R&D expenditure.[18] Between 2000 and 2003, the top 100 domestic electronics and information enterprises spent on average about 3 percent of annual sales revenue on R&D, with telecom equipment manufacturers Huawei Technologies, Datang Telecommunications and Zhongxing Telecommunications leading the way, each devoting about 10 percent of the sales revenue to R&D.[19] Nationwide, of the more than 10 million medium- and small-sized firms, 150,000 allocate more than 5 percent of sales to technological development.[20]

---

[17] For a discussion about the creation of productive systems in China, see Rigas Arvanitis, Pierre Miège and Wei Zhao, "A Fresh Look at the Development of a Market Economy in China," *China Perspectives*, No. 48 (2003): 51–62.

[18] Albert Guangzhou Hu, "Ownership, Government R&D, Private R&D and Productivity in Chinese Industry," *Journal of Comparative Economics* 29, no. 1 (2001): 136–157.

[19] See http://www.mii.gov.cn (June 10, 2003).

[20] *Kexue shibao (Science Times)*, March 11, 2002.

Some of the most technology-intensive companies have taken the R&D issue seriously by establishing or reinforcing their R&D institutes.[21] For example, in Shenzhen, China's Open-door Policy "window", 477 (91.7 percent) of the 521 R&D institutes are associated with enterprises, and 90 percent of the R&D personnel work in enterprises.[22] Legend, Founder, Chunlan, among others, have central research academies oriented towards developing process and product technologies, and long-term technology strategies. Several Chinese corporations have also set up R&D centres abroad as they expand internationally.[23]

Huawei, a non-state-owned telecom equipment maker, is a particular case in point. Founded in 1988, its charter specified that it would devote 10 percent of its sales revenue to R&D, and increase the expenditure if necessary. Forty percent of the company's employees are engaged in R&D, and the company is also involved in exploratory and pre-competitive research.[24] In 2006, Huawei earned sales revenues of RMB65.9 billion, of which RMB5.9 billion (8.9 percent) were spent on R&D. The company now owns 3,335 patented technologies with a significant percentage being invention patents, and its intelligence network won the first-class prize of China's Scientific and Technological Progress Award in 2002, a rare but impressive achievement for an enterprise.[25]

HIGH-TECH EXPORTS: COMPARATIVE OR COMPETITIVE ADVANTAGES?

A high-tech industry is, loosely speaking, one whose success depends largely on the ability to keep up with rapid innovations in

---

[21] *Beijing qingnian bao (Beijing Youth Daily)*, March 22, 1999, 6.

[22] Yang Shenghua, *Zhongguo: Chuangxin shengchun*, 60.

[23] Research Group, *Zhongguo keji fazhan yanjiu baogao 2000: Kexue jishu de quanqiuhua yu zhongguo mianling de tiaozhan (A Research Report on China's S&T Development (2000): The Globalization of Science and Technology and Its Challenges for China)* (Beijing: Social Science Literature Press, 2000), 298.

[24] Yang, *Zhongguo: Chuangxin shengchun*, 253, 262.

[25] See http://www.huawei.com.cn (October 19, 2007).

products, production processes, or both.[26] Microelectronics, biotechnology, new materials, telecommunications, civilian aviation, robotics plus machine tools and computer hardware and software are considered to be crucial in the global competition.[27] Statistical classifications of high-tech industry typically rely on such indicators as the ratio of R&D expenditures to sales, share of scientists and engineers in the labour force, etc. The US Bureau of Census has adopted a separate classification code, "advanced technology", in reporting merchandise trade. Products within the classification are supposed to meet the following criteria: (a) the underlined technology is from a recognised high technology field (e.g., biotechnology, information technology); (b) products represent leading-edge technology in that field and (c) such products constitute a significant part of all items covered in the "advanced technology" classification.[28]

In China, a firm can register and be certified as "high-tech" only if it falls into the above-mentioned categories and meets the following requirements: at least 30 percent of its employees have college or above education, more than 5 percent of its sales are spent on R&D and more than 60 percent of its sales are related to technology

---

[26] For a survey and discussion on the analysis of high-tech trade statistics, see J. A. D. Holbrook, "High-Tech Trade Pattern Analysis: Its Use and Application for Industry Competitiveness Response and Government Policy Development," *CPROST Report # 95-11* (Ottawa: The Canadian Advanced Technology Association/Industry Canada Workshop on High-Tech Trade Statistics, 1995).

[27] Lester C. Thurow, *Head to Head: The Coming Economic Battle among Japan, Europe, and America* (New York: William Morrow, 1992).

[28] Robert H. McGuckin, Thomas A. Abbott, III, Paul E. Herrick and Leroy Norfolk, "Measuring the Trade Balance in Advanced Technology," *Center for Economic Studies Report, no. 89-11* (Washington: US Bureau of Census, 1989); US Bureau of Census, "US International Trade in Goods and Services: Information on Goods and Services," at http://www.census.gov/foreign-trade/Press-elease/current_press_release/explain.txt (November 15, 2001); John Sullivan Wilson, "The US 1982–1993 Performance in Advanced Technology Trade," *Challenge*, no. 1 (1994): 11–16.

services and high-tech products.[29] "High-tech," in China's trade statistical reporting system until 1998, referred to computers and telecommunications, life sciences, aerospace and aeronautics, electronics, weapons, opto-electronics, computer integrated manufacturing, nuclear technology, biotechnology and materials. Since 1998, China has reported high-tech trade statistics under a new scheme, which omits weapons and nuclear technology, but introduces a new "other" technology category, presumably a combination of the weapons and nuclear technology categories.

Each high-tech category can be further divided into different levels according to technological intensity and the resulting profit and added value. For example, in the PC category, the first level is CPUs and core software, which has been dominated by the Wintel model (microprocessors from Intel and operating systems and major applications packages from Microsoft). The second, which includes such critical elements as integrated circuits, memory chips and displayers, has both a higher level of risk as well as profit. The third and lowest level is the assembling and manufacturing of terminal products, which have lower levels of technological intensity but higher logistic costs and whose advantages are reflected through economies of scale and localised sales and services.[30] Apparently, China has been stuck mainly in the lowest level of the high-tech value chain.

One measure of the high-tech industry is trade statistics. However, comparable high-tech trade data are difficult to locate not only because the "high-tech" definition is dynamic but also because it varies across countries. Here, two sets of data are used, one from official Chinese sources and the other from the United States. Although there are discrepancies between these, which may come

---

[29] Ministry of Science and Technology, "Guojia gaoxin jishu chanye kaifaqu gaoxin jishu qiye rending diaojian he banfa" (Conditions and Methods of Certifying High- and New-Technology Enterprises in National High- and New-Tech Industrial Development Zones), in Ministry of Science and Technology (comp.), *Zhongguo jishu chuangxin zhengce (Policies on Technological Innovation in China)* (Beijing: Kexue jishu wenxian chubanshe, 2000), 78–79.

[30] Yuko Arayama and Panos Mourdoukoutas, *China against Herself: Innovation or Imitation in Global Business?* (Westport, CT: Quorum Books, 1999), 107.

from different statistical specifications, different currency exchange rates during different periods, etc., both illustrate the positions, trends and changes of China's high-tech trade. The data from the American source provides further comparable high technology trade statistics of, and specific categories for, economies in the world between 1980 and 1998[31] so that it is possible to calculate Trade Competitiveness (TC)[32] and Revealed Comparative Advantage (RCA).[33]

Having experienced a steady increase, high-tech exports seem to be an important growth engine in the Chinese economy (see Figure 1.1). As measured by TC, China's high-tech competitiveness in trade has improved from −0.53 in 1991 to −0.04 in 2003 according to the Chinese data. If the data from the American source is used, however, China's TC in high-tech declined slightly from −0.11 in 1980 to −0.14 in 1998 (see Figure 1.2). Among the nine high-tech

---

[31] The data are compiled by the US National Science Foundation from the WEFA/ICF World Industry Service database. See National Science Board, *Science and Engineering Indicators* (Arlington, VA: National Science Foundation, 2002), Appendix Table 6-1: World Industry and Trade Data for Selected Countries or Economies and Industries: 1980–1998.

[32] Trade competitiveness (TC) measures the share of a nation's difference in exports and imports in the nation's trade:

$$TC = (X - M)/(X + M),$$

where X is nation's exports and M is nation's imports. A positive TC displays a competitiveness of a nation's good, with a greater than 0.5 reading meaning comparative advantage and a less than −0.5 reading indicating comparative disadvantage.

[33] Revealed comparative advantage (RCA) measures a nation's share in world exports of a good in the nation's share of total world exports:

$$RCA_j = (X_j/X_{wj})/(X_t/X_{wt}),$$

where X_j is a nation's exports of good j, X_{wj} is world's total exports of good j, X_t is a nation's total exports and X_{wt} is world's total exports. A greater than 2.5 RCA measure demonstrates that a nation has a very strong competitive edge in producing and trading a good, a reading between 1.25 and 2.5 means a strong competitiveness of a nation in a good and a lower than 0.8 RCA index signifies that the nation is less competitive in its particular product. See Bela Balassa, "Trade Liberalization and 'Revealed' Comparative Advantage," *The Manchester School of Economics and Social Studies* 33, no. 2 (1965): 99–123.

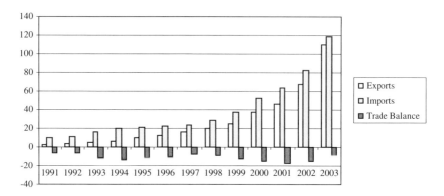

Figure 1.1: China's High-Tech Trade (US$ billion, 1991–2003)

Source: National Bureau of Statistics and Ministry of Science and Technology (ed.), *China Statistical Yearbook of Science and Technology* (Beijing: China Statistics Press, 2003).

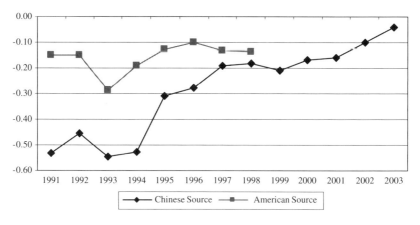

Figure 1.2: Trade Competitiveness (TC) of China's High-Tech Trade (1991–2003)

Source: National Bureau of Statistics and Ministry of Science and Technology (ed.), *China Statistical Yearbook of Science and Technology* (Beijing: China Statistics Press, 2003); National Science Board, *Science and Engineering Indicators* (Arlington, VA: National Science Foundation, 2002).

categories defined by the Chinese statistics, computers and tele-communications, aerospace and advanced materials have gained international competitiveness; opto-electronics and the 'other' technology category have lost competitive advantages, while electronics, computer-integrated manufacturing, life sciences and biotechnology have not seen much change in the trade pattern. As a whole, computer-integrated manufacturing, 'other' technology, aerospace and electronics are the least competitive.

China's high-tech trade deficits have been fluctuating but increasing, reflecting the high demand for, and dependence upon, advanced foreign technology. Although China has enjoyed a trade surplus in computer and telecommunications technology for several years, TC (0.39 for 2003) is less than the critical 0.5 threshold, suggesting that China is still left behind in this largest trading area which accounted for 83.3 percent of the high-tech exports in 2003. Trade deficits have been growing gradually in almost all other high-tech areas, especially in electronics and computer-integrated manufacturing, except in biotechnology whose trade surplus has been too small to form a critical mass. Similar results can be obtained by using American data as well, with "office and computing machinery" and "communications equipment" gaining ground but still being far from the 0.5 reading. "Drugs and medicines" suffered a dramatic loss while there was not much change in "aerospace".

Next, RCA is used to further measure how competitive China's particular high-tech fields are in the world (see Figure 1.3). The "office and computing machinery" category had been the only high-tech area in which China made strong international gains, as indicated by the remarkable increase of RCA from 0.076 (a very low competitiveness reading) in 1980, to the level of 1.30 in 1998 (strong TC). RCA for "communications equipment" increased between 1980 and 1990 and declined thereafter, and the competitiveness of the "aerospace" industry had improved but not that well. However, the RCA for "drugs and medicines" eroded significantly over the period in which comparable data are available, from a very competitive industry to not competitive.

Over the 1990s, China made progress in international high-tech exports and commanded competitiveness in some high-tech areas. But what are behind these impressive trade statistics? First, obviously, while the export-oriented strategy has shown results, processing and assembling using materials from abroad for export purposes

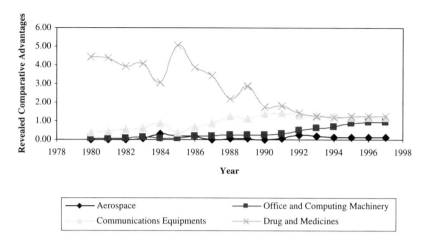

Figure 1.3: Revealed Comparative Advantages (RCA) of China's High-Tech Trade (1980–1998)

Source: National Science Board, *Science and Engineering Indicators* (Arlington, VA: National Science Foundation, 2002).

accounted for about 90 percent of China's high-tech exports in 2006.[34] It is doubtful that China has acquired much advanced technology through assembling activity, although in terms of technology content, FDI in China in the early 21st century was much different from that in 1985 or even the early 1990s.[35]

Second, the export-led high-tech industry has been based on low labour costs and imported foreign technologies or even components. China has become a big assembly line for products made of critical high-tech parts from abroad plus some low-tech domestic components. Most of the Chinese exports are lower-end products involving basic processing and manufacturing techniques, while imports in general are much more sophisticated.[36] There has

---

[34] See http://www.sts.org.cn/tjbg/gjscy/documents/2007/070618.htm (October 19, 2007).

[35] For a similar finding through the use of a different set of international trade statistics, see Francoise Lemoine and Deniz Unal-Kesenci, "Assembly Trade and Technology Transfer: The Case of China," *World Development* 32, no. 5 (2004): 829–850.

[36] Denis Fred Simon, "The Microelectronics Industry Crosses a Critical Threshold," *China Business Review* 28, no. 6 (2001): 8–20.

been a tendency for the world's leading MNCs, especially those in the ICT area, to move their manufacturing facilities (to outsource production) to China, which, unfortunately, is not due to the nation's competitiveness in technology, but largely because of its comparative advantage in labour.[37] China has moved, and will steadily upmarket anything, either high- or low-tech, that requires many pieces to be assembled in an efficient manner at low cost. Investors can find attractive production bases in China, and this is globalisation at work in the purest sense.[38] Being labour- rather than technology-intensive, those so-called "high-tech" gadgets have a profit margin sometimes as low as 2–3 percent. For example, Wanda, a wireless mouse manufactured by Logitech International SA, a Swiss-American company, sells in the United States for around US$40. Of this, China takes a meagre US$3 for wages, power, transport and other overhead costs.[39] In a word, located at the lower end of the international division of labour, the nation has yet to achieve much in added value and raise its competitive advantage significantly. This may also explain the discrepancy of trade statistics between the Chinese and American sources: products considered as "high-tech" in China may not be considered so elsewhere.

Third, in areas where China is enjoying a certain level of competitiveness, much of it has come from foreign-invested enterprises (*Sanzi qiye*). In 2000, for example, 92.5 percent of computer systems and 96.4 percent of mobile communications equipment were exported by

---

[37] There are conflicting views about China's comparative advantage in labour. Some believe that such a situation is expected to exist for at least 10 years, given China's large pool of cheap labour in the central regions. See *Asian Wall Street Journal*, March 15–17, 2001, 1, 8. Others think that China may lose such a comparative advantage because in some Chinese cities, labour costs are as high as those in some Southeast Asian countries. See *Asian Wall Street Journal*, December 30, 2002, A1, A2.

[38] Joe Studwell, *The China Dream: The Elusive Quest for the Great Untapped Market on Earth* (London: Profile Books, 2002), 225.

[39] Andrew Higgins, "Symbiotic Ties to China Are a Boon and a Burden for American Economy," *Asian Wall Street Journal*, February 2, 2004, A1, A5B.

foreign-invested enterprises.[40] In 2006, foreign-invested enterprises contributed 88.1 percent of China's high-tech exports, while state-owned enterprises (SOEs) have seen its portion continuously declining.[41] FDI to China is supposed to diffuse advanced technology to Chinese enterprises and make them technologically competitive. Unfortunately, the high-tech export statistics show a different picture.

The above analysis seems to indicate another reality about China's high-tech sector and industry: they have developed rapidly, but they are structurally risky, e.g., processing- and assembling-focused, low-end product-oriented and low value-added, and foreign-invested enterprises-led. Because of this, China may make and export "high-tech" products in large quantities, but may not enjoy higher added value as high-tech products are supposed to do, as a larger share of its companies' hard-earned profits go to owners of core-high technologies. The situation has not been improved, and therefore the growth is probably unsustainable. To become a high-tech power, China has to move beyond comparative advantage in labour to gain competitive edge in a "cluster" of technologies so as to climb the technology value chain.

CHALLENGES

Although technological development seems a priority, Chinese firms have many difficulties in attaining sophistication in technology, mainly because they lack the technological capability. This has lead to price wars, patent infringements and generally speaking, difficulties in upgrading its technologies.

Continuous Price Wars: The TV Sector

China's TV sector has recently received enormous attention. In November 2003, TCL, a consumer electronics producer in China,

---

[40] Jiang Xiaojuan, "Zhongguo de waizi jingji dui zhengzhang, jiegou shengji he jingzhengli de gongxian" (Contributions of Foreign Invested Enterprises in China to Local Economic Growth, Structural Upgrading and Competitiveness), *Zhongguo shehui kexue (Social Sciences in China)*, no. 6 (2002): 4–14.

[41] See http://www.sts.org.cn/tjbg/gjscy/documents/2007/070618.htm (October 19, 2007).

merged its TV manufacturing facilities with those of its French counterpart, Thomson. The combined company, in which TCL holds a 67 percent share, is expected to export 18 million TVs in 2004, thus becoming the world's number one, with 10 percent of the market. But in the meantime, TCL, along with fellow Chinese TV makers Changhong, Konka and Xoceco, lost in the US Department of Commerce anti-dumping case.

Using price as a weapon, i.e., anti-dumping being a countermeasure, in the TV sector is nothing new in China. Since 1996, the Chinese market has witnessed a series of TV price wars. In the name of defending the indigenous industry, price wars do help domestic firms gain market shares over their foreign competitors. But the rising market shares of some of the Chinese firms are often at the expense of their domestic peers or even themselves.[42] As price wars ate up their profit margins, many TV makers could not even maintain a price that is higher than the cost. In fact, in 2001, TV manufacturers saw the average profit level fall from 2.26 percent in 1999 to 2.05 percent and suffered losses of nearly RMB3 billion.[43]

The intense price wars must have something to do with supply and demand. When demand for TV sets exceeded supply in China, local governments piled into this sector which had an artificially low market entry barrier, but actually a high technology entry barrier, and then used a high degree of protection to ensure captive markets for local products and prevent unprofitable firms under their jurisdictions from being acquired. Then, overcapacity occurred as a result of duplicate economic activity at many Chinese firms that had been set up just for the sake of creating employment for the excessive labour.[44] However, it is argued here that such interpretations miss a vital point, or at least an important factor: China's TV makers do not possess core technologies in very large-scale integrated circuits, tubes, displays and others.

---

[42] At one point, Changhong TV sets were sold according to their weight: a 29-inch (52.5 kg) sold at RMB1,575 or RMB30 per kilogram. See *Zhongguao jingji shibao (China Economic Times)*, June 12, 2002.

[43] *Hong Kong iMail*, April 26, 2002, 2.

[44] *Financial Times*, October 19, 2001, 13.

Infringement of Foreign Patents:
The Case of DVD Players

In early 2002, China-made DVD players were impounded by customs in several European countries with the charge that their makers had not paid for the patents used. Later, Philips, Sony and Pioneer (or so-called 3C) waged a legal battle in the European Union court, pressuring Chinese DVD player makers to pay royalties for the technologies. Initially, payment was requested at US$20 per DVD machine, which the Chinese side claimed to be too high given that the sales price of a player was only US$90.[45] Through negotiation, these firms settled the case by agreeing to pay US$5 per machine to 3C. Later, they also reached agreements with other foreign companies on royalty payments: 4 percent of the sales price, or US$4, whichever is higher, for each player to the 6C alliance of NEC, Panasonic, Toshiba, JVC, Mitsubishi and Time Warner, US$10 to DTS, US$4.95 to Dolby Laboratories and US$2.5 to MPEG LA. Most recently, Thomson, the partner of TCL, requested a payment of US$1 or US$1.50, depending upon where the player is sold, i.e., in China or abroad. With the number of DVD players made in China in 2003 being at least 50 million, the total payment was huge.[46]

Such incidents have been typical of Chinese industry in the past decade. From the product life cycle perspective, MNCs have gradually moved the production of consumer electronics products from the United States and Japan to Singapore, South Korea, Taiwan and Hong Kong, and then to China and other countries with low labour costs. However, they use critical technology patents as leverages and also focus on developing next-generation products or technology embodied in the existing products. China is supposed to absorb and assimilate such technology and gradually develop indigenous products and climb the ladder of technological learning. Unfortunately, this has not happened. Thus, located at the downstream of the global value chain, China has no

---

[45] *Beijing qingnianbao (Beijing Youth Daily)*, March 11, 2002.
[46] See http://tech.sina.com.cn/it/2004-03-11/0712303633.shtml (March 11, 2004).

choice but to continue paying for the use of foreign technology. In the meantime, the homogenisation and commoditisation of these products have inevitably dragged Chinese firms into price competition. As such, their earning power has been diminished significantly. The profits that TV producer Changhong made from sales of 6.94 million sets was about equal to what Sony earned selling half a million sets.[47]

Moreover, the phenomenon is not limited to the consumer electronics industry. Take Legend, China's largest PC maker, as an example.[48] In 1998, it took over IBM to become the leader in China's PC market (it acquired the PC business from IBM in 2004). But as Liu Chuanzhi, Legend's chairman, acknowledged, the company has merely played the role of a "mover" (*banyungong*) for foreign technology.[49] Similarly, having spent several billion dollars importing first-generation analog technology and second-generation global mobile communications (GSM) technology, China's mobile communications industry is still under the shadow of foreign technology. Although home-made mobile handsets held a market share of more than 50 percent in 2003, a dramatic increase from 5 percent in 2000, Motorola and Nokia have sold more phones to Chinese customers while many of those shipped by Bird, China's top handset maker, are still sitting in warehouses or on store shelves.[50] Moreover, as few firms have devoted themselves to technological development, each and every mobile phone made in China has critical components imported from abroad.[51]

---

[47] *Financial Times*, October 19, 2001, 13.

[48] Although its Chinese name is still *liangxiang*, "Legend" recently changed its English name into "Lenova." "Legend" is used here as it will take time for "Lenova" to be known worldwide.

[49] Fang Zhou, Guo Tianxiang and Tian Yishan, *Jinggao weiji: Zhongguo jiaru shijie maoyi zhuzhi qianxi* (*Crisis Warning: Self Examination of Chinese CEO on the Eve of China's WTO Accession*) (Kunming: Yunnan renmin chubanshe, 2001), 45.

[50] See http://www.emtchina.com/eNews/emt_200302a.htm (March 5, 2004); Evan Ramstad, "Amid Tech Boom, Chinese Stalwarts Scrape for Gains," *Asian Wall Street Journal*, February 27–29, 2004, A1, A8.

[51] *Ershiyi shiji jingji daobao (21st Century Economic News)*, December 30, 2002; January 10, 2003.

China's handset market has also been experiencing disastrous price wars and profit erosion.[52] And although the exact amount of money that China Unicom paid for Qualcomm's CDMA technology is unknown, it includes an entry fee, a software license fee and a fee linked to the number of subscribers or revenues. Recently, Cisco Systems, the world's leading networking and communications manufacturer, accused China's switcher/router developer Huawei Technologies of patent infringement.[53] Future areas of contention involving intellectual property rights in China include automobiles and digital TV.

BROADER AND DEEPER PROBLEMS

Since the early 1980s, in an effort to explore the Chinese way of technology diffusion, new technology enterprises have spun off from China's research institutes, while universities have competed with MNCs. Many have been successful because of their strong connection with the institutions from which they were spun off, for example the Chinese Academy of Sciences' (CAS) "Legend," Beijing University's "Founder," etc. Although they were financially humble at the beginning, they were very successful in getting access to staffing and facilities. Significantly, the roots of these research achievements were formed as a result of state investment during the planned economy period.[54]

It seems that the strategy has been working well thus far. But further development of these young technology enterprises, and the high-tech sector as a whole, which has been viewed as key to China's future, will depend more on an indigenous technological capability. Sadly, such a capability is quite weak for the following reasons.

---

[52] See for example, *Shichang bao (Market News)*, September 27, 2003; *Zhongguo gongshang shibao (China Business Times)*, February 11, 2004.

[53] Bruce Einhorn, "China: Too Fast a Learner?," *Business Week*, February 3, 2003.

[54] Qiwen Lu, *China's Leap into the Information Age: Innovation and Organization in the Computer Industry* (New York: Oxford University Press, 2000).

First, many of China's industrial firms have few financial resources to carry out innovative R&D activities. Large- and medium-sized enterprises have spent on average 0.5–0.8 percent of their sales on R&D (see Table 1.1).[55] According to a more comprehensive survey of the nation's R&D resources in 2000, firms within high-tech parks spent an average 1.9 percent of their sales on R&D, far below the 5 percent standard by the Chinese definition of a high-tech firm, noted above, while those outside the parks a mere 0.63 percent.[56] As enterprises have been cautious in R&D spending, a fair guess would be that the industry cannot afford to spend money on technology.[57]

Second is the serious lack of qualified personnel because of a severe "brain drain" of Chinese talent to foreign countries and foreign-invested enterprises in China. In 2002, personnel involved in technological development in large- and medium-sized SOEs accounted for 5 percent of the total employees, and only about a quarter had technological development units, representing a steady decline since the 1990s.[58] As a result, even after acquiring designs from MNCs, SOEs still lack the depth of engineering expertise necessary to fully exploit the technology and become competitive globally.[59]

---

[55] National Bureau of Statistics and Ministry of Science and Technology (comp.), *China Statistical Yearbook on Science and Technology* (Beijing: China Statistics Press, 2003), 94–95.

[56] See http://www.china.org.cn/chinese (June 8, 2002).

[57] One may argue that given its complex, uncertain, prolonged and even risky nature, R&D does not guarantee an immediate return to the investment or an increase in the firms' competitiveness. See Sanjaya Lall, "Technological Change and Industrialization in the Asian Newly Industrializing Economies: Achievements and Challenges," in *Technology, Learning, and Innovation*, ed. Linsu Kim and Richard R. Nelson (New York: Cambridge University, 2000), 13–68. For a recent news report on the Japanese case, see "Japan Asks Why More Yen Don't Yield More Products," *Science*, 296 (May 17, 2002): 1230–1231. One may also argue that Dell has not relied on technology to achieve its status as the world's largest PC maker. The fact of matter is that in the US there are Intel, Microsoft, Hewlett-Packard and many other technology-intensive firms, while Chinese high-tech firms such as Legend, Founder, Huawei, etc., are mandated to become technologically innovative.

[58] *China Statistical Yearbook of Science and Technology*, 2003, 94–95.

[59] Kathryn Kranhold, "China Makes Power Play to Score Technology from Foreign Partners," *Asian Wall Street Journal*, February 26, 2004, A1, A7.

Table 1.1: Enterprise Technology-Related Expenditure (RBM100 million, percent, 1991–2002)

	1991	1992	1993	1994	1995	1996	1997	1998	1999	2000	2001	2002
R&D Expenditure	58.6	76.1	95.2	122.0	141.7	160.5	191.3	197.1	249.9	353.6	442.3	560.2
Technology Importation	90.2	116.1	159.2	266.7	360.9	322.1	236.5	214.8	207.5	245.4	285.9	372.5
Absorption and Assimilation	n.a.	n.a.	0.6	n.a.	n.a.	1.4	1.4	1.5	1.8	18.2	19.6	25.7
Purchase of Domestic Technology	3.7	n.a.	4.7	13.2	25.5	25.8	16.6	18.2	13.8	26.4	36.3	42.9
Enterprise/National R&D Expenditure (percent)	38.86	36.3	37.2	39.4	40.6	39.7	37.6	35.8	36.8	60.0	60.4	61.2
R&D Expenditure/Sales Revenue (percent)	0.49	0.50	0.50	0.51	0.46	0.48	0.52	0.53	0.60	0.71	0.76	0.83

Source: National Bureau of Statistics and Ministry of Science and Technology (ed.), *China Statistical Yearbook of Science and Technology* (Beijing: China Statistics Press, various years).

Third, there is always the question of how the limited amount of resources is utilised. In pursuing a quick and short-term pay-off, almost all Chinese enterprises are keen to import foreign technology as a way to upgrade production technology. In the past, the focus has been on obtaining hardware instead of software, i.e., patents, know-how, blueprints, etc. Between 1991 and 2002, 95 percent of the spending on technology imports was devoted to hardware with very little devoted to obtaining technology licenses. At large- and medium-sized enterprises, more money was spent on technology importation than on R&D until 1999 (see Table 1.1). And once the equipment was imported, almost no financial resources were devoted to absorption, assimilation and innovation, thus resulting in a vicious cycle of "importing, lagging behind, importing again, and lagging behind again."[60]

Fourth, enterprises also lack interest in engaging domestic learning institutions with respect to R&D efforts. The reforms in the science and technology system since the mid-1980s have to some extent activated the enthusiasm of researchers in these institutions (the supply side of technology), but enterprises (the demand side) have been reluctant to acquire technology from domestic sources. That is to say, the deeply-rooted problems of separation between innovation and the economy, and of organisational rigidity between enterprises and institutions of learning, have not been solved.[61] Such a problem may be due to the culture conflict between industry and academia. For example, in late 1998 when the CAS set out to make its "Knowledge Innovation Programme" the nation's centre in basic research and

---

[60] An analysis of the Chinese statistics indicates that imported technologies are more likely to lead to market success in new product sales through their absorption. See Yifei Sun, "Sources of Innovation in China's Manufacturing Sector: Imported or In-house Developed?," *Environment and Planning A* 34, no. 6 (2002): 1059–1072.

[61] For the structural difficulties that China needs to overcome in order to respond to the innovation challenge, especially the *danwei* effect, referring to the fact that the work unit is still very much the unit of reference of the governments (local and national) as well as the companies themselves, see Rigas Arvanitis, Pierre Miège and Wei Zhao, "A Fresh Look at the Development of a Market Economy in China," *China Perspectives*, no. 48 (2003): 51–62.

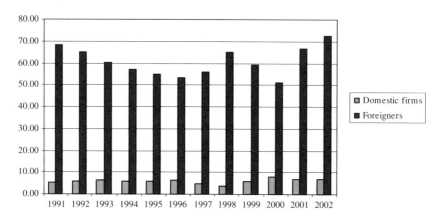

Figure 1.4: Invention Patents Granted in China (percent, 1991–2002)

Source: National Bureau of Statistics and Ministry of Science and Technology (ed.), *China Statistical Yearbook of Science and Technology* (Beijing: China Statistical Press, 2003), 434.

high-tech development, one of the measures was a reverse takeover by Legend of CAS' Institute of Computing Technology which had spun off the Institute 14 years earlier. But the marriage ended in divorce because both sides had difficulty accommodating each other in research focus and technological development strategy.[62]

Fifth, inevitably and consequently, fewer Chinese enterprises own independent intellectual property rights in core technologies, as the data on patent (an important benchmark for the level of industrial technology) suggest (see Figures 1.4 and 1.5).[63] Chinese firms seem to be more interested in utility model and design patents that link to unsubstantial modification, but lag far behind their foreign counterparts in invention patents. Since the 1990s, out of the more than 273,000 invention patent applications, only 47,452 (17.4 percent) were from Chinese firms, which were granted 5,876

---

[62] *Jishuanji shijie (China Computer World)*, no. 1 (January 3, 2000): A17–A24.

[63] Although the economy has been struggling worldwide, one would never know it by looking at the booming patent activity, especially in information technology and telecommunications, in the US. See Erika Jonietz, "Economic Bust, Patent Boom," *Technology Review* (May 2002): 71–77.

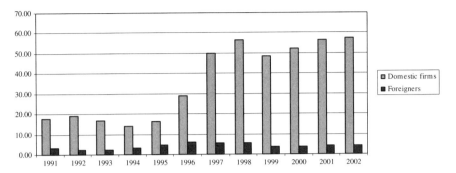

Figure 1.5: Utility Model and Design Patents Granted in China (percent, 1991–2002)

Source: National Bureau of Statistics and Ministry of Science and Technology (ed.), *China Statistical Yearbook of Science and Technology* (Beijing: China Statistical Press, 2003), 434.

(6.4 percent) of the total. While Chinese enterprises have been busy importing technology, foreign entities, most likely MNCs, have grabbed 63.2 percent of the total invention patents from China. This may further restrain China's industrial technology. For example, China's pharmaceutical industry is built on modelling generic or off-patent drugs from abroad.[64] Of the more than 1,000 core patents on colour TVs, none belongs to China; 92 percent of the 426 3G mobile communications invention patent applications filed in China were from abroad, while China's Huawei Technologies ranked eighth with 23 applications, about a quarter of Samsung's.[65] In the petrochemicals industry, patent applications from MNCs accounted for 90 percent of the total; and in the aerospace industry, invention patents filed by foreign firms are 30 times more than those by domestic ones.[66] Of the invention patents received by China's Patent

---

[64] Recently, China issued a new regulation on new medicine approval, according to which, a new medicine is defined as one appearing in China for the first time. See *Beijing xiandai shangbao (Beijing Business Daily)*, December 26, 2002, 5.

[65] *Renmin ribao and Huanan xinwen (People's Daily — Southern China News)*, June 21, 2002, 1.

[66] *Jingji guanchabao (The Economic Observer)*, April 22, 2002, 1.

Administration between 1987 and 2002 in the areas of optical technology, photography and information storage, 75, 81 and 89 percent, respectively, were from foreigners.[67] The serious question is what the bottom line for the Chinese economy will be if MNCs continue to define the technological agenda and set the tone for the path of economic development.

As a result, a yawning gap remains between the finest corporations in China and the world. The nation has yet to come up with a China-created product as Japan did in the early 1970s, or as South Korea did in the 1990s,[68] and not one of China's largest SOEs, or "national teams" as they are always referred to, have become a globally competitive giant with a global market, global brand or global procurement system.[69] This seems to be a bitter but fair technological assessment of the current situation in the Chinese industry.

CONCLUSION AND DISCUSSION

China's high-tech sector and industry have gained vitality in the past two decades, but much of the development has been built on a massive infusion of foreign capital and FDI-embodied technology. It is quite understandable for a developing country like China to follow the technology importation path in its economic and technological development. However, to what extent should China be dependent on foreign sources for technology and for how long should China adopt such a development strategy?

Historically, Japan, Taiwan and South Korea all experienced the lag between technology importation and indigenous innovation. For example, when South Korea started its heavy-and-chemical-industry-led industrialisation in the 1960s, it chose the importation of foreign

---

[67] See http://www.blogchina.com/new/display/24128.html (February 26, 2004).

[68] See http://peopledaily.com.cn/GB/jinji (March 23, 2002); Arayama and Mourdoukoutas, *China Against Herself*, 8.

[69] Peter Nolan, "China and the Global Business Revolution," *Cambridge Journal of Economics* 26, no. 1 (2002): 119–137; Evaluation Association for China's Enterprises (comp.), *Shiji zhijiao de Zhongguo daxing gongye qiye (China's Large Industrial Enterprises at the Turn of the Century)* (Beijing: Jingji ribao chubanshe, 2000).

technology. Later on, through establishing enterprises as the important player in the national innovation system and providing policy guidance, the country has seen endogenous innovation-driven development.[70] Korean firms have gradually moved from original equipment manufacturing (OEM) to own-design manufacturing (ODM) and own-brand manufacturing (OBM) so as to garner much added value.[71] One would expect China to develop along the same trajectory.

In the meantime, the experiences of Asia's newly industrialised economies also suggest that it is not technology importation, but rather the lack of local absorptive capacity to assimilate, adapt and improve imported technology, that leads to dependency on foreign technology. Heavy reliance on FDI as a means of technology transfer may to some extent reinforce such dependency.[72] China's economic development seems to be at a critical juncture in that it is facing the danger of dependency.

Notwithstanding the many advantages that would push China to overcome its current technological slump and nurture a knowledge-based economy in the 21st century, the creation of new products and services resulting from innovations will be easily accommodated by a large domestic market that has started to be affluent, thus paving the way for even more innovations. However, the market advantage as well as comparative advantage in labour in many years to come could also discourage Chinese firms from being innovative. For one thing, by combining its strengths in low cost manufacturing and marketing channels with after-sales service capabilities, China has successfully overcome its weaknesses in quality, which probably gives firms less incentive to do well in the first place. With its

---

[70] See for example, Linsu Kim, *Imitation to Innovation: The Dynamics of Korea's Technological Learning* (Boston, MA: Harvard Business School Press, 1997).

[71] Jin W. Cyhn, *Technology Transfer and International Production: The Development of the Electronics Industry in Korea* (Cheltenham, UK: Edward Elgar, 2002).

[72] Linsu Kim, "Pros and Cons of International Technology Transfer: A Developing Country's View," in *Technology Transfer in International Business*, ed. Tamir Agmon and Mary Ann Von Glinow (New York: Oxford University Press, 1991), 223–239.

market leverage, China will likely continue having access to foreign technology. But only through its enhanced technological capacity can China assume a leading position in the world market and enhance the position of indigenous firms vis-à-vis those from the advanced industrialised nations.[73]

Moreover, the ability to attain sustainable development can only be achieved through absorbing and assimilating imported technology and then turning out new products bearing such technology in the near term. China's technological capability in industry is still weak, which, plus the lack of urgency to pay attention to innovation among Chinese firms, makes the outlook not that optimistic. The current technology policy, namely, playing the standards game, is in fact a sign of its weakness rather than strength, as China in the globalisation process has gained little in its indigenous capability.

Of course, while it may be tempting to attribute the lack of technological innovation in Chinese enterprises to the bottleneck that inhibits or impedes China's industrial development, technology is one of the determining factors. If some of China's high-tech enterprises at the very beginning were successful in exploiting and commercialising research results, they now run the risk of becoming so large and bureaucratic that they are unable to continue as they previously did or even lose entrepreneurial spirits, as has happened to large corporations elsewhere.[74] In the name of diversification and joining the "Fortune 500 Club", for example, Legend had expanded its business into system integration and services as well as areas in which the company does not have enough expertise to compete with established firms, such as mobile phone handsets, digital cameras, management consulting and even real estate.[75] It turned out to

---

[73] Alberto Gabriele, "S&T Policies and Technical Progress in China's Industry," *Review of International Political Economy* 9, no. 2 (2002): 333–373.

[74] Jay B. Barnet and Barry Baysinger, "The Organization of Schumpeterian Innovations," in *Strategic Management in High Technology Firms (Monographs in Organization Behavior and Industrial Relations*, vol. 12), ed. Michael W. Lawless and Luis R. Comez-Mejia (Greenwish, CT: JAI Press, 1990), 3–14.

[75] *Lianhe zhaobao* (Singapore), March 11, 2002, 17; *Nanfang zhoumo (Nanfang Weekend)*, March 28, 2002; *Beijing Chengbao (Beijing Morning Post)*, April 22, 2002.

be a painful move and the firm recently had to re-focus on its PC business.

Emphasising innovation and indigenous technological capability build-up does not mean that institutional arrangements (including industrial policy, venture capital, stock market, etc.), ownership and enterprise culture are secondary. But it remains to be seen whether China's recently initiated standards-centred technology policy will stimulate innovation or protect less advanced domestic technology and hinder technological development in China.

Since the whole issue of technological development in industry boils down to development of an indigenous technological capability, the ultimate question is whether or not this capacity can be created by enterprises alone. The creation of this technological capability is country-, region-, or history-specific: many Silicon Valley firms have close relations with Stanford University; Japanese capability began in the pre-Meiji era; and South Korea has emphasised the importance of the educational system and construction of a structure that massively supports technology and engineering.[76] Of course, firm-specific characteristics also explain some push toward technological development. Though what has proved successful in other countries may not be necessarily applicable to China, many of its high-tech enterprises did spin off from institutions of learning in the 1980s. In the meantime, the Chinese Government has granted institutions of learning more leeway in transferring research results achieved through government funding. With large increases in investment in R&D and minimal increases in personnel, Chinese enterprises can develop an indigenous technological capability

---

[76] See for example, James F. Gibbons, "The Role of Stanford University: A Dean's Reflections," in *The Silicon Valley Edge: A Habitat for Innovation and Entrepreneurship*, ed. Chong-Moon Lee, William F. Miller, Marguerite Gong Hancock and Henry S. Rowen (Stanford, CA: Stanford University Press, 2000), 200–217; Hiroyuki Odagiri and Akira Goto, "The Japanese System of Innovation: Past, Present and Future," in *National Innovation Systems: A Comparative Analysis*, ed. Richard R. Nelson (New York: Oxford University Press, 1993), 76–114; Linsu Kim, "National System of Industrial Innovation: Dynamics of Capability Building in Korea," in *National Innovation Systems*, ed. Richard R. Nelson, 357–382.

through collaborating with universities and research institutes. It should also organise firms and institutions of learning to tackle common technology.[77]

ACKNOWLEDGEMENTS

The author would like to thank Professors Richard P. Suttmeier and Jon Sigurdson for their critical and constructive comments on an early version of this chapter.

---

[77] For a recent case in which the US Semiconductor Industry Association sought federal assistance to help create and fund a Nanoelectronics Research Institute, see Don Clark, "US Chip Makers Want to Create Research Institute," *Asian Wall Street Journal,* June 11–13, 2004, M8.

Chapter 2

China's Regional Variations in Patenting

Ding Lu and Albert G. Hu

The technological intensity of Chinese products has been rapidly rising. Between 1985 and 2004, China's share of the world's high-tech products rose from a mere 0.4 to 6 percent while the share of high-tech products in its manufactured exports increased from 2.6 to 29.9 percent.[1] In terms of high-tech intensity of manufactured exports, China had already reached the level of the high-income countries by 2002.[2]

However, China's indigenous R&D capability remains weak. In 1996, foreign affiliates accounted for 59 percent of China's technology-intensive exports. The share went up to nearly 90 percent in 2004.[3] Chinese inventors were granted 404 patents by the US Patent and

---

[1] UNCTAD, *World Investment Report*, 2002 and National Bureau of Statistics of China, www.sts.org.cn/sjkl/gjscy/data2005/2005-2.htm (February 20, 2007)

[2] Albert G. Hu and Gary H. Jefferson, "Science and Technology in China," paper presented at the Conference China's Economic Transition: Origins, Mechanisms, and Consequences, Pittsburgh, November 5–7, 2004.

[3] M. Felicia Fai, "China's Growing Technological Capabilities: Opportunities and Threats for Foreign Multinational Enterprises," paper presented at the Conference Mapping the Territory for Chinese Management Research, Beijing, June 17–20, 2004. See the sources in Footnote 1.

Trademark Office in 2003. Although this number was about 10 times what China had achieved a decade earlier, it still paled in significance compared to that of Japan (35,350), Taiwan (5,938) and Korea (4,428).[4]

China has noticeably intensified its R&D efforts in recent years. The country's R&D to GDP ratio has nearly doubled since the mid-1990s reaching 1.35 percent in 2004, the highest among developing countries.[5] This surge is driven by both domestic and foreign firms. The painful experience of paying exorbitant amounts for licensing fees to foreign patent holders has motivated many Chinese companies to actively build their own intellectual property portfolios. This can be achieved by either investing heavily in their own R&D or aggressively acquiring intellectual property from foreign inventors.[6] On the other hand, many multinational companies have been increasingly outsourcing R&D activities to China after the country became a member of WTO. According to a global survey of 104 senior executives of multinational companies, China has emerged as the number one location choice for offshore investment in R&D, ahead of the US, India, UK, Germany and others.[7]

It is against this quickly changing landscape of technological transformation in China that the authors examine how various institutions have, through their interaction with local R&D performers, affected research orientation in China's regions. By estimating a regional knowledge production function and using patents as a proxy of proprietary technologies, the results provide useful policy implications by identifying crucial institutional and policy reforms that may influence applied research orientation and intensity. In doing so, this

---

[4] Albert G. Hu and Gary H. Jefferson, "Science and Technology in China."

[5] China's National Statistical Bureau, www.sts.org.cn/nwdt/gndt/document/052.htm (May 5, 2005). The Chinese Government's upward revision of the GDP figure in late 2005 should reduce the ratio but it would still remain among the highest in the developing world.

[6] He Yizan, "Fortune 500 Companies' Patenting Behaviour in China," 2004, www.surfip. gov.sg/sip/site/focus/surfip_focus__200403016859.htm (March 25, 2004).

[7] Economic Intelligence Unit (EIU), "Scattering the Seeds of Invention: The Globalisation of Research and Development," Hong Kong, 2004.

study also maps out substantial regional variations in acquiring proprietary technologies, an empirical observation interesting to business
practitioners for decisions on location choice of R&D investment.

Patenting in China has received scant academic examination.
Wu estimated a knowledge production function using provincial
level patent data.[8] Sun studied the regional variation of spatial distribution of Chinese patents across provinces.[9] Hu was the first to esti-
mate a patents production function using firm-level data.[10] He
showed that establishing formal R&D organisation substantially
improves patents production. Cheung and Lin also estimated a
knowledge production function using provincial level patent applications data to examine whether there is technology spillover from
foreign direct investment.[11]

This chapter contributes to this small but growing literature by
linking regional variation in patenting to local economic institutions
such as business participation and technology market development.
The next section discusses the institutional features of China's science-
and-technology research and its distribution across Chinese provinces.
This is followed by some econometric analysis and conclusions.

FEATURES OF CHINA'S SCIENCE AND TECHNOLOGY RESEARCH ACTIVITIES

China's national system of science and technology has undergone
drastic transformation in the reform era. The pre-reform system of
central planning and administration has given way to a hybrid system
consisting of both state patronage and a market-driven incentive

---

[8] Wu Changqi, "Innovation, Patenting, and International Competitiveness: Empirical
Evidence from China," *Seoul Journal of Economics* 8, no. 2 (1995): 231–250.

[9] Sun Yifei, "Spatial Distribution of Patents in China," *Regional Studies,* 34, No. 5
(2000): 441–454.

[10] Albert G. Hu, "R&D Organization, Monitoring Intensity, and Innovation Performance in Chinese Industry," *Economics of Innovation and New Technology* 12, no. 2
(2004): 117–144.

[11] K. Y. Cheung and P. Lin, "Spillover Effects of FDI on Innovation in China: Evidence
from the Provincial Data," *China Economic Review*, 15, No. 1 (2004): 25–44.

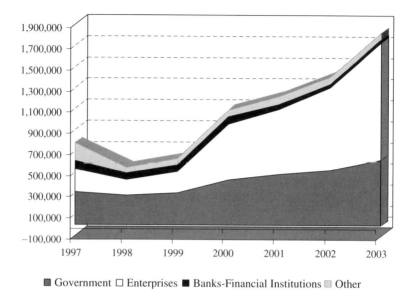

■ Government □ Enterprises ■ Banks-Financial Institutions ▨ Other

Figure 2.1: Sources of Science and Technology Research Funds (Thousand RMB)

Source: National Bureau of Statistics of China and Ministry of Science and Technology, *China Statistical Yearbook of Science and Technology* (Beijing: China Statistics Press, various years).

structure. Enterprises have become the most critical element in the chain of technological innovation.

Elevation of enterprises' role in technological innovation is reflected in the changing funding structure of science and technology in China. As shown in Figure 2.1, the share of science and technology activity funded by enterprises increased from 28 to 60 percent between 1997 and 2003. Meanwhile, the share of government funding declined from about 40–50 percent in 1997–1999 to 34.1 percent in 2003. The greater role of business in research and development is also highlighted by the growing share of the large-and-medium-sized enterprises in fund uses (Figure 2.2).

The research institutes still perform considerable R&D despite their declining share of the overall science and technology expenditure. The Chinese government began in the early 1990s to influence the research orientation of these institutions by reducing grants and

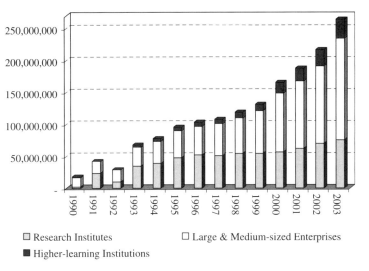

Figure 2.2: Users of Science and Technology Research Funds (Thousand RMB)

Source: National Bureau of Statistics of China and Ministry of Science and Technology, *China Statistical Yearbook of Science and Technology* (Beijing: China Statistics Press, various years).

other kinds of direct financial support and, therefore, forcing them to support themselves through consulting and technology service activities. The objective was to forge a closer tie between them and the enterprise sector. By 1999, a total of 243 research institutes under the supervision of various ministries of the central government had been converted into corporate entities.

In a parallel development, Chinese universities have also been active in commercialising technologies that they have developed. The amount of research funds used by higher learning institutions has risen substantially in recent years. Both the research institutes and universities have intensified their research in technologies of commercial potential as they actively seek collaborations with business firms.

China's integration into the global economy has raised the stakes of foreign companies in protecting their intellectual property rights (IPR) in the country. The pressure from developed countries has brought urgency to the issue. China's Patent Law was first enacted in 1984.

The Copyright Law was enacted six years later in 1990. The Patent Law underwent substantial revisions in 1992 to expand the scope of patent protection. When China joined the WTO in 2001, it made further commitments to improve protection for intellectual property. Since then, China has made a series of moves to fulfil its commitments in accordance with the Agreement on Trade-Related Aspects of Intellectual Property Rights (TRIPS). Following the TRIPS Agreement, China took on the obligations to protect and enforce the IPRs in accordance with internationally accepted norms.[12] Although intellectual property protection has been far from perfect in China, these newly created institutions have served to enhance the value of intellectual property and have also helped to create markets for technology and innovations.

China's market for technology transfer has been booming. Figure 2.3 shows that, between 1991 and 2003, the size of China's technology market grew more than 10 times in terms of transaction value while the number of deals displayed a much more moderate trend of growth. The implied rise in the value per transfer deal suggests that increasingly more technology contracts traded on the market were of higher values over these years.

Local capability and intensity of scientific-and-technological research vary enormously across China. Differences in human capital, legacies of the pre-reform centrally planned system, initial development conditions, proximity and accessibility to international markets, the central government's regional policies and different paces of economic reforms, etc., have all contributed to regional variations in R&D activity and productivity.

---

[12] The TRIPS Agreement established the minimum standards for the protection of various intellectual property rights, such as copyrights and neighbouring rights, trademarks, geographical indications, industrial designs, patents, integrated-circuit layout designs and undisclosed information. It also specified the standards for enforcing intellectual property rights in administrative and civil services particularly the rules against copyright piracy and trademark counterfeiting.

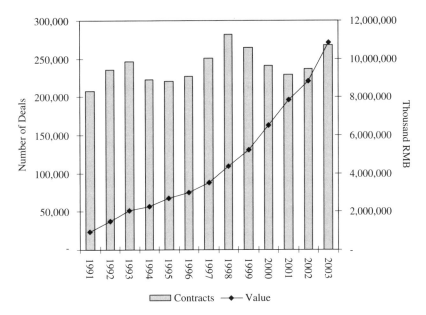

Figure 2.3: Growth of Market for Technology Transfer

Source: National Bureau of Statistics of China and Ministry of Science and Technology, *China Statistical Yearbook of Science and Technology* (Beijing: China Statistics Press, various years).

Figure 2.4 plots the average annual number of patents granted to domestic applicants against the average annual value of research fund use in China's provincial economies from 2001 to 2003. The top 10 provincial economies that produced the most patents are labelled. It appears that Guangdong and Zhejiang not only generated the most patents, but did so with relatively less research money. In contrast, Beijing, although a forerunner in patent production, spent relatively more money on science-and-technology research.

Why has there been such a wide inter-regional variation in the numbers of patents generated and fund uses? Differences may arise due to research productivity, such as capability of science-and-technology research and quality of human capital. Another important factor is researchers' incentives to seek out legal protection of their proprietary technologies, or the propensity to patent. Patent is an IPR that may give rise to economic rents from monopoly control of the

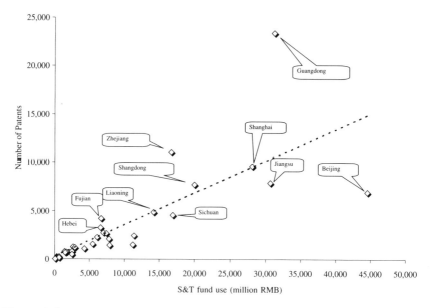

Figure 2.4: Science and Technology Fund Use vs. Number of Patents Granted, 2001–2003 (Average Annual Value)

Source: National Bureau of Statistics of China and Ministry of Science and Technology, *China.Statistical Yearbook of Science and Technology* (Beijing: China Statistics Press, various years).

patented technology. The incentive to patent one's technology — whether it is generated by one's own research or purchased from the market — may depend on factors such as enforcement of proprietary rights, technology market conditions, and the extent of international transactions.

Figure 2.5 shows large variation in the number of patents generated per million RMB of research funds across provinces.[13] It also suggests a loose but positive correlation between patents per million RMB of R&D and the enterprise share of science-and-technology research fund uses.

The role of the technology market may be crucial in determining the direction of research activities. The total technology transfer

---

[13] Figures 2.5 and 2.6 do not include Hainan, Ningxia, Qinghai and Tibet, each of which spent less than RMB1 billion annually on science-and-technology research from 2001 to 2003.

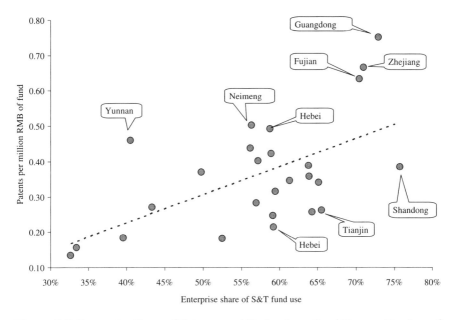

Figure 2.5: Enterprise Share of Science and Technology Fund Use vs. Number of Patents per Million RMB of Fund Use, 2001–2003 (Average Annual Value)

Source: National Bureau of Statistics of China and Ministry of Science and Technology, *China Statistical Yearbook of Science and Technology* (Beijing: China Statistics Press, various years).

contract value registered in a province indicates the size of the local market. The ratio between the total contract value and the research fund use can serve as a rough indicator for the relative importance of the technology market. As shown in Figure 2.6, the contract value to fund use ratio varies widely across regions and its correlation with the patents per million RMB of research money spent is rather weak. More rigorous analysis is therefore necessary.

A PRELIMINARY ANALYSIS

Based on the preliminary observations in the previous section, it is hypothesised here that the re-orientation of China's national innovation system from a centrally planned system towards a market-driven one is critical in explaining the variation in patent output across China's regions. The focus here is on two factors: the more prominent

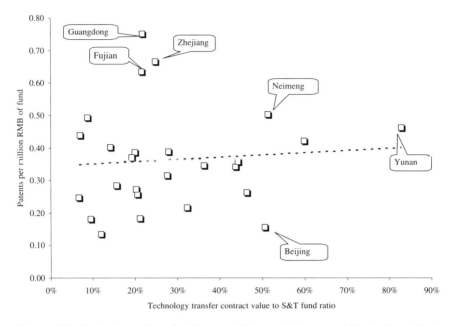

Figure 2.6: Technology Transfer Contract Value to Science and Technology Fund Ratio vs. Number of Patents per Million RMB of Fund Use, 2001–2003 (Average Annual Value)

Source: National Bureau of Statistics of China and Ministry of Science and Technology, *China Statistical Yearbook of Science and Technology* (Beijing: China Statistics Press, various years).

role of the enterprises in technological innovation and the presence and extent of market-based technology transfer. To test this hypothesis in a rigorous way, a patent production function is estimated in the tradition of Griliches, Jaffe, and Henderson and Cockburn.[14] Production of patents is characterised by a Poisson process:

$$E(P_{it}) = \exp(\alpha + \gamma \log R_{it}), \qquad (2.1)$$

[14] Zvi Griliches, *R&D, Patents, and Productivity* (Chicago: University of Chicago Press, 1984); Adam B. Jaffe, "Technological Opportunity and Spillovers of R&D: Evidence from Firms' Patents, Profits, and Market Value," *American Economic Review* 76, No. 5 (1984): 984–1001; and Rebecca Henderson and Iain Cockburn, "Scale, Scope, and Spillovers: The Determinants of Productivity in Drug Discovery," *The Rand Journal of Economics* 27, No. 1 (1996): 32–59.

where P_{it} is the patent count in region i at time t and R_{it} is region i's R&D stock at time t. Therefore, γ is elasticity of patent production with respect to R&D stock.

To account for the learning-by-doing characteristic of R&D and inter-temporal knowledge spillover, a measure of knowledge stock is constructed and used as the innovation input in the patent production function.[15] The perpetual inventory method is applied to construct the knowledge stock using past research expenditures:

$$R_t = (1 - \delta) R_{t-1} + F_{t-1}, \tag{2.2}$$

where F is the annual flow expenditure or funds raised and δ is the assumed depreciation rate of the knowledge capital.[16] The starting stock is assumed to be:

$$R_0 = F_0/(\delta + \mu), \tag{2.3}$$

where μ is the growth rate of F.

We capture the role of the enterprises in innovation activity with f, the large- and medium-sized firms' share of research fund use. The extent of market-based technology transfer is measured by m, the total contractual value registered in the local market for technology transfer divided by the provincial stock of research fund estimated by (2.2).

It is hypothesised here that both of these proxies have effects on elasticity of patent production with respect to R&D stock:

$$\gamma = \beta + \lambda_f f_{it} + \lambda_m \, m_{it} \,. \tag{2.4}$$

Substitute that into (2.1), we have

$$\begin{aligned} E(P_{it}) &= \exp\left(\alpha + (\beta + \lambda_f f_{it} + \lambda_m \, m_{it}) \log R_{it}\right) \\ &= \exp\left(\alpha + \beta \log R_{it} + \lambda_f (f_{it} \log R_{it}) + \lambda_m (m_{it} \log R_{it})\right). \end{aligned} \tag{2.5}$$

---

[15] Zvi Griliches, "Issues in Assessing the Contribution of Research and Development to Productivity Growth," *Bell Journal of Economics* 10, No. 1 (1979): 92–116.

[16] As in most studies about knowledge capital, it is assumed that $\delta = 15\%$.

Formally, our hypotheses are:

H1:   Patent output is proportionally related to knowledge (capital) stock through a Poisson process, i.e., $\gamma > 0$.

H2:   Participation of enterprises raises elasticity of patent production with respect to knowledge stock, i.e., $\lambda_f > 0$ significantly.

H3:   Development of the technology market also raises elasticity of patent production with respect to knowledge stock, i.e., $\lambda_m > 0$ significantly.

Data was collected from the *China Statistical Yearbook of Science and Technology* (various years) to compile the values of R_{it}, m_{it} and f_{it} for the 1990–2003 period. Table 2.1 presents the descriptive statistics of the key variables. Provincial and year dummies are included to control for region specific effects and economy-wide shocks respectively:

$$E(P_{it}) = \exp\left(\alpha + \beta \log R_{it} + \lambda_f \left(f_{it} \log R_{it}\right)\right.$$
$$\left. + \lambda_m \left(m_{it} \log R_{it}\right) + \theta_i D_i + \theta_t D_t\right). \tag{2.6}$$

Results of the Poisson estimation of Eq. (2.6) are reported in Table 2.2. The z-statistics in Table 2.2 are based on Huber–White robust variance estimation.

All estimated coefficients have the expected signs. All estimated coefficients, except that for λ_m in the case of regression including both year and provincial dummies, are highly significant over 99 percent. The estimated λ_m in the last regression with both year and provincial dummies is reasonably significant over 90 percent. Thus, all our hypotheses are supported by the empirical evidence.

Figure 2.7 plots the year dummy estimates using year 2003 as the reference group. There appears to be two sharp rises during the period under study. The first surge occurred in 1993, reflecting the effect of a substantial revision of the Patent Law in 1992 to expand the scope of protection for intellectual property. The second surge occurred in 1999 when the government accelerated the restructuring of large-and medium-sized state-owned enterprises. The level of patent production remained high in the subsequent years and

Table 2.1: Descriptive Statistics of the Key Variables

Variable	Observations	Mean	Standard deviation	Minimum	Maximum
Patent grants	420	1,947	2,942	1	29,235
Patent applications	420	3,276	4,581	2	43,186
Invention patent grants	409	105	179	0	2,261
Knowledge stock: Research institutions	420	3,633,495	5,849,993	17,079	48,800,000
Knowledge stock: Higher education	420	443,599	726,353	117	6,274,764
Knowledge stock: Large- and medium-sized Enterprises	392	4,085,242	4,440,794	259,034	26,400,000
S&T funds: Research institutions	420	825,248	1,414,753	9436	11,200,000
S&T funds: Higher education	414	166,880	287,871	29	2,380,672
S&T funds: Large- and medium-sized enterprises	408	1,105,273	1,572,915	0	13,400,000
Technology market transactions	372	809,901	1,305,107	0	12,431,180
F	392	0.53	0.13	0.11	0.82
M	372	0.04	0.04	0.001	0.46

Note: All monetary variables are measured in thousand RMB.

reached another peak in 2003. Enhanced confidence in China's effectiveness in dealing with IPR protection after its accession to the WTO in 2001 apparently has been a great stimulus to patent application and patent-related research in this period.

Table 2.2: Poisson Regression Estimations of Equation 2.6

	With year dummies only (1990–2003)	With year and provincial dummies (1990–2003)	With year dummies only (1991–2003)	With year and provincial dummies (1991–2003)
	Coefficient	Coefficient	Coefficient	Coefficient
$\log R_{it}$	0.7764	1.2597	0.7997	0.5970
	18.73*****	*11.70******	*20.01******	*2.78******
$f_{it} \log R_{it}$			0.1430	0.1310
			8.05*****	*4.06******
$m_{it} \log R_{it}$			0.2900	0.1145
			4.55*****	*1.74****
Mean θ_t	−0.5525	−0.1173	−0.2725	−0.3792
Mean θ_i		0.4246		−0.1988
Pseudo R^2	0.69	0.97	0.78	0.97
Wald chi^2	525	26,918	708	33,948
Log likelihood	−150,915	−17,006	−10,3491	−13,988
N	392	392	361	361

Note: Italic figures are z-statistics.
***** significant at 99%; **** significant at 95%; *** significant at 90%.

CONCLUDING REMARKS

We estimated a patent production function to investigate the determinants of the variation in the number of patents granted by China's State Intellectual Property Office across the provincial economies. The conventionally assumed proportional relationship between patents and knowledge stock leaves a significant proportion of the variation unexplained. Thus, a simple theoretical model was built to identify other possible causes of such variation and data was collected for 1990–2003 to test the validity of these hypothesised causes. Several preliminary but important findings were made: (a) higher participation of enterprises has facilitated research on proprietary technologies; (b) a more developed technology market

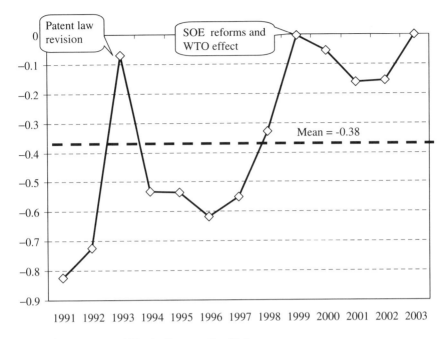

Figure 2.7: Estimated Yearly Dummy Coefficients

has had similar effects; (c) better patent protection for proprietary technology, accelerated reforms of state-owned enterprises in the late 1990s and China's accession to the WTO have all had a positive impact on such research. These findings may provide useful information for public policy making about science-and-technology research. They may also be a useful input in business decision making pertaining to investment choice of R&D locations.

The methodology used here can be extended to explore other unexplained causes of inter-regional variation in patent generation across the provinces of China. Using pseudo-R-square values in Table 2.2 as a rough guide, the basic model estimated with knowledge stock and yearly dummies can explain about 69 percent of inter-regional differences in (patented) technology output. Adding the two proxy variables, i.e., the participation of enterprises and technology-market deepening, increases the model's explanatory power to 78 percent. With provincial "dummies" added, the percent-age of inter-regional differences explained by the model is further raised to 97 percent. Therefore about 19 percent of inter-regional performance variations can be potentially explained by other region-specific factors. To study these factors, the simple (patent) technology-production function used here needs to be enriched with more theoretical hypotheses and data to analyse what are behind the impacts of these provincial dummies.

Chapter 3

R&D Incentives, Industrial Structure and Technology Transfer in China

Ping Lin and Jing A. Zhang

INTRODUCTION

The Chinese Government launched a nationwide drive towards introducing foreign technology on a vast scale over 20 years ago, in the hope that Chinese firms, after absorbing the imported technologies, would eventually be able to innovate on their own and compete with firms from developed countries. How successful has China's "market-for-technology" policy been? How willing have Chinese enterprises been to imitate advanced foreign products and technologies? How willing and effective have they been in the area of inventing new products and technologies on their own?

Using data on domestic patent applications and approvals published by the Chinese Government, this chapter aims to provide a systematic analysis of innovation activity in China since its first Patent Law came into force in 1985. It investigates the extent to which Chinese innovators are willing to spend resources to conduct R&D activity, identifies major obstacles that have hindered Chinese enterprises' incentive to innovate, and examines the implications of the findings for further economic restructuring in China, particularly after its accession to the WTO in December 2001. This chapter focuses on structural factors, such as the degree of industrial concentration and vertical integration that might have hindered Chinese firms' incentive to innovate.

In recent years there have been a few empirical studies on innovation in China. Jefferson *et al.* examined a set of panel data for approximately 20,000 large- and medium-sized Chinese enterprises over the 1995–1999 period.[1] These authors studied the impact of industrial concentration, firm ownership and capital intensity on R&D incentives for Chinese enterprises. While their findings on the relationship between R&D incentives and industrial concentration are similar to those presented here, their approach differed in two ways. First, Jefferson *et al.* did not look at the composition of patent applications and innovators, as done here. Second, they were not concerned with the vertical aspects of industrial structure. Other studies focus on various aspects of R&D in China. For example, Liu and White both examined the impact of regional variables on innovation activity in China, whereas Hu analysed the relationship between R&D and productivity growth in Chinese industries.[2]

THE SHORT HISTORY OF LEGAL PROTECTION FOR INNOVATIONS IN CHINA

China has made tremendous progress in establishing a legal system for the protection of innovations. Historically, the concepts of rewarding individuality and originality were not easily embraced under the old Chinese system of central planning. Patent rights

---

[1] See G. Jefferson, H. Bai, X. Guan and X. Yu, "R&D Performance in China's Large and Medium-size Enterprise Sector," Working Paper, Brandeis University, 2001. Their model uses one-firm and two-firm concentration ratios.

[2] X. Liu and S. White, "An Exploration into Regional Variation in Innovative Activity in China," *International Journal of Technology Management* 21, no. 1/2 (2001): 114–129; Albert Hu, "Ownership, Government R&D, Private R&D, and Productivity in Chinese Industry," *Journal of Comparative Economics* 29, no.1 (2001): 136–157.

introduced after the founding of the People's Republic of China in 1949 were abolished in 1954 and replaced by a system of awards for inventions under which inventions belonged to the state and could be used free of charge.[3]

In 1984, the Patent Law and its implementing regulations were enacted and came into effect in 1985. On the very first day of the enactments of the Patent Law in April 1985, as many as 3,455 patent applications were filed, setting a world record in the history of IP protection. The Patent Law has since been amended twice. The first revision took place in 1992 when the patent length was extended (from 15 to 20 years for invention patents and from 5 to 10 years for utility model and external design patents). The second revision, which was completed in September 2000, eliminated the provisions under the old law that discriminated against the state-owned enterprises, and introduced new provisions designed to make it more rewarding for enterprise employees to innovate. Since the passage of the 1984 Patent Law, the Central Government has issued over 20 regulations and guidelines so as to promote innovation activity in China. Today's Patent Law in China is almost in line with international standards. Up till now, China has acceded to all the international patent treaties, and its laws on intellectual property rights (IPR) meet the requirements of WTO's agreement on trade related intellectual property rights (TRIPS).

Since the passage of its first Patent Law in 1985, China has put in place a fairly effective system for enforcement of the laws. China has adopted two procedural systems: judicially through the People's Court and administratively through the relevant administrative authorities at the central, city, provincial and county levels throughout the country. Intellectual property divisions have been established in the court of law in many major cities. Enforcement of the Patent Law, in particular, and of the intellectual property right laws, in general, have been greatly improved in China since the early 1990s due to both the internal interest of China and external pressures from its major trading partners, such as the United States.

---

[3] Michael D. Pendleton, "China's Intellectual Property Law," Occasional Paper, Centre for Contemporary Asian Studies, Chinese University of Hong Kong, 1985.

R&D AND TECHNOLOGY TRANSFER IN CHINA: FROM 1991 TO 2004

R&D Incentives in China

Although still low relative to other countries, the ratio of the R&D expenditures to GDP in China has been growing steadily in recent years. Table 3.1 shows that the China's R&D expenditures increased significantly from RMB15.97 billion in 1991 to RMB196.63 billion in 2004. The figures include the R&D projects self-financed by firms as well as those supported by the government and foreign investors. In relative terms, R&D expenditures reached the lowest level in 1995 and 1996, amounting to only 0.6 percent of China's GDP. This was partially due to the rapid expansion of GDP in these two years. Following 1995, however, the R&D/GDP ratio has been growing at a quite impressive rate.

China's success in establishing a modern IP protection system is naturally reflected in the real numbers of patents. Figure 3.1 shows the number of domestic patent applications filed from 1985 to 2005. In 1985, a total of 14,372 applications were filed. The number reached 170,682 in 2000, increasing at an average annual rate of roughly 18.0 percent, and reached 476,264 in 2005, at an average annual growth rate of 22.8 percent. The annual growth rate was 20.4 percent for those filed by domestic inventors and 15.8 percent for patent applications filed by foreign inventors. The faster growth in foreign patent applications, as shown in Figure 3.1, can be attributed to several factors. First, China's first revision of its Patent Law in 1992 substantially extended the protection period. Second, China has greatly improved its enforcement of IPR laws since the early 1990s.[4] As a result, the number of patent applications filed from overseas, most of which were for patents of inventions, was 5,347 in 1992, but rose to 93,107 in 2005, growing at an average annual rate of 24.6 percent.

---

[4] Another contributing factor is China's entry into the Patent Cooperation Treaty in 1994, which further facilitates overseas patent applications in China.

Table 3.1: R&D Expenditures (100 Million RMB, Current Prices)

	1991	1992	1993	1994	1995	1996	1997	1998	1999	2000	2001	2002	2003	2004
R&D expenditures	159.7	197.8	248.3	306.2	348.7	404.5	509.2	551.1	678.9	895.7	1,042.5	1,287.6	1,539.6	1,966.3
R&D/ GDP (percent)	0.74	0.74	0.72	0.65	0.60	0.60	0.68	0.70	0.76	0.90	0.95	1.07	1.13	1.23

Sources: *China Statistical Year Book on Science and Technology*, various years; *China Science and Technology Statistical Data Book*, 2005; and *China Science and Technology Indicators*, various years.

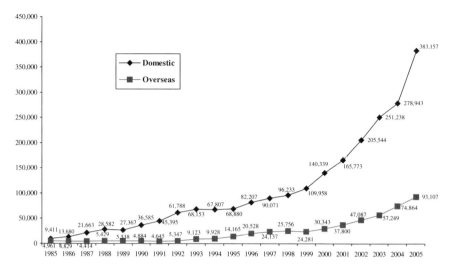

Figure 3.1: Patent Applications, 1985–2005

Sources: *China Statistical Year Book on Science and Technology*, various years; *China Science and Technology Statistical Data Book*, various years; and *China Science and Technology Indicators*, various years.

Types of Innovations Undertaken

The current Patent Law of China divides patentable innovations into three categories: invention, which is a new technical solution relating to a product, process or improvement thereof; utility model, which means a new technical solution relating to the shape or structure of a product that is not directly related to its aesthetic properties; and external design, which involves a new design of shape, pattern or combination, or of colour or aesthetic properties. The patent duration is 20 years for inventions and 10 years for the other two types of patents. Innovations that can be classified as inventions are regarded as major innovations. To obtain a patent for an invention, the applicant must meet the "novelty, inventiveness and practical applicability" requirements. The applications for patenting of utility models or design, on the other hand, need only to pass an "initial examination", wherein the patent office simply checks on the

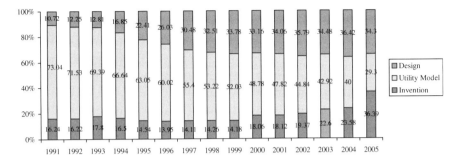

Figure 3.2: Distribution of Three Types of Domestic Patent Applications, 1991–2005
Sources: Same as for Figure 3.1.

completeness of the files and makes sure the same object has not been patented before.

Figure 3.2 portrays the distribution of applications for the three types of patents filed from 1991 to 2005. One striking observation is that the applications for major innovations (invention patents) accounted for less than 20 percent of the total number and were declining during the 1990s, dropping to only 14.2 percent in 1999. However, the share of applications for major innovations has significantly increased since 2000. In 2005, the applications for invention patents accounted for 36.4 percent of the total patent applications. Applications for utility models have correspondingly decreased during the same period. The share of applications for utility models to the total number dropped from 73.1 percent in 1991 to 29.3 percent in 2005. Applications for external designs have continued to increase and represented over 30 percent of the total applications in 2005. Overall, one can roughly conclude that since the passage in China of the first Patent Law in 1985, Chinese innovators have devoted most of their R&D resources to small R&D projects and generated minor innovations such as utility models and external designs during the 1990s. One cannot help but notice the very low and declining percentage of major innovations (patent for inventions) over the past one-and-a-half decades. However, after China's entry into the WTO, Chinese innovators must struggle for competitive advantage in both the international and domestic markets and follow some common market principles. As a result, Chinese innovators are beginning to put more emphasis on major innovations.

Types of Innovators

Under the current Chinese system, applicants for patents are divided into three basic categories: industrial enterprises (IEs), university and research institutions (URIs), and individuals. IEs devote resources to their R&D activity in order to come up with new products or new technologies. The inventions of the IEs, if patented, belong to the enterprises that discovered them. Usually, the output of the R&D activity by IEs can be readily used for production and leads to immediate commercial benefits to the innovators.

URIs are mostly funded by the Central or Provincial Governments, although funding from contracting with industrial enterprises has been increasing in recent years. These institutions employ well-trained scientists and engineers to conduct basic and applied research. The R&D output of the URIs can be of either academic or commercial value.

The third category of inventors is individuals who use their own resources rather than their employers' to engage in innovative activity. If successful, they can file, as they almost always do, for patent protection for their discoveries. Patents belonging to the first two categories of inventors are called service-patents. To exploit their discoveries' commercial uses, the individual inventors need to either sell their patents to commercial users or develop these inventions by setting up their own business.

Figure 3.3 depicts the shares of patents filed from 1991 to 2005 by each of the three types of inventors. As can be seen, the primary suppliers of patents in China were the individual inventors who provided over 60 percent of the patent applications filed every year during that period. The IEs, which the Government has been hoping would become the main force of innovation, contributed less than 17 percent of the total patent applications filed before the mid-1990s and less than 35 percent afterwards. Although the share of IEs increased after 1995, this change was mostly due to the decline in

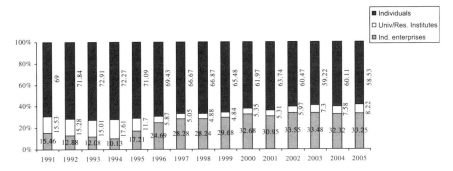

Figure 3.3: Patent Applications by Different Types of Innovators, 1991–2005
Sources: Same as for Figure 3.1.

the contribution of the URIs.[5] Individual inventors were consistently the main force of innovation, at least in terms of the number of patent applications filed.[6]

In terms of patents granted, individuals are also the largest contributors of patents. In particular, as shown in Figure 3.4, over 60 percent of approved patents went to individuals from 1991 to 2004. URIs each received less than 10 percent of the total number of patents granted from 1997. The share of patents granted to IEs increased from 19.1 percent in 1991 to 34.5 percent in 2004.

The information garnered from Figures 3.2–3.4 can be summarised as:

- More than 70 percent of the domestic patent applications filed were for small innovations (utility models and external designs) since the passage of China's Patent Law in 1985.

---

[5] A plausible explanation for the increasing share of the IEs and the decreasing share of the URIs after the mid-1990s is the Government's efforts in recent years to encourage research institutes to merge with industrial enterprises. This explanation also applies to Figure 3.4.

[6] Note that service inventors (such as business firms) may choose not to file patent applications for reasons such as their desire not to reveal technical details of their discovery to their competitors. Individual inventors do not seem to have such qualms. The propensity to file patents is higher for individual inventors as they usually do not have the capacity to commercialise their inventions by themselves.

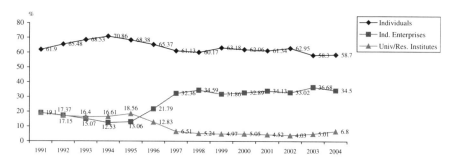

Figure 3.4: Patents Granted to Different Types of Innovators, 1995–2004
Sources: Same as for Figure 3.1.

- Since 1990, over 60 percent of the domestic patent applications filed came from individuals, and more than 60 percent of the patents granted domestically went to individuals.
- While the above patterns were fairly steady during the 1990s, China's patented innovations have improved in recent years with a bigger proportion of major innovations (invention patents).

Given the above patterns, one might be tempted to think that the dominant position of the individual inventors may simply reflect the low quality of R&D projects undertaken by these individual inventors. This, however, is not necessarily the case.

As Figure 3.5 shows, individuals supplied over 60 percent of the patent applications for invention patents (major innovations) throughout the 1990s until 2000 when their share dropped to 50 percent and dropped further to 36.5 percent in 2004. In other words, individuals are as dominant in producing major inventions as they are in accounting for the three types of patents as a whole.[7] The relative contribution of the IEs, while increasing after 1995, was consistently below 30 percent before 2000. Since 2000, IEs have become the first contributor of major innovations in 2004.

---

[7] Of course, the number of patents is a crude measure of R&D productivity as it does not fully reflect the quality and commercial value of the patents.

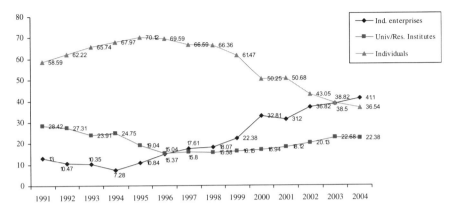

Figure 3.5: Invention Patent Applications by Types of Innovators, 1991–2004
Sources: Same as for Figure 3.1.

TECHNOLOGICAL INNOVATION BY THE LARGE- AND MEDIUM-SIZED ENTERPRISES (LMEs)

In 2004, there were a total of 27,692 large- and medium-sized enterprises in China, of which 18,791 were domestic funded (3,681 were state owned) and 4,700 were the so-called "San Zi" enterprises (wholly foreign owned, equity joint ventures and contractual joint ventures between foreign firms and Mainland Chinese firms). The rest included collectively owned and privately owned enterprises. In terms of production activity and output, the LMEs are undoubtedly the main force in China's economy today. R&D performance of the LMEs, however, is perhaps not as impressive as one would expect.

Table 3.2 contains information regarding the technological innovation of the LMEs from 1991 to 2004.

While the number of LMEs grew fairly fast during the time period, especially in the second half of the 1990s, the number of LMEs that had their own technology development research institutes actually declined, until 2003.[8] In 1991, 52.9 percent of the LMEs had

---

[8] This decline was likely due to the reorganisation and consolidation of SOEs initiated by the Central Government in the middle 1990s. While the number of LMEs was growing, certain existing firms (including their research institutes) may have merged with one another. In fact, the number of technical engineering personnel employed by the LMEs increased between 1991 and 1998.

Table 3.2: Technological Innovation by the LMEs

	1991	1992	1993	1994	1995	1996	1997	1998	1999	2000	2001	2002	2003	2004
Number of LMEs	14,935	16,991	15,000	20,162	23,026	24,061	24,024	23,577	22,276	21,776	22,904	23,096	22,276	23,267
of which having tech-institutes	7,899	8,576	9,503	8,817	9,165	8,179	7,313	7,220	7,120	6,187	6,000	5,836	6,424	6,467
S&T expenditures/ national total (%)	42.7	42.7	38.5	43.5	43.2	41.3	41.2	42.4	44.1	40.2	42.3	42.3	47.0	50.0
S&T expenditures/ sales (%)	1.39	1.37	1.26	1.34	1.19	1.15	1.21	1.28	1.35	1.65	1.67	1.73	1.52	1.49
R&D expenditure (100 million RMB)	58.6	76.1	95.2	122.0	141.7	160.5	188.3	197.1	249.9	353.6	442.3	560.2	720.8	954.4
R&D expenditure/ national total (%)	41.2	45	48.6	55	40.6	39.7	37	35.8	36.8	39.5	42.4	43.5	46.8	48.5
R&D expenditures/ sales (%)	0.49	0.50	0.50	0.51	0.46	0.30	0.52	0.53	0.60	0.71	0.76	0.83	0.75	0.71
New products/sales revenue (%)	9.9	10.5	10.7	10.2	8.50	10.0	10.0	11.7	13.2	15.3	15.0	16.1	14.6	15.1
Number of patent applications	—	—	—	—	—	4,936	5,896	6,317	7,884	11,819	15,339	21,297	31,382	42,318
Applications per firm	—	—	—	—	—	0.205	0.2454	0.268	0.354	0.543	0.670	0.922	1.409	1.819
Patent applications/ national total (%)	—	—	—	—	12.2	12.7	10.3	8.56	12.4	15.5	19.0	12.5	10.2	12.0
Buying foreign technology (100 million RMB)	90.2	116.1	159.2	266.7	360.9	322.1	236.5	412.4	207.6	245.4	285.9	372.5	405.4	368.0
R&D: buying technology	0.7:1	0.7:1	0.6:1	0.5:1	0.4:1	0.3:1	0.8:1	0.5:1	1.2:1	1.4:1	1.5:1	1.5:1	1.8:1	2.6:1
Absorbing technology (100 million RMB)	4.1	—	6.2	—	13.1	13.6	13.6	14.6	18.1	18.2	19.6	25.7	27.1	56.0
Buying tech: absorbing tech	22.0:1	—	25.7:1	—	27.5:1	23.7:1	17.4:1	28.2:1	11.5:1	13.5:1	14.6:1	14.5:1	15.0:1	6.6:1

Sources: Same as for Table 3.1.

their own technology institutes but after 2000, less than 30 percent had them. In terms of R&D intensity, though the level has improved over the past 15 years, the LMEs spent less than 1 percent of their annual revenues on R&D activities.[9]

Thus, it is not surprising that the R&D output of the LMEs was also low. In particular, in 1996 the number of patents applied per firm (for all three types of patents) was only 0.21. Though the figure improved after 1996, still only about one out of every three LMEs filed a patent during the entire year of 1999. By 2004, each LME applied for 1.82 patents, a significant increase. One way to measure the value of the R&D output of the LMEs is to look at the ratio of new product sales to the total revenues of the LMEs. As can be seen from Table 3.2, about 10 percent of the LMEs' revenues were derived from new products sales from 1991 to 1997. The ratio exceeded 15 percent in 2000.

It has been claimed that Chinese enterprises are much more willing to purchase technologies from abroad (technology introduction) than to innovate on their own. This claim is certainly supported by the 1990s data in Table 3.2. Specifically, in all but the late 1990s, the LMEs spent more money buying technologies from abroad than on developing their own R&D activities. The ratio of expenditures on R&D to that of introducing technologies from abroad was 0.65:1 in 1991. What is more striking is that this ratio declined throughout the first half of the decade and bottomed out at 0.31:1 in 1996 before climbing in 1997. The year 1999 was the first time that the LMEs spent more on their own R&D than on purchasing foreign technologies.[10] By 2004, the LMEs spent 2.6 times as much on R&D as they did on buying foreign technologies.

---

[9] Historically, the Chinese Government also publishes data on science and technical (S&T) expenditures which are broader than what R&D expenditures cover.

[10] However, the figure for 1999 may not be comparable with those in the previous years due to institutional changes in China. In 1999, about 242 research institutes formerly relating to Government ministries or provinces were spun off to merge with existing enterprises or become independent entities as part of China's efforts to transform its centrally planned research institute system into a market-oriented one. R&D expenditures for those research institutes were not included in the figures for the LMEs for the years prior to 1999.

Chinese firms are trying to buy less technology and do more of their own innovation, but their innovation performance is still at a relatively low level. Table 3.2 also reveals that the relative contribution of the LMEs to the national innovative activity has not risen much over the past one-and-a-half decades. In particular, while investing more of their annual sale revenues on scientific and technical development (and on R&D), the LMEs' contribution to the nation's total expenditures has remained fairly steady at about 45 percent. In terms of the R&D output, however, the share of the LMEs' patent applications (invention, utility model and external design) has increased from 12.2 percent in 1996 to 19.0 percent in 2001, but dropped to 12 percent in 2004.

Year 2000 seems to have been a special year for Chinese LMEs. Most of the indicators in Table 3.2 showed great improvement in 2000. This may have been due to the anticipation of China's entry to the WTO in December 2001, i.e., the Government efforts to improve technological levels and the performance of China's large enterprises, especially state-owned enterprises (SOEs).

R&D INCENTIVE AND INDUSTRIAL STRUCTURE

The Schumpeterian View

The degree of horizontal concentration is a measure of how intense competition is in a given industry. The conventional wisdom (or the Schumpeterian view) is that firms in more concentrated industries are more likely to conduct R&D because the not-so-severe competition in the product market guarantees an attractive return on R&D investments.[11] Arguments in support of the Schumpeterian view also include the following: (1) large companies have the resources needed to undertake innovation projects (the "deep pocket" argument); (2) with large research teams, big firms can enjoy economies of scale in

---

[11] Schumpeter (1950) initiated modern research concerning the effects of market structure on innovation by stressing the role of large companies in R&D activity. See Joseph Schumpeter, *Capitalism, Socialism, and Democracy*, 3rd edn. (New York: Harper & Row, 1950).

knowledge production; (3) being more diversified, larger companies are more able to absorb the risks of R&D; (4) the R&D output in one business line of a giant company can be used in other lines of its business; and (5) large companies often have a longer time horizon, which is particularly important for undertaking R&D projects.

Different from, but not contrary to, the Schumpeterian view is the view that a firm's incentive to innovate depends on the types of R&D projects to be conducted. For drastic innovations (those that can drive competitors out of business), smaller firms (or firms in industries with a lower degree of concentration) tend to have a stronger incentive to innovate. This is because the lower the degree of concentration, the lower the current profits of each firm and thus the greater the gain from innovation.[12]

Low Degree of Industrial Concentration in China

The Chinese Government does not systematically publish the data on the degree of concentration of its industries. Table 3.3 contains some information about the eight-firm concentration ratios (CR8) in two-digit Chinese manufacturing industries in 1995 and 2000, respectively. As can be seen, the Chinese manufacturing industries generally have a low degree of concentration. In 1995, for example, no two-digit manufacturing sector had a CR8 ratio above 50 percent; only four sectors had a CR8 ratio exceeding 30 percent. The CR8 ratios were below 20 percent for most of the manufacturing sectors. Consistent with Schumpeter's hypothesis, the R&D expenditures of Chinese firms were very low as a percentage of their annual sale revenues in 1995, with no single industry investing more than 1 percent and most investing less than 0.5 percent of their annual sales in R&D activity.

A primary reason for a low degree of concentration is regional competition and the regional protectionism that has accompanied

---

[12] On the other hand, for incremental (or non-drastic) innovations, the larger the number of firms in the industry, the lower the profit post-innovation and hence the less attractive the R&D projects to a given firm. Thus, consistent with the conventional view, for incremental innovations the incentive to innovate is negatively related to the degree of competition in an industry.

Table 3.3: Eight-Firm Concentration Ratio and R&D Intensity in Chinese
Manufacturing (percent)

Industry	1995		2000	
	CR8	R&D/Sale	CR8	R&D/Sale
Food processing	5.28	0.04	7.51	0.10
Food production	9.91	0.07	13.10	0.19
Beverage production	8.64	0.13	20.39	0.30
Tobacco processing	32.97	0.12	54.01	0.11
Textiles	2.77	0.12	6.59	0.19
Garments and fibre products	3.76	0.08	9.30	0.06
Leather, furs and related products	2.94	0.15	n.a.	0.06
Timber and straw products	5.73	0.06	n.a.	0.10
Furniture manufacturing	5.36	0.04	n.a.	0.06
Paper making and paper products	5.34	0.22	10.90	0.26
Printing and record medium products	5.11	0.09	n.a.	0.22
Educational and sports products	8.06	0.02	n.a.	0.15
Petroleum processing and coking	44.85	0.19	82.84	0.16
Chemical materials and products	11.26	0.35	7.94	0.55
Pharmaceutical products	11.77	0.77	28.81	1.12
Chemical fibres	37.60	0.12	13.83	0.42
Rubber products	18.27	0.61	36.40	0.42
Plastic products	3.64	0.27	6.02	0.33
Nonmetal mineral products	2.44	0.28	6.13	0.29
Ferrous metals processing	30.16	0.17	39.51	0.29
Nonferrous metals processing	13.31	0.20	10.32	0.38
Metals products	4.64	0.25	9.48	0.33
Ordinary machinery	6.52	0.62	9.90	0.76
Equipment for special purposes	6.18	0.60	11.65	0.95
Transportation equipment	20.86	0.55	28.92	0.75
Electric equipment and machinery	8.80	0.37	30.75	0.68
Electronic and telecommunications equipment	14.65	0.38	23.07	1.18

Note: The CR8 for 2000 were calculated from the *China Large Enterprises Groups Yearbook*, 2001, for sales exceeding RMB500 million. The CR8 for 1995 were calculated from the *China Large and Medium-sized Enterprises Yearbook*, 1996. The R&D data for 1995 are from China's Third Industrial Census and that for 2000 are from R&D Census Data 2000.

China's opening up in the past two decades. With huge amounts of foreign capital flowing in, regional (provincial and municipal) governments have had strong economic and political incentives to compete for foreign capital. Various preferential policies (tax holidays, land support, etc.) were offered by various regions in order to attract foreign investors. As a result, a larger number of firms have been established in almost all industries, many of which operate below their efficient scale. For instance, the total market share of the top 300 companies in the machinery industry in China was only 30 percent in 1998.[13]

In the second half of the 1990s, the Chinese Government encouraged mergers and acquisitions with the ambition of establishing Korea-type large-scale companies, and allowed the exit of firms unable to compete with more efficient firms.[14] This has caused the degree of industrial concentration to rise rapidly. By 2000, the CR8 ratio exceeded 30 percent in several Chinese manufacturing industries (and 80 percent for petroleum processing and coking). This concentration ratio increased significantly for many industries, and for some industries even doubled within five years' time. There was also a significant increase in R&D intensity during that period. In 2000, the R&D/sale ratio exceeded 1 percent for electronic and telecommunications equipment and pharmaceuticals, and was much higher for most industries compared to 1995. While still low in absolute terms, the substantial increase in R&D investment by Chinese firms is a result, on the one hand, of the Government's efforts to encourage innovation, and the rise in industrial concentration on the other, as suggested by Schumpeter's hypothesis.

Availability of Foreign Technologies and Strategic Considerations

One feature of the Chinese economy today is the persistently high availability of foreign technologies ready to be imported as

---

[13] Chinese Academy of Social Sciences, *Report on China's Industrial Development* (Beijing: Zhigong Press, 1999).

[14] See P. Lin, "Merger Control in China," in *New Development in Competition Law under Globalization* (in Chinese), *China Forum on the Rule of Law Series*, ed. X. Y. Wang (Beijing: Social Sciences Academic Press, 2005), 25–38.

multinational companies all try to enter the China market. In fact the Government, on many occasions, has required technological licensing as a precondition for foreign firms to enter China's market. This abundant supply of foreign technologies has shifted the trade-off between buying technology and innovating on one's own in favour of the purchasing option. Relative to innovating on one's own, purchasing technology is less risky and the returns can be realised quickly. Because of this, a "crowding out effect" may exist in China: importing foreign technologies has "squeezed out" domestic innovation projects. The propensity to purchase foreign technologies is thus very high for Chinese firms. If all rival firms choose to buy technologies, it does not make sense for a firm to conduct its own R&D projects because these often take a long time to finish. Undertaking independent R&D projects would likely mean a loss of market share to rival firms in the short run. Therefore, the corresponding Nash equilibrium is that all firms choose to buy technologies. According to a recent survey of the automobile industry, purchasing equipment was ranked as *the* most important channel of obtaining advanced technology.[15]

TECHNOLOGY TRANSFER TO CHINA

There are five different ways to transfer foreign technologies to China: (1) technology transactions under which foreign patent holders sell their patent rights to Chinese manufactures; (2) technology licensing whereby foreign patent holders grant permission to Chinese firms to use their patented technology by paying a fee; (3) joint venture technology licensing; (4) purchasing equipment

---

[15] The survey covered a range of 131 auto/auto part makers in China. Besides purchasing equipment, other means to acquire technology included, in order of importance, exchange with other enterprises, purchase of patents and contract R&D. For further details, see N. Zhang, "On the Technological Development System of China's Automobile Industry," *Science and Technology Management* 3 (1998): 49–54.

(complete set or key equipment) in which foreign technologies are embodied; and (5) co-production. The first three are related to direct knowledge transfer, while the last two are related to the so-called hardware transfer.

From Table 3.4, one can see that purchasing equipment was the dominant means of acquiring foreign technology from 1991 to 1998, accounting for over 80 percent of the total value of imported technology each year except in 1992 and 1998. As some observers have pointed out, technology transfer to China in the 1990s was largely in the form of hardware transfer, rather than direct transfer of knowledge (in the form of technology licensing or technology transactions). Some have blamed the foreign suppliers for this imbalance, saying they have been unwilling to transfer technologies in such a way that make it easier for the Chinese counterparts to catch up with them. Others have blamed the Chinese buyers for putting too much emphasis on purchasing ready-to-use equipment, rather than on the "basic knowledge" behind them. Since 1999, the share of purchasing equipment has rapidly declined to less than 40 percent.[16]

Another important way of transferring technology, especially high technology, is high-tech product imports. From 1991 to 2004, high-tech product imports accounted for an increasing share of the total product imports, moving from 14.8 percent in 1991, to 20.8 percent in 1998 and over 28 percent in 2004.

However, as shown in Table 3.4, trade in high-tech products has been making a negative contribution to the overall balance of trade during the last 15 years. In contrast, manufactured goods in total have made a positive contribution to the overall balance of trade during the same period. In other words, China's overall positive balance of trade is attributed to the positive contribution of lower technology-intensive manufactured products rather than high-tech products.

---

[16] This is partially due to the change in indicators of technology transfer statistics. For example, the relevant statistics before 2000 did not cover patent technology licensing and transactions computer software transfers and trademark licensing.

Table 3.4: Technology Imports (US$100 Million)

	1991	1992	1993	1994	1995	1996	1997	1998	1999	2000	2001	2002	2003	2004
High-tech product imports	94.4	107.1	159.1	206.0	218.3	224.7	238.9	292.0	376.0	525.1	641.1	828.4	1,193.0	1,613.4
As % of total imports (%)	14.8	13.3	15.3	17.8	16.5	16.2	16.8	20.8	22.7	23.3	26.3	28.1	28.9	28.7
Balance	−65.6	−67.2	−112.3	−142.5	−117.4	−98.1	−75.8	−89.5	−128.9	−154.6	−176.6	−149.8	−89.8	40.2
Balance of manufactured products	27.4	6.1	−146.7	21.7	196.3	157.3	450.9	459.3	361.4	453.9	419.5	511.6	634.2	1088.2
Technology imports														
Total	34.6	65.9	61.1	41.1	130.3	152.6	159.2	163.7	171.6	181.7	90.9	173.9	134.5	138.6
Technology licensing and transaction	4.8	6.0	4.5	3.9	14.7	16.8	17.1	37.1	47.5	—	17.6	107.5	57.6	51.6
As percentage of total	13.82	9.16	7.34	9.50	11.31	10.98	10.76	22.64	27.67	—	19.35	61.79	42.81	37.22
Equipment	29.0	47.0	53.8	36.2	112.5	124.4	136.8	112.4	69.3	—	33.6	18.5	29.7	37.8
As percentage of total	83.94	71.33	87.99	88.29	86.30	81.52	85.93	68.64	40.34	—	56.94	10.66	22.05	27.31

Sources: Same as for Table 3.1.

The high-tech product balance (import/export) represents the impact of national innovation capabilities and efforts on a nation's technology change and economic base.[17] The analyses of China's technology transfer and high-technology products presented above suggest that China still needs to expend much effort to become true innovators, especially in the high-tech area, and to benefit from the large amount of investment in the development of more technology-incentive innovation resources and capabilities.

Sources of Technology Transfer to China

The data presented in Table 3.5 show that throughout the last 15 years, Japan, the US and Germany were consistently the top three technology suppliers to China, accounting for around 50 percent of the total import value.

During the first half of the 1990s, Japan was the biggest supplier, followed by the US and Germany, whereas in the second half Japan fell to third place, with the US taking the lead. A major reason for the decline in Japan's ranking was the negative impact of the Asian Financial Crisis on Japan's economy which inevitably affected its FDI to China and also to the region as a whole. This negative effect is reflected in the decline in the total volume of Japan's technology exports to China.

---

[17] J. L. Furman, M. E. Porter and S. Stern, "The Determinants of National Innovative Capacity," *Research Policy* 31 (2002): 899–933; H. Grupp, S. Maital, A. Frenkel and K. Koschatzky, "A Data Envelopment Model to Compare Technological Excellence and Export Sales in Israel and European Community Countries," *Research Evaluation* 2 (1992): 87–101; S. Maital, A. Frenkel, H. Grupp and K. Kochatzky, "Relation between Scientific and Technological Excellence and Export Performance: Theoretical Model and Empirical Test for EC Countries," *Science and Public Policy* (June 1994): 138–146; W. Nasierowski and F. J. Arcelus, "Interrelationships among the Elements of National Innovation Systems: A Statistical Evaluation," *European Journal of Operational Research* 119 (1999): 235–253; E. B. Viotti, "National Learning Systems: A New Approach on Technological Change in Late Industrializing Economies and Evidences from the Cases of Brazil and South Korea," *Technological Forecasting and Social Change* 69 (2002): 653–680.

Table 3.5: Technology Exports to China by Country (US$10,000)

	1991	1992	1993	1994	1995	1996	1997	1998	1999	2000	2001	2002	2003	2004
Total	345,953	658,988	610,943	410,575	1,303,264	1,525,700	1,592,312	1,637,510	1,716,221	1,817,596	909 090	1,738,920	1,345,121	1,385,558
Japan	26,928	13,7606	174,557	76,911	224,862	240,400	339,058	208,831	194,399	337,771	112 935	298,031	351,481	293,790
%	7.78	20.88	28.57	18.73	17.25	15.76	21.29	12.75	11.33	18.58	12.42	17.14	26.13	21.20
US	13,509	143,164	50,654	59,406	227,187	213,000	181,627	300,030	334,154	316,266	181,532	700,985	326,555	292,109
%	3.90	21.72	8.29	14.47	17.43	13.96	11.41	18.32	19.47	17.40	19.97	40.31	24.28	21.08
Germany	26,486	73,260	74,789	123,199	189,207	490,700	158,431	235,117	274,956	279,807	182,542	153,387	113,578	219,307
%	7.66	11.12	12.24	30.01	14.52	32.16	9.95	14.36	16.02	15.39	20.08	8.82	8.44	15.83
France	19,359	38,274	17,510	19,488	170,573	61,400	66,701	76,199	80,771	65,649	104,353	42,349	42,881	129,214
%	5.60	5.81	2.87	4.75	13.09	4.02	4.19	4.65	4.71	3.61	11.48	2.44	3.19	9.33
Russia	137,355	24,535	38,270	356	75,899	117,700	107,754	192,147	7,836	35,916	1,176	2,536	2,373	2,129
%	39.70	3.72	6.26	0.09	5.82	7.71	6.77	11.73	0.46	1.98	0.13	0.15	0.18	0.15
Sweden	1,790	996	1130	10,515	21,038	32,600	65,285	92,657	227,170	135,308	70,C40	96,348	10,203	53,445
%	0.52	0.15	0.18	2.56	1.61	2.14	4.10	5.66	13.24	7.44	7.70	5.54	0.76	3.86
South Korea		1,703	30,430	8,376	10,264	15,000	86,635	27,158	78,794	57,798	21,588	96,449	141,127	80,726
%		0.26	4.98	2.04	0.79	0.98	5.44	1.66	4.59	3.18	2.37	5.55	10.49	5.83
Hong Kong	1,997	7,564	4,170	13,418	58,648	92,200	53,244	74,641	90,724	124,178	55,778	59,784	51,468	67,755
%	0.58	1.15	0.68	3.27	4.50	6.04	3.34	4.56	5.29	6.83	6.14	3.44	3.38	4.89
Others														
%	34.26	35.19	35.92	24.09	24.98	17.22	33.51	26.30	24.90	25.58	19.71	16.62	22.71	17.83

Sources: Same as for Table 3.1.

WTO REQUIREMENTS FOR IPR AND TECHNOLOGY TRANSFER

WTO general agreements, such as the Agreement on Trade Related Investment Measures (TRIMs) and the Agreement on Trade Related Intellectual Property Rights (TRIPS), must be observed by all member countries of the WTO.

The TRIPS

The TRIPS Agreement, which came into effect on January 1, 1995, is to date the most comprehensive multinational agreement on intellectual property. As in the General Agreement on Tariffs and Trade and the General Agreement on Trade in Services, the starting point is the two basic principles: national treatment (treating foreigners and one's own nationals equally) and most-favoured-nation treatment (equal treatment for nationals of all trading partners in the WTO).[18]

The TRIPS Agreement has three main features: standards, enforcement and dispute settlement. The agreement sets out the minimum standards of protection to be provided by each member country for each category of intellectual property including copyrights, patents, trademarks, geographical indications,[19] industrial designs and the layout design of integrated circuits. For patents, in particular, the TRIPS agreement requires member countries to make patents available for any invention, whether products or processes, in all fields of technology without discrimination, subject to the normal texts of novelty, inventiveness and industrial applicability. The protection duration for patents should be at least 20 years counted from the filing date (Article 33). The protection period for industrial designs is at least 10 years (Article 16.3).

---

[18] National treatment is also a key principle in other intellectual agreements outside the WTO.

[19] A geographical indication is a name or sign used on certain products which corresponds to a specific geographical location or origin (e.g., a town, region or country). The use of a geographical indication may act as a certification that the product possesses certain qualities or enjoys a certain reputation due to its geographical origin.

When the WTO agreement took effect in 1995, developed countries were given one year to ensure that their laws and practices confirmed with the TRIPS Agreement. Developing countries were given five years while the least developed countries have 11 years.

Second, the TRIPS agreement requires that member countries have to ensure that IPRs can be enforced under their laws and that the penalties for infringement be tough enough to deter further violations. The procedure must be fair and equitable, and not unnecessarily complicated or costly. People involved should be able either to ask a court to review administrative decisions on their cases or to appeal to a lower court's ruling.

Third, the TRIPS agreement makes IPR-related disputes between the WTO members subject to the WTO's dispute settlement procedures.

The TRIMS

The Agreement on Trade Related Investment Measures (TRIMS), negotiated in the Uruguay Round, prohibits measures that are inconsistent with the national treatment principle or involve the use of quantitative restrictions. The TRIMS not allowed include local content, trade-balancing, foreign exchange-balancing and domestic sale requirements. The Agreement requires that all policies not in conformity with it be eliminated within two, five or seven years, for developed, developing and least developed countries, respectively.

No More "Force-Technology Transfer"

For many years, the Chinese Government imposed local content requirements on inward foreign investment in many industries, most notably the automobile industry and on electronics products as a means to encourage technology transfer and expand the benefit of FDI to domestic upstream suppliers.

Various laws and regulations have required technology transfer from foreign companies. China's FDI and industrial policies have frequently included explicit provisions for technology transfer in the form of local content requirements, production export quotas and/or collaboration in production, research or training. There have been reports over the past several years of some foreign companies being "forced" to transfer technology to China in exchange for access to its enormous market.[20] A recent survey of some EU firms revealed that 46 percent of the technology transfers to China by these EU firms were the result of Government policies and regulations requiring local sources and/or technology transfer.[21]

China had agreed to eliminate local content requirements immediately after it acceded to the WTO and not to enforce provisions in existing contracts that imposed this requirement. It had also agreed to eliminate technology transfer requirements as a condition for investment approval.[22] Inward FDI is no longer conditioned on conducting R&D in China.

With China's accession to the WTO, existing barriers to foreign investments are to be removed. For example, in the bilateral agreement between China and the US, China agreed not to make conditions with respect to foreign investment, import approvals on technology transfer or on conducting R&D in China. It also agreed that any prerequisites for investment approval or importation, and the terms and conditions of any transfer of technology would be settled between the parties in a contract and not be imposed by the Government. China also agreed to eliminate requirements mandating that the Chinese partners in a joint venture gain ownership of trade

---

[20] See "US Commercial Technology Transfers to the PRC," a research report by the US Bureau of Export Administration and the Office of Strategic Industries and Economic Security, 1999.

[21] D. Bennett, X. Liu, D. Parker, F. Steward and K. Vaidya, "Technology Transfer to China: A Study of Strategy in 20 EU Industrial Countries," Aston Business School, Aston University, 2000.

[22] China also agreed to eliminate other TRIMs not directly related to IPRs, such as export performance requirements and foreign exchange- and trade-balancing requirements.

secrets after a certain number of years.[23] Local content requirements are not permitted under the TRIMs. With these changes, Chinese enterprises will lose an important channel for obtaining foreign technologies, namely the "forced technology transfer".

However, it would be wrong to draw the conclusion that China's entry into the WTO hampers technology transfer to China. There are positive forces that work to facilitate technology transfer to China. Firstly, without doubt, the enforcement of the IPR laws is greatly improving with entry into the WTO. The government has a stronger incentive to strengthen IPR law enforcement, because, on the one hand, its credibility is at stake and, on the other, violations are subject to the dispute settlement mechanisms of the WTO. Improved law enforcement reduces the risk of transferring advanced technologies to China.

Secondly, with accession to the WTO and the removal of various trade and investment barriers, foreign firms enjoy a freer and wider range of business opportunities in China. This certainly increases the benefit of transferring technology. For example, China has become an increasingly attractive place for multinational corporations to establish R&D centres. By 2000, about 60 foreign companies had established such centres in China, and by 2004, 700.[24]

Thirdly, there is also a competition-induced incentive for technology transfer and FDI. In addition to being required by government regulations, technology transfer to China in the past was also motivated by normal business considerations such as market expansion or responses to pressures from rival firms. According to an EU survey, when asked what were the reasons for technology transfer to China, 80 percent of the companies cited market access, 57 percent cited cost advantage, 48 percent cited "part of company globalisation strategy" and 33 percent cited response to competitors'

---

[23] See the sector papers by the Washington Council on International Trade at http://www.wcit.org/topics/china/chi_intro.htm (April 2, 2007).

[24] Ministry of Commerce, *2005 Report of Transnational Corporations in China* (Beijing: China Economic Publishing House, 2005).

moves (actual or potential).[25] These factors, especially the last, competition-induced factor, will continue to be the main motivations for foreign technology transfer to China.

With free entry to the China market, more foreign investors and capital will come. As competition intensifies, foreign investors will face stronger market pressure to transfer advanced technologies. This will increase the quality of technology transfer to China. In addition to bringing in a larger number of and more advanced technologies to China, foreign companies may find it more necessary to set up their own research centres within the country, as has been taking place in recent years in order for them to be able to more closely follow the market situations and increase their advantage over their competitors.

There is another interesting channel for technology transfer to China, namely overseas acquisition of advanced technology by the emerging Chinese multinationals. As competition in the domestic markets intensifies, some Chinese firms have begun to seek strategic assets outside in order to strengthen their competitiveness both in and outside China's markets. Such competition-driven importation of technology to China is reflected in Lenovo's acquisition of IBM's PC production line and TCL's acquisition of RCA and Thomson brands.[26]

Finally, technology transfer and FDI to China in the past two decades have significantly helped improve the technology and innovation base of Chinese industries. The economy is at a much more advanced stage than before. Domestic suppliers are now capable of producing higher quality products, and customers are more sophisticated. These will raise the standard for and increase the benefits of technology transfer and FDI to China.

---

[25] D. Bennett *et al.*, "Technology Transfer to China: A Study of Strategy in 20 EU Industrial Countries."

[26] For more discussion on the strategic asset seeking motive of Chinese multinationals, see K. Y. Edward Chen and P. Lin, "Emerging Chinese Multinational Corporations," mimeo, Lingnan University, 2006.

R&D Induced by Industry Structural Changes

Increased competition will further erode the profitability of many already struggling Chinese firms. In the short run, Chinese industries will become less concentrated as new firms enter. If the positive relationship between industrial concentration and incentive for R&D really holds in China, one would expect the R&D incentive to drop following China's entry to the WTO. However, there have been noticeable signs of consolidation among Chinese industries. For example, there have been merger frenzies within the automobile and electronic appliance industries since early 2000. Mergers and acquisitions will help firms realise economies of scale in R&D activity, enabling them to more effectively absorb foreign technologies. The increasing degree of concentration will also promote innovation.[27]

Industrial Policy-Based Approach vs. Market Failure-Based Approach

Over the past two decades, China's policy on science and technology, technology transfer and innovation has been dominated by the logic of industrial policy. The Government has regarded its innovation policy as a means to direct and guide resources, and especially FDI, towards pillar industries. Huge amounts of resources have been invested directly in selected industries (for example, the information industry, computer sciences, new materials, aerospace, etc.),[28] to designated projects (such as the "863" and "973" Programme),[29] and to

---

[27] For an analysis of recent merger and acquisition activities in China, see P. Lin, "Merger Control in China."

[28] See *The Decisions Regarding Enhancing Innovation, Developing High-Tech Industries, and Commercialization of Technology Discoveries*, The Central Committee of China's Communist Party and the State Council, 1999.

[29] In March 1986, the National High-Tech Research and Development Programme (863 Programme) was launched, after exhaustive examination by scientists. The Programme set 20 themes in biology, spaceflight, information, laser, automation, energy, new materials and oceanography. The Government's role is one of

the establishment of "Science Parks" at both the state and the provincial levels. With respect to foreign investment, China's policies are explicit in the types of investment "prohibited", "permitted" or "encouraged" with the last category focusing on advanced technologies. Foreign investors in high-tech industries are given preferential treatment, such as tax rebates and lower tariff rates as incentive to transfer technology.

Government support to industrial innovation, based instead on the grounds of market failure associated with R&D activity, is entirely justified by economic theory and fully consistent with fair and efficient competition. Modern economics informs us that there exist systematic barriers in a free market system to innovative activities. In particular, innovation suffers from the so-called "appropriability problem". This refers to fact that innovators in general are not able to capture the entire benefit of their R&D investments.

The invention of new products or processes results in a greater consumer surplus which is not captured by the inventor. Also, the innovation may also benefit the inventor's competitors through knowledge spillovers. Unable to capture the entire benefits of their investments, but yet having to bear all the risks involved, private firms may invest less in R&D compared to the social optimum. Government support, in the form of R&D subsidies or tax credits for

---

macro-control and support. The general research is decided on by scientific discussion, and specific projects are determined by a committee of experts responsible for keeping abreast of international research developments and reporting annually on their own fields so as to set new research directions. Another distinctive feature of the Programme is that its results can be quickly industrialised. As a key measure for development of basic scientific research, the 973 Programme was launched in 1998. It mainly involves multi-disciplinary, comprehensive research on important scientific issues in such fields as agriculture, energy, information, resources, population, health and materials, providing theoretical basis and scientific foundations for solving problems. The programme encourages outstanding scientists to carry out key research in cutting-edge science and important sci-tech issues in fields with a major bearing on socio-economic development. Representing China's national goals, it aims to provide strong scientific and technological support for significant issues in China's 21st century socio-economic development.

example, can enhance firms' R&D incentive and thus help overcome the "appropriability problem". Other means of promoting R&D include allowing firms to set up R&D joint ventures, strengthening patent protection, etc.

This market failure-based approach towards promoting innovation has been actively pursued by almost all developed countries within the WTO rules.[30] China must abandon the traditional industrial policy approach to both designing and implementing its national innovation policy and upgrade it to one based on market failure considerations. Under WTO rules, the Government can still support industrial R&D, but not by selecting specific sectors and not just the projects of domestic firms. Rather, market forces should guide resource allocation towards the industries needing R&D investment the most, with the Government role solely being to correct R&D market failures instead of selecting the "leading sectors for the future". All firms operated in China should be treated equally in seeking Government funding. R&D joint ventures or strategic alliances should be encouraged, regardless of the nationality of the participants. The Government can play an important role in facilitating the "cluster effect" of innovation by providing quality infrastructure and coordinating the locations of firms' research activities. Government procurement, whereby the Government purchases certain newly invented products as a means to boost demand and lower the market risk of innovation, is still allowed under the WTO as long as the selection procedure obeys the principles of "national treatment".

CONCLUDING REMARKS

China's establishing of a modern patent system in 20 years is a remarkable achievement. However, a patent system itself, though necessary, is not sufficient for enterprises to undertake innovation

---

[30] R&D subsidisation is permitted under the WTO's Agreement on Subsidies and Countervailing Measures, up to a maximum of 75 percent of the costs of industrial research and up to 50 percent of "pre-competitive development activity" (Article 8.2.a).

activity. China's innovation activity in recent years has been primarily on a small scale, aimed at small R&D projects (utility models and external designs, as opposed to inventions). Industrial enterprises have not yet become the main force of innovation. Even when they are equipped with technology purchased from abroad, Chinese firms must develop the capability to innovate on their own in order to compete successfully in the world's markets. There are yet to be any indications of this happening persistently and on a reasonable scale in China.

China must now obey WTO rules. One immediate consequence of this is that forced technology transfer, which had been such an effective means for China to obtain advanced technologies from abroad in the past, is no longer feasible. This certainly tends to lower the supply of technology. On the other hand, accession to the WTO is bringing abundant business opportunities, including technology transfer. A rule-based business environment, an improved IPR protection system and a more level playing field for international competitors, in particular, is greatly stimulating FDI to China and trade flows with the rest of the world. Promising business perspectives will increase foreign investors' "stand-alone" incentive for technology transfer by making it more attractive. At the same time, and perhaps more importantly, increased competition will also raise the need for foreign firms to transfer better technologies so as to secure their market advantage and induce Chinese firms to seek advanced technologies abroad. In fact, the strategic-asset-seeking motive is a major push factor for emerging Chinese multinational corporations to go abroad.[31]

The Chinese Government should abandon its long-time industrial policy-based innovation and technology policy and instead adopt market failure-based polices. Consistent with the WTO rule of free and fair competition, the Government has an important role to play in overcoming the "appropriability problem" associated with innovation activity, by means of R&D subsidies, coordinating and facilitating R&D cooperation and alliances among firms, whether

---

[31] K. Y. Edward Chen and P. Lin, "Emerging Chinese Multinational Corporations."

they are Chinese or foreign, and by designing sensible regional poli-cies so as to promote the "clustering effect" of R&D. With China's accession to the WTO, R&D activity and technology transfer to China is increasingly being guided by the invisible hand, rather than by the visible hand, perhaps in a more effective way.

Standards and the State: Chinese Technology Policy in an Age of Globalisation

Richard P. Suttmeier and Xiangkui Yao

As China's economy has grown and become more technologically complex, the nature of Chinese industrial policy has become a matter of widespread international interest. With China's accession to the WTO, the crafting of industrial policy has had to find a middle ground between adherence to WTO norms and the introduction of measures to enhance Chinese competitiveness and ability to move up the international value chain. The search for this middle ground has inevitably called attention — both within China and in the international community — to the proper role of government in the Chinese economy.

The state's involvement in the economy is, of course, complicated by 25 years of reform experience designed to redefine that involvement and by Chinese aspirations to move the economy to higher levels of value added production through programmes to encourage technological innovation. A strong government commitment to technological development in support of industrial strength encourages views of the Chinese state as highly techno-nationalist. On the other hand, the complex patterns of relationships with foreign technology and international innovation systems constrain government action and suggest that China's technological development experience might be more aptly described as techno-globalist. In this view, government is seen as increasingly ceding responsibilities for the technological development of the economy to market-driven enterprises involved in global business transactions.

China's efforts to promote its own technical standards provide an especially interesting case for exploring this techno-nationalist/techno-globalist tension, and more generally, the role of the state in industrial development in the post WTO era.[1] China's interest in standards is driven by a need to modernise the Chinese domestic standards regime and bring it into conformity with China's WTO obligations, while at the same time, utilising China's growing technological capabilities and market power to develop technical standards that will enhance the competitiveness of Chinese firms. Given the growing importance of standards in the international economy as well as China's rapid emergence as a major player in the world's economic activities, these standardisation initiatives have attracted considerable international attention both from foreign companies operating in China and from foreign governments: Chinese standard setting efforts have the potential to shape the direction of technological development in the Chinese domestic market and to influence the acceptability of Chinese goods abroad.

As China seeks to increase the relative gains that the nation receives from its participation in the international economy, Beijing has attempted to craft an ambitious national technology policy that features expanded commitments to domestic research and development and the use of measures to capture value from successful R&D

---

[1] For an expanded discussion, see Richard P. Suttmeier, Xiangkui Yao and Alex Zixiang Tan, *Standards of Power? Technology, Institutions, and Politics in the Development of China's National Standards Strategy* (Seattle: National Bureau of Asian Research, 2006).

through the building of a Chinese intellectual property (IP) portfolio and the incorporation of Chinese IP into Chinese-developed standards. Foreign corporations and governments have been concerned that these policy initiatives could be implemented in ways which would produce barriers to trade and investment, leading ultimately to Chinese standards that are incompatible both with international standards and with the principles of interoperability upon which the global economy depends. With the stakes so high, the role of the state in standards development has become a matter of considerable international policy importance.

A DRIFT TOWARDS TECHNO-NATIONALISM?

In November 2003, Beijing announced that China's indigenously developed encryption standard for wireless communication was being adopted as a "national standard" and that, in the future, all wireless devices sold in China would have to adhere to it. This WLAN Authentication and Privacy Infrastructure (WAPI) standard was reportedly developed to overcome known security problems with the existing, widely used 802.11x "wi-fi" standard developed by the Institute of Electrical and Electronics Engineers (IEEE).[2] Beijing announced that the technology supporting the standard was to be protected and made available only to a limited number of Chinese companies. Gaining access to the technology, which would be necessary for meeting the standard, would not only require that foreign firms partner with Chinese firms but would also increase the chances that valuable intellectual property would diffuse to the Chinese partners. This important Chinese initiative to promote national standards therefore created deep concern — which rapidly escalated into alarm — among foreign companies

---

[2] This discussion of WAPI is drawn from Ping Gao, "Elements Influencing Standardisation in Developing Countries: A Case of Wireless Security Standard Disputes," *SIIT2005 Proceedings* (September 2005): 115–124; and Scott Kennedy, "The Political Economy of Standards Coalitions: Explaining China's Involvement in High-Tech Standards Wars," *Asia Policy* 2 (July 2006): 42–62.

and foreign governments that China seemed to be using standards as a form of protectionism in violation of the terms of the Technical Barriers to Trade (TBT) provisions of the WTO. The dispute over WAPI has led to mistrust and ill will between segments of the Chinese and foreign information technology communities — feelings that are yet to dissipate.

The WAPI story illustrates the importance of standards in the international economy and how what had once seemed like an obscure technical matter can become a high-level diplomatic issue relevant to China's rise as a great trading nation. As the saga unfolded, the high technology community in the United States, aided by the Department of Commerce and the US Trade Representative, made extraordinary efforts to reverse Chinese policy both through representations with the Chinese government and by enlisting Cabinet-level political support to pressure Beijing to recon-sider the Chinese position. The US side seemed to have succeeded in this endeavour when, in April 2004 at the meeting of the US–China Joint Commission on Commerce and Trade, State Counsellor Wu Yi announced that China would suspend the requirement that the WAPI standard be met.[3]

The story did not end with the Wu Yi announcement, however. Instead, the forces supporting WAPI within China revised their approach and sought to advance the cause of the standard through more established international standard-setting procedures. Advocates of this new tact have been frustrated and disappointed, however. A revised version of WAPI was to be discussed in December 2004 at a meeting of the Joint Technical Committee, Subcommittee 6, of the International Organisation for Standardisation and the International Electrochemical Commission (ISO/IEC JTC1 S6) in Orlando, Florida. Some of the key technical personnel from the Chinese delegation were, however, unable to get visas in time for the

---

[3] Wu Yi announced that the suspension would be indefinite, that the standard would be revised in response to comments from Chinese and foreign firms and that China would attempt to advance the standard through participation in international standards bodies. See Gao, "Wireless Security Standard Disputes," 119.

meeting. A follow-on session of ISO/IEC JTC1 S6 in February 2005 in Frankfurt, Germany ended with the Chinese delegation marching out of the meeting in anger, alleging that American companies had taken control of the agenda to promote the revised IEEE 802.11i against Chinese interests.

ISO/IEC JTC1 S6 began to formally consider WAPI in October 2005 when the standard, along with 802.11i, was placed on a ballot for approval by ISO/IEC members. During the balloting period, which ended in March 2006, voting members of ISO/IEC JTC1 S6 could choose to approve both standards, neither, WAPI only, nor 802.11i only. The six-month voting period was characterised by aggressive lobbying from both sides and by acrimonious charges levelled against the US by the Chinese.[4] In the end, 802.11i was selected by a convincing margin, thus apparently marking WAPI's defeat as an international standard. However, whether this setback marks the end of the WAPI saga remains to be seen. In December 2005, Beijing announced that WAPI-compliant devices would be given preferential consideration in government procurement and subsequently announced the formation of a new WAPI industrial alliance of Chinese companies to promote the standard.[5] WAPI's defenders in China have launched new criticisms of the process leading to the approval of 802.11i, and the defeat of the Chinese standard, and filed an appeal with ISO/IEC. The appeal was rejected, with the Chinese again walking out of the meeting at which it was being considered, and vowing to raise the matter to the diplomatic level.

---

[4] The IEEE issued a "WAPI Position Paper" in November 2005 that laid out in considerable detail an assessment of the pros and cons of the two standards. In response to this and other IEEE initiatives, the Chinese side issued an "Urgent Alert on IEEE's Recent Unethical Activities." A sub-theme amid all this acrimony was the status enjoyed by the two sides. China is represented at ISO/IEC by its "national body" the Standards Administration China (SAC), which entitles it to permanent membership ("P member") on JTC1, whereas IEEE is only a "C" liaison organisation, not having "national body" status (the US is represented at ISO and IEC by ANSI as its national body).

[5] See Joe McDonald, "China Touts Wireless Encryption Standard," *Business Week*, March 8, 2006.

The saga of WAPI has done much to focus attention on China's approach to standardisation, leading many observers to wonder whether WAPI is a harbinger of a new techno-nationalist standards strategy that is likely to lead to ongoing conflicts with the international community over standard setting.[6] WAPI, however, is not the only high-profile standards initiative to come out of China within the past five years. A review of these other cases, and the broader context in which standards initiatives are occurring, indicates that technical standard-setting for high-technology industry in China is a more complex, variegated affair than the WAPI case alone would suggest.

INNOVATION, STANDARDS AND STRATEGY

China's efforts to develop a national standards strategy should be seen in the context of the major themes of its technology policy. The current interest in standards, for example, is rooted in long-held aspirations for Chinese technology and the belief that through technological development, China can reclaim a position of wealth and power lost to technologically superior countries over the course of the past 150 years. According to this view, as a great country, China should of course have its own technical standards. Chinese technology policy, as developed over the past six years, seeks to lay the foundation for these standards, and build Chinese capabilities for indigenous innovation over the next 15 years.

Toward this end, China recently announced a new medium- and long-term plan (MLP) for scientific and technological development which covers a variety of research objectives, institutional reform measures and policy instruments intended to make China an "innovation-oriented society" by the year 2020. A central objective of the plan is the promotion of *zizhu chuangxin*, translated variously as "indigenous," "independent," or "homegrown innovation," and the development of technologies based on Chinese intellectual

---

[6] Richard P. Suttmeier and Xiangkui Yao, "China's Post-WTO Technology Policy: Standards, Software, and the Changing Nature of Techno-Nationalism," *NBR Special Report*, no. 7 (May 2004).

property and employing Chinese developed standards.[7] China's standards strategy, therefore, lies at the core of Beijing's technology policy objectives for the next 15 years.

The timing of China's emerging new technology policy is also closely related to China's anticipation of WTO membership and subsequent accession. With new WTO commitments, China faced the loss of established industrial policy tools while at the same time having to confront new foreign competition in China's more liberalised markets. WTO accession also carried an obligation both to modernise the national standards system and to attempt to harmonise this system with international practices. Standards have thus moved toward the centre of the policy agenda both as a possible WTO-compliant tool of industrial policy[8] and as a challenge to modernise and internationalise the inherited standards system.[9]

This new concern for standards is reflected in the special attention given the topic by the Ministry of Science and Technology (MOST), which has included both generous support for research on standards in its portfolio of high priority R&D projects during the 10th five-year plan period (2000–2005), the commissioning of a major national policy study on standards and the drafting of a national standards strategy under the leadership of the China National Institute of Standardisation (CNIS).[10]

---

[7] This term encompasses genuinely "original innovation" (*yuanshi chuangxin*), "integrated innovation" (*jicheng chuangxin*, or the fusing of existing technologies in new ways) and "re-innovation" (*yinjin xiaohua xishou zaichuangxin*) which involves the assimilation and improvement of imported technologies.

[8] In a 2004 draft of China's standards strategy paper, the authors discuss the need to "formulate China's own technical standards, build the technical barriers to trade that can achieve the justifiable objectives, reasonably protect the domestic market, ward off the impact of foreign products and technologies and take a critical position and initiative in international competition while abiding by the international rules." Cited in Magnus Breidne and Anders Hektor, "Standards Battle for Competition — ICT Strategies in China and Japan," unpublished paper, Swedish Institute for Growth Policy Studies, April 2006.

[9] Suttmeier and Yao, "China's Post-WTO Technology Policy."

[10] During the 10th five-year period, MOST sponsored a series of "megaprojects" in conjunction with its "863" High Technology Programme. Among the megaprojects

The strategy paper defines the responsibilities of various parties in the national standards system and lays out a series of principles and objectives for the system.[11] The complex role of the state in technology policy is evident in this architecture of jurisdictions. Standards are categorised hierarchically both by levels of responsibility and by whether the standards are voluntary or mandatory (the latter applying mainly to matters of health and safety). With regard to the former, national standards — both mandatory and voluntary — are at the top of the hierarchy and are responsible for the Standardisation Administration of China (SAC).[12] SAC serves as China's "national body" at most international standards organisations (such as the ISO and IEC) and oversees the administration of the national standards system.[13]

Industry standards (also known as "trade" standards) represent the second tier of the hierarchy. Responsibility for the development, approval and propagation of standards at this level is entrusted to relevant government bodies under the State Council and approved trade associations. The former includes industrial ministries such as

---

was a major initiative on standards titled "Key Technical Standards Project," which included R&D support for WAPI, AVS, 3G telephony, optical networks, IP technologies and other standards that have gained prominence. Reportedly, some 29 standards have resulted from this work, of which 13 have been submitted to ISO, IEC or ITU for consideration. See Breidne and Hektor, "Standards Battle for Competition." The project also included the policy study supporting the standards strategy through a project entitled "Study on the Development Strategies for China's Technical Standards." See Chaoyi Zhao, "China's Evolving Standards System: Institutions and Strategy," paper prepared for the China's High-Technology Standards Workshop, sponsored by the National Bureau of Asian Research and Tsinghua University, Beijing, January 6, 2006, 14.

[11] The discussion here is drawn from Chaoyi Zhao and John M. Graham, "The PRC's Evolving Standards System: Institutions and Strategy," *Asia Policy* 2 (July 2006): 63–87.

[12] SAC, which has vice ministerial status, is part of the Chinese General Administration of Quality Supervision Inspection and Quarantine (AQSIQ). AQSIQ emerged out of the reorganisation of China's standards system in 2001 that followed WTO accession. Suttmeier and Yao, "China's Post-WTO Technology Policy."

[13] The Ministry of Information Industry, however, represents China at the ITU.

the Ministry of Information Industry (MII), the National Development and Reform Commission (NDRC)[14] and the Commission of Science, Technology and Industry for National Defence (COSTIND).[15] By 2004, more than 37,850 industry standards had been registered with the SAC.

The third tier of the hierarchy is represented by local standards that are the responsibility of local governments. One of the objectives of China's standards strategy has been to overcome excessive diversity in local standards and harmonise these with national standards. As a result, local standards are to be superseded by national and industry standards once they are available and established. Enterprise standards constitute the fourth and bottom rung.

The operation of the standards system involves 264 technical committees and 386 subcommittees involving some 30,000 technical experts. The standards system also includes the work of more than 25 standardisation research institutes at the national level and 158 local institutes. In the field of electronics, for instance, the China Electronic Standardisation Institute (CESI) supports the industry standards work of MII. In recent years, some 12 national level and 257 local level standardisation associations have also emerged, including the China Association for Standardisation, as well as industry-focused groups such as the China Electronics Standardisation Association (CESA) and China Communications Standards Association (CCSA).[16] Thus, the evolving Chinese standards system is usefully understood as being constituted by a series of industry specific subsystems involving parent government agencies, technical committees, standards research institutes and standards associations whose members are drawn from industry and academia.

---

[14] Having responsibilities for standards in 17 areas of industry, NDRC increasingly works with trade associations (such as the China Machinery Industrial Federation) and enterprises (such as China National Offshore Oil Corporation) in standards development.

[15] COSTIND oversees standards work in five industries, including shipbuilding, nuclear power, aviation, space and civilian products manufactured by the arms industry.

[16] Zhao, "China's Evolving Standards System," 11–12.

In addition to laying out the structure and organisation of the standards system, the standards strategy also seeks to integrate standardisation efforts with technology policy. The strategy paper recognises that WTO obligations have eliminated many policy tools for protecting national industries, that the players in the international economy who control standards also enjoy many competitive benefits and that a number of countries around the world are, therefore, adopting national standards strategies. It tries to establish a workable set of relationships between government and industry under the rubric of a standards strategy that is guided by government, yet takes enterprises as the major player, and is market-oriented. Following the time line of the MLP, the paper envisions a phased development of Chinese standards that will allow for the new standards system to be institutionalised by 2010 with the expectation that by 2020 China would have become one of the leaders in international standard-setting, with Chinese standards becoming the basis for international standards. China thus hopes to move from the current phase of localising international standards to the internationalisation of national standards.[17]

As in other countries, the standards strategy calls for an increasing effort at coordinating R&D activities with standards development, with particular emphasis placed upon ensuring that the products of programmes for *zizhu chuangxin* get translated into Chinese standards incorporating Chinese intellectual property. The strategy calls for the commitment of resources to ensure that "scientific and technological achievements" lead to "experimental demonstration" and then to "technical standards development" and "application and promotion".[18] To support the "internationalisation of national standards," the paper recognises that special measures will be necessary to enhance China's effective participation in international standard-setting bodies. These include the development of expert teams who have the language ability, knowledge of

---

[17] Ibid., 15–16.
[18] Ibid., 17.

how international standardisation bodies operate and technical expertise to represent China effectively in these forums.

The strategy document has attempted to reconcile what are often contradictory impulses in Chinese thinking regarding standards: attempting to apportion the proper roles for government in terms of standard-setting and for enterprises in terms of responding to market signals, clarifying the distinction between voluntary and mandatory standards, deciding the proper balance between domestic standard-setting and international standardisation. It has also grappled with competing preferences for formal international standards bodies (in keeping with European and Japanese preferences) as opposed to more informal market-oriented working groups and consortia that have become so important in the fast-moving world of ICT (and which are more in keeping with US approaches). The thinking evident in the standards strategy document reflects the inherent tension visible in other countries — and in international standardisation more generally. On one side is cooperative behaviour to produce a public good or common benefit that facilitates technological progress and economic activities. On the other is strategic behaviour that seeks to enhance self-interest by becoming a standard-setter who uses control over standards, and the intellectual property embedded in them, to seek competitive advantage.

A DIVERSITY OF CASES

China's standards strategy is still a work in progress, and many adjustments are likely to be made during the actual implementation of the strategy over the coming 15 years. It is impossible to predict how successful this strategy will be and what consequences the strategy will hold for China's interactions with other members of the international community. Nevertheless, we are beginning to accumulate experience with other cases, and as noted above, the WAPI experience may not be an adequate guide to Chinese standard setting practices. These other prominent cases include the following.

TD-SCDMA

China's efforts at standardisation for third-generation (3G) mobile telephony centres on the TD-SCDMA (Time Division-Synchronous Code Division Multiple Access) standard developed by the Datang Corporation in cooperation with Siemens.[19] TD-SCDMA was formally submitted to the International Telecommunications Union (ITU) in 1998 for acceptance as an international 3G standard. It was recognised as such in May 2000, with the result that TD-SCDMA joined the European-backed WCDMA and the US-backed CDMA 2000 as competing standards for the next generation of mobile phones.

TD-SCDMA is said to offer technical advantages over WCDMA and CDMA 2000 that relate to higher spectrum efficiency, asymmetric downloading and uploading data rates and the utilisation of smart antennas.[20] Apart from technical advantages, however, the story of TD-SCDMA is closely related to the influence of government policy and market size in a wireless telecommunications market that has now become the largest in the world.

TD-SCDMA[21] is based on technology developed at the parent of Datang, the China Academy of Telecommunication Technology (CATT), which was under the former Ministry of Posts and

---

[19] The discussion below is derived from Alex Zixiang Tan, "Competition and Collaboration among 3-D Wireless Standards in China," paper prepared for the China's High-Technology Standards Workshop, sponsored by the National Bureau of Asian Research and Tsinghua University, Beijing, January 6, 2006.

[20] Tan, "Wireless Standards in China."

[21] SCDMA-WLL was developed by Beijing Xinwei, a joint venture established in November 1995 by the State Planning and Reform Commission, the Ministry of Posts and Telecom and CWill, a US company created by Chinese students. In 1999, Xinwei reportedly drafted the TD-SCDMA standard. See Haifeng Yang, "Chen Wei and His Story with Wireless Communication," *Tongxin shijie wang* (Communications World), July 30, 2003, http://www.cww.net.cn/Technique/getmsg.asp?id=24&articleID=3944 (May 30, 2006). This report has detailed information regarding SCDMA-WLL's origin and relations to TD-SCDMA. See also United States Information Technology Office, "Listing Plans to Buoy Chinese Telecom," http://www.usito.org/USITO/uploads/258/weekly_sep10.htm (May 30, 2006); and United States Information Technology Office, "Recent Developments in SCDMA," http://www.usito.org/USITO/uploads/41/weekly_dec5.html (May 30, 2006).

Telecommunications.[22] CATT's work on SCDMA, using "smart antenna" technology, began in 1994. It was approved by the Ministry of Posts and Telecommunications in 1997 and later won a first class prize for technological progress awarded by MII. CATT first proposed a Chinese 3G standard on the basis of SCDMA when in 1997 ITU solicited a draft proposal for IMT-2000.[23]

The commercial promotion of the standard began in October 2002 with the establishment of the TD-SCDMA Industry Alliance (composed of 17 domestic firms and eight joint ventures) and the TD-SCDMA Forum in December 2002 (now with a total membership of approximately 420 Chinese and international firms). In October 2002, MII issued a notice on frequency planning for 3G telephony, reserving the 155 MHz frequency for TD-SCDMA. Since 2002 there has been a steady growth both in the establishment of partnerships between Chinese and foreign companies and in the gradual intro-duction of devices designed for the TD-SCDMA architecture, and in December 2004 Chinese Prime Minister Wen Jiabao made the first international call using TD-SCDMA technology. Though having selected TD-SCDMA as a national standard in January 2006, MII has yet to issue any licenses for 3G operations. Meanwhile, network tri-als of the technology are being conducted in five locations by China's three telecom operators: China Telecom, China Netcom and China Mobile.[24]

---

[22] For more information about Datang and CATT, see Datang's homepage at http://www.catt.ac.cn/intro/fzlc.asp (May 30, 2006).

[23] Chunhua Liu, "Historic Overpassing: the Path of TD-SCDMA's Indigenous Innovation," *People's Post and Telecommunication*, December 27, 2005, http://www.cnii.com.cn/20050801/ca330265.htm (May 30, 2006); See also "Keynote Speakers: Li Shihe," IEE Mobility Conference 2005, http://www.mobility05.org/keynote (May 30, 2006); Professor Li is Chief Technology Officer of Datang and leader of the TD-SCDMA research team.

[24] See "Chinese Carriers Finalise Locations for TD-SCDMA Testing," *Xinhua*, March 6, 2006, http://www.tdscdma-forum.org/EN/news/see.asp?id=2720 (May 30, 2006); see also "China to End Testing on TD-SCDMA Network in Q3," *SinoCast*, April 24, 2006, http://www.tmcnet.com/usubmit/-china-end-testing-td-scdma-network-q3-/2006/04/24/1600347.htm (May 30, 2006).

The Chinese government has supported the development of TD-SCDMA with R&D support and preferential financing for domestic firms. The most important role for government in this particular case of standards, however, will be the government's licensing decision, a decision that MII has delayed until now. In the view of some observers, the delay has been due to MII's judgement that TD-SCDMA is not yet technologically mature and thus could not be favourably licensed on technical grounds. Delay, therefore, would give the Chinese proponents more time to refine the technology. Others, however, have pointed to the complex politics in which the TD-SCDMA licensing decision is embedded. Given the declarative themes of technology policy as discussed above, it would be reasonable to expect strong pressure from parts of the technical community to use the license decisions to advance a Chinese developed standard, perhaps through an exclusive license. Such a decision, however, would certainly not be welcomed by the domestic and foreign firms, which have substantial interests in the other two standards.

As Alex Tan has clearly shown, foreign firms would not be the only companies to be negatively affected by the failure to license CDMA 2000 and WCDMA. China's equipment manufacturers and service providers also have strong interests in the latter two standards due to the fact that current 2G operations are grounded in technologies from which the 3G technology has evolved. A degree of technical "lock in" thus factors into industry decision-making, with China Mobile, for instance, more inclined to favour WCDMA (because of the company's experience with the 2G GSM standard) and China Unicom more oriented toward CDMA 2000 (due to the company's current use of CDMA). In actuality, of course, both international and domestic firms have hedged somewhat and are preparing to work within whatever standards are selected. Nevertheless, the complex politics of the case have suggested to some that all these standards will eventually be licensed.[25] An additional factor influencing the licensing decision is that China will want to have a functioning 3G system in operation in time for the 2008 Olympics.

---

[25] Tan, "Wireless Standards in China."

As with other standards reviewed in this paper, the TD-SCDMA initiative is strongly influenced by concerns over the importance of using technologies that incorporate Chinese-developed intellectual property as well as the avoidance of burdensome licensing fees. Tan's analysis suggests, however, that meeting these objectives may be more difficult than previously thought. Qualcomm patents still underlie much of the technology behind wireless telephony, and Qualcomm has indicated an intention to pursue fair payment for its IP with TD-SCDMA manufacturers. In addition, as noted above, many of the products that have begun to appear using the TD-SCDMA architecture involve the active participation of multinational companies with Chinese firms, with the former bringing their own IP to these collaborations.[26]

AVS

A working group on standards for Audio Video Coding (AVS) was established in June 2002 upon the initiative of MII's Department of Science and Technology.[27] The group's current members include both Chinese and foreign companies and research entities. The work on AVS actually includes four separate technical standards (for the integration of the system, audio, video and digital copyright management).[28] The AVS standard for video compression became a national standard in April 2005.

Work on advanced audio and video coding systems began in 1996 under the leadership of Professor Gao Wen, with support from

---

[26] Ibid.

[27] This discussion of AVS draws on Gao Wen, "AVS — An Open and Cost-Efficient Chinese National Standard on Audio Video Coding Tools," opening address at China's High-Technology Standards Workshop, sponsored by the National Bureau of Asian Research and Tsinghua University, Beijing, January 6, 2006; Jun Su and Min Du, "Market Failure and Government Failure: Research on the Mechanism of AVS Standard-Setting," paper prepared for the China's High-Technology Standards Workshop, sponsored by the National Bureau of Asian Research and Tsinghua University, Beijing, January 6, 2006.

[28] For more information about AVS, visit the AVS homepage at http://www.avs.org. cn/en/ (May 30, 2006).

the Multimedia Subcommittee of the National Committee for Information Technology Standardisation and with funding from the 863 National High Technology Programme's "Intelligent Computing" project. Much of this early work was focused on support of the MPEG standard and led to the formation of a MPEG-China group in 1998. With support from "863", China sent a delegation to present four proposals to the 48th MPEG meeting in July 1999.

By 2001, China (with representatives from the Institute of Computer Technology of the Chinese Academy of Sciences, Tsinghua University and Microsoft Research Asia) began to participate in the work of the Joint Video Team (JVT) of the ITU. A central concern of the Chinese specialists in these activities was control over intellectual property and the excessive license fees that seemed to attend to the next generation of audio video standards. In May 2002 a group comprised of 24 international companies and seven Chinese firms began to explore the possibilities of developing a royalty-free standard. The establishment of the AVS Working Group followed shortly thereafter with the expectation that close cooperation with MPEG-China would be maintained. At the June 2003 meeting of JVT, Gao Wen's group at the CAS Institute of Computer Science was given the lead for the development of video coding software.

The development of AVS has received high-level review and approval from the Ministry of Science and Technology's Department of High and New Technology, CAS's Bureau of High Technology Research and Development, the Chinese Academy of Engineering's Division of Information and Electronic Engineering and MII's Department of Science and Technology. Progress has continued on the various standards that comprise the AVS package and, as noted above, the video standard has now been approved as a national standard.

Many observers of Chinese standardisation activities call attention to the work of AVS as a particularly positive example of a technically advanced and procedurally fair standards body, one that is open and internationalised in its proceedings, and which has devised a progressive set of policies for managing IPR issues through its patent pool system. Nevertheless, in 2003 the AVS programme received a significant setback when the State Administration of Radio, Film and Television (SARFT) rejected the AVS system in favour of MPEG-4, thus failing to use a government procurement tool to further the Chinese developed standard.

EVD

EVD (enhanced versatile disk) is a standard for high-definition optical disc players, targeted for use in the greater China region, created by the Beijing E-world Technology Company. MII has approved it as a recommended national standard, but as with other standards initiatives, EVD has an interesting and complicated history.[29]

In May 1999 the major players in China doing research on digital optical discs made a proposal to the State Economic and Trade Commission (SETC) for National Key Technological Innovation Project support for R&D on a "Special Project on a New-Generation High Definition Digital Laser Video Disc System." The Science and Technology Office of the Ministry of Information Industry took the lead in organising the project and, in October, the SETC approved the formation of the China Digital Optical Disk Technology Consortium (made up of several enterprises and research institutes) and allocated RMB10 million for the project.

With permission from the MII Department of Science and Technology, Beijing E-World Technology was established as a spin-off from the Consortium in March 2000, with all members of the consortium becoming stockholders of E-World. In April 2000, following the establishment of Beijing E-World, China's National Audio Video and Multimedia Systems and Devices Standardisation Committee (under the State Bureau of Quality and Technical Supervision and MII)

---

[29] See "Jiu tuo reng bu jue: guojia gaoqing dieji biaozhun daodi shi zenme le" (Long Time but No Decision — What Happened to National High Definition Optical Disc Standards?) *Sina Sci&Tech News*, February 2, 2005, http://www.ynkaiyuan.gov.cn/news/show.asp?url=TechNews/it/2005-02-02/1342521840.shtml (May 30, 2006); "EVD jishi" (EVD Milestones), http://www.davworld.net/productsystem/EVD/js.htm (May 30, 2006); "EVD xiangmu jianjie" (Brief Introduction of EVD Project), *EVD.org.cn*, http://www.evd.org.cn/evd/ReadNews.asp?NewsID=310 (May 30, 2006).

approved the formation of a "New-Generation Digital Optical Disk Standardisation Working Group" to be led by Beijing E-World. The working group was charged with developing the specifications for a next-generation laser video disc system, and in September 2000 the first draft of the specifications had been finished.

By July 2001, E-World Technology had finished the design for its EVD Digital Video Disc System and two manufacturers from Guangdong had begun making EVD discs using E-World's technology. That same month the Working Group met and approved EVD as a draft standard. In December, on behalf of the Consortium, E-World signed an agreement for cooperation on next-generation HD discs with a group composed of research institutes and DVD manufacturers from Taiwan. At the end of December, the EVD system received a positive evaluation at a "new technology product appraisal meeting" organised by the Ministry of Information Industry.

In March 2003, E-World signed an agreement with LSI Logic of the US to establish a joint research lab in Beijing for EVD chip development and design. On July 8, 2004 the EVD standard was published on the homepage of the Chinese Electronics Standardisation Association in an effort to promote the standard's adoption. After a month of promotion, the standard still had not generated much enthusiasm, in part because MII had concluded that EVD should be subject to further evaluation in comparison with the competing HDV[30] and HVD[31] standards. Working with the EVD, HVD and HDV consortiums, both MII's Offices of Science and Technology and New Products and MII's Testing and Evaluation Centre agreed in mid-July 2004 to entrust the testing and evaluation of the three standards to the National Testing and Inspection Centre for Radio and TV Products. Following this evaluation, in February 2005 MII announced

---

[30] HVD (High-definition Versatile Disc) is mainly supported by AMLOGIC (Shanghai) Inc. and Skyworth, Changhong, TCL, and Konka. See AMLOGIC, press release, "HVD Alliance is Founded in Shanghai, China," April 28, 2004, http://www.amlogic.com/News/News_042804.pdf (May 30, 2006).

[31] HDV (High Definition Video) is mainly promoted by KHD (Beijing Kaicheng High-Clarity Electronics Technology Co. Ltd). Interestingly, KHD is a member of the EVD Consortium and one of the stock-holders of E-World.

its approval of EVD as a national standard for the next-generation high-definition optical disk technology.[32]

The approval of EVD as a national standard, however, does not secure EVD's place in the electronics industry. EVD is classified as a voluntary standard and continues to face stiff competition in the marketplace. On April 23, 2005 the Shanghai-based HVD Consortium announced that HVD would become the standard for the Shanghai Information Electronics Association and would be supported by the relevant agencies of the Shanghai government and the TV and Electro-Acoustic Institute of the Beijing-based No. 3 Research Institute of the China Electronics Group Corporation, which drafted the HVD specifications.[33]

EVD, of course, also faces daunting competition from the international heavyweights — Sony's Blu-ray consortium (which includes Panasonic, Samsung, Dell, HP and Philips among others) and Toshiba's HD–DVD alliance (which includes NEC and others).[34] Both Blu-ray and HD–DVD represent efforts to replace the current DVD technology and are seen by some to be technically superior both to EVD and to HVD.[35] In the face of such competition, some in the Chinese media have begun to question the rationale behind the EVD initiative:

---

[32] See "Zhongguo gaoqing dieji biaozhun chutai, EDV wei xingye tuijianxing biaozhun" (EVD Becomes China's Recommended Industrial Standard for High Definition Optical Discs), *Sina.com*, February 24, 2005, http://tech.sina.com.cn/it/2005-02-24/1649534940.shtml (May 30, 2006).

[33] Meiying Yu, "Zhang Baoquan: Fangdichan bu neng chi tai jiu, biaozhun ke chi yi beizi" (Zhang Baoquan: You Can Live on Standards Your Whole Life), *Sina.com*, June 1, 2005, http://tech.sina.com.cn/it/2005-06-01/0616623129.shtml (30 May, 2006).

[34] David Carnoy, "Fully Equipped: HD-DVD vs. Blu-ray: Who Cares?" *CNet Reviews*, December 7, 2004, http://reviews.cnet.com/4520-8900_7-5600201-1.html. Toshiba's HD-DVD appearance recently has left some observers underwhelmed. See David Pogue, "Why the World Doesn't Need Hi-Def DVDs," *New York Times*, May 11, 2006.

[35] Zhenpeng Liang, "Jieli Yingguo cunchu jutou, EVD juji Riben liang da languang zhenying" (EVD Takes Advantage of UK NME Technology and Challenges Two Japanese Blue-ray Consortium), *NetEase*, September 9, 2005, http://tech.163.com/05/0909/05/1T6DPJ9A000915BD.html (30 May, 2006).

... at its very beginning, EVD was designed to avoid the patent trap of DVD technology. Chinese developers own only 20 percent of the IPR of EVD technology, however, and could not break away from DVD patents. EVD is not a break-through in key technology and doesn't fundamentally improve storage capacity of optical discs.[36]

The EVD initiative has also encountered problems in cooperation with international companies. The early prototype of EVD, for instance, used LSI Logic's MPEG-2 based technology.[37] In order to save on royalties, however, the EVD group sought to use On2 Technology's VP5 and VP6 data compression technology as a substitution of MPEG-2; this attempt quickly led to a contract dispute with On2.[38] One purported reason for E-World's new relationship with the United Kingdom's New Media Enterprise (NME) (discussed further below) is that E-World wanted access to NME's VMD technology in order to compensate for the small storage capacity problems in E-World's own technology.[39]

In addition to technological shortcomings, EVD also suffers from institutional problems evident in other high technology initiatives. Although organised by the government at the outset, the EVD standardisation effort quickly evolved into a commercial activity through the formation of E-World. In the absence of the administrative authority of the government, however, the conflicts of interest among

---

[36] "EVD: Jishu qixing de dianxing shibai?" (EVD: A Typical Failure of Technological Malformation?), *NetEase* at http://tech.163.com/special/E/000915LH/EVD_DIE.html (May 30, 2006).

[37] See LSI Logic, "Enhanced Versatile Disc (EVD): Developed by Leading Chinese Consumer OEMs for Use in Greater China Region," http://www.lsilogic.com/technologies/industry_standards/enhanced_versatile_disc_evd.html (May 30, 2006).

[38] See On2 Technologies press release, "Beijing E-world and On2 Announce the Inclusion of VP5 and VP6 in the People's Republic of China EVD Standard," November 18, 2003, http://www.on2.com/company/news-room/press-releases/?id=199; On2 Technologies press release, "On2 Technologies, Inc. Will File for Arbitration against Beijing E-World," April 29, 2004, http://www.on2.com/company/news-room/press-releases/?id=222 (May 30, 2006).

[39] Liang, "EVD Takes Advantage." For detailed information about VMD technology, see New Medium Enterprises, "Significant Technology for Future High Definition Systems," http://www.nmeinc.com/vmd.htm (May 30, 2006).

the commercial stakeholders have become unmanageable. For example, Beijing Kaicen High Definition Technology (KHD), a member of the EVD consortium and one of the stockholders of E-World, appears to harbour little reluctance to introduce and promote the competing HDV standard.

In addition, a high-profile conflict involving E-World's relationship with NME has recently developed. The conflict involves a dispute between E-world and Zhang Baoquan, the president of the Antaeus Corporation, a joint venture Zhang established with E-world. Zhang has been a vocal supporter of EVD and a major investor in the building of cinemas that use EVD technology.[40] However, because E-World has sold approximately 70 percent of its stock (including ownership of the EVD standard) to NME, Zhang has accused E-World of national betrayal.[41] Continuing controversies over the E-World-NME deal have further clouded the future of EVD.[42]

Home Networking

With the accumulation of digitally based smart devices in the modern home, industrialised countries around the world have a growing interest in technologies that will allow these devices to be linked together in a network. In China, interest in home-networking began in 1999 when, with the blessing of the State Economic and Trade Commission, 12 Chinese companies joined together to form the Home Informationisation Network System Structure and Product

---

[40] "Surprise at E-Worlds UK Deal," *People's Daily*, December 1, 2005, http://english.people.com.cn/200512/01/eng20051201_224906.html (May 30, 2006).

[41] See "Dujia: Fuguo bomai shenji jiulun, Zhang Baoquan nu chi Hao Jie yanxing" (E-World Deny Selling itself to NME, Zhang Baoquan Denounce Hao Jie's Words and Behaviour), *Sohu IT*, December 1, 2005, http://it.sohu.com/20051201/n240849552.shtml (May 30, 2006) (Hao Jie is E-World's CEO).

[42] On January 1, 2006, Hao Jie, E-world's CEO, was arrested for embezzling Antaeus property. For more details, see "Ma Jian: Hao Jie bei ju, EVD biaozhun he qu he cong" (Hao Jie Arrested: Where Will EVD Standard Go?), *ChinaByte*, January 16, 2006, http://tech.sina.com.cn/it/2006-01-16/1156821235.shtml (May 30, 2006).

Development Platform Working Group.[43] In 2001, MII took the initiative to establish a Digital TV Receiver Equipment and Home Network Platform Interface Standards Working Group, which included the members of the former group plus 11 new companies. In August 2005, the working group was renamed as Ministry of Information Industry Home Networking Standards Working Group.[44]

The Digital TV Receiver Equipment and Home Network Platform Interface Standards Working Group in effect superseded the former. By October 2003, the working group had considered four standards proposals from its members, two of which were accepted and submitted to MII for approval. Lenovo expressed dissatisfaction with the direction of the group's work and lobbied MII to allow Lenovo to set up another working group. MII approved the suggestion on the condition that the new group would focus more on the digital office and allow the original group to focus on the home. The Lenovo-led group became known as the Intelligent Group and Resource Sharing (IGRS) Working Group (or *shanlian*). The original group, now led by Haier, became known as the ItopHome Alliance (e-*jiajia*). Both groups have now submitted standards that have been approved by MII and are in the process of commercialising them. Konka and TCL, for instance, are now producing IGRS compliant televisions.[45]

Both groups have expanded, with IGRS now having some 50 members and ItopHome having 244. Though both permit foreign members, IGRS has become the more internationalised, with member companies from Japan, South Korea and Taiwan, and memoranda of understanding for technical cooperation with home-networking groups in Japan and Korea.[46] IGRS requests that its members disclose

---

[43] The discussion below draws on Kennedy, "Political Economy of Standards Coalitions."

[44] See MII China Home Network Working Group's homepage at http://www.china homenetwork.org/aboutus/aboutus.htm (May 30, 2006).

[45] Kennedy, "Political Economy of Standards Coalitions."

[46] On November 17, 2005 IGRS, ECHONET Consortium of Japan and the Home Network Forum of Korea together established the Asia Home Network Council (ANHC), the first cross-region standard organisation in East Asia.

relevant patents for contributed technology that can be made available to other members on the basis of the RAND ("reasonable and nondiscriminatory") principal. IGRS also employs a patent pool for the licensing of technology to non-member companies.[47]

As in other cases, the Chinese initiatives are being undertaken in the face of ongoing standards development in the international economy. In this case, the Digital Living Network Alliance (DLNA), formed in 2004 out of the Digital Home Working Group (DHWG), has been promoting its DLNA Home Networked Interoperability Guidelines v1.0. The alliance has approximately 238 members from relevant industries around the world and has begun to certify products as DLNA compliant. Interestingly, Lenovo was a founding member of DLNA, and TCL and Huawei have subsequently joined. Products from MNCs that comply with the DLNA guidelines have begun to enter China and have stimulated the accelerated commercialisation of the Chinese standards. The cross-membership phenomenon represented by Lenovo, TCL and Huawei, however, also suggests possibilities for cooperation.[48] On January 9, 2004, IGRS Working Group and Digital Living Network Alliance (DLNA) met in Beijing and explored a common vision for IPR management, technical frameworks and marketing. This led to the July 27, 2005 IGRS–DLNA Cooperation Summit in Beijing, at which the two organisations expressed enthusiasm to cooperate based on the common goal of the two parties' standard interoperability and compatibility in the future.

RFID

An especially important Chinese standards initiative, still in its early stages, concerns radio frequency identification (RFID) technology. Industry analysts predict that the demand for systems employing

---

[47] Kennedy, "Political Economy of Standards Coalitions."

[48] Kennedy notes that Intel is interested in introducing its "Viiv" home entertainment system into China, a move that has led to the opening of discussions between IGRS and DLNA. See Kennedy, "Political Economy of Standards Coalitions."

RFID is likely to grow into a $5.9 billion business within the next two years, with China playing a major part in this growth story.[49] The importance of this technology for China is due to the nation's rapidly growing adoption in supply-chain management and inventory control, particularly by such major retailers as Wal-Mart, which sourced over $20 billion worth of products from China last year.[50] Although Wal-Mart is supportive of the existing international standard, Electronic Product Code (EPC, the so-called "Gen2" standard developed by EPCGlobal), China, as with other standards, has expressed concern over having to pay royalties to EPCGlobal on a technology that will have such a ubiquitous presence in China's foreign trade.

China's interest in RFID, however, is not limited to supply-chain management. Having already experimented with the use of RFID technology in its "golden card" initiative of the early 1990s, China will reportedly be issuing approximately 900 million RFID-enabled identification cards by the end of 2008.[51] In light of the diffusion of bags of blood contaminated with AIDS and hepatitis, there is also interest in using RFID to monitor blood supply and track blood products. Thus, the interest in the technology is closely intertwined with aspects of social policy and the promotion of the "informatisation" of Chinese society. As with other technologies relating to radio transmissions, RFID is also one in which China's security apparatus takes an interest.

RFID technology consists of a "tag" (a transponder located in the object to be identified), a reader of the signal coming from the tag, a database that enables identification and software to operate the system. For supply-chain management in particular, a standardised system is important in order to realise the many advantages of RFID

---

[49] Fred Stakelback, "RFID: New Markets for an Old Technology," *Asia Times*, April 29, 2006, http://www.atimes.com/atimes/China_Business/HD29Cb02.html (May 30, 2006).

[50] Ibid.

[51] Stackelback, "New Markets for an Old Technology." The "Golden Card" project was intended to promote the use of credit cards, and more generally, e-banking and e-commerce.

at locations around the world.[52] This is the reason why China's RFID initiative is causing some concern — there are indications that the Chinese approach may diverge from what is becoming the international standard.

China's worries about the direction of international standardisation for RFID seem to turn on three issues. The first involves intellectual property and royalty questions. Although EPCGlobal has indicated the possibility of licensing its technology on a royalty-free basis, other companies making products employing the Gen2 standard have indicated an intention to charge royalties. The second issue concerns the numbering system used to identify objects with embedded RFID tags. The EPCGlobal approach, which is becoming adopted internationally, uses a fairly simple coding system that allows authorised parties to acquire information about the tagged object from the EPC database. Companies wishing to use the system must register with EPC and pay an annual fee for the service. China, on the other hand, uses its own coding system (the National Product Code) and has been reluctant to accept the idea that Chinese manufacturers should have to pay for the EPC system and adopt an additional numbering scheme. Finally, the EPCGlobal system is designed to allow participating supply-chain partners to share information about products through an open registry. EPC has subcontracted the maintenance of the registry to an American company, Verisign. Some in China believe that control over information resources of this sort, which pertain to commercial success, would violate national security norms.[53]

There also seems to be some confusion regarding China's management of its RFID initiatives. SAC reportedly supports EPCGlobal. Yet MII has recently indicated that research on RFID will be one of six major projects on information technology during the 11th five-year

---

[52] Jonathan Collins, "Metro Calls for Action on RFID Standards," *RFID Journal*, February 13, 2006, http://www.rfidjournal.com/article/articleprint/2150/-1/1 (May 30, 2006).

[53] Craig Harmon and Leslie Downey, "RFID: Will China Throw in a Monkey Wrench?," *BusinessWeek*, September 12, 2005, http://www.businessweek.com/technology/content/sep2005/tc20050912_6790.htm (May 30, 2006).

plan (2006–2010). In addition, the Ministry of Science and Technology is currently taking the lead in an interagency project to draft an RFID strategy paper that will chart a course for technological development in this area.[54] Until now, however, there seems to have been some confusion as to who has the lead on promoting the standard. Though a working group on RFID was established in November 2003, SAC suspended this group in October 2004 on the grounds that it duplicated the work of another working group on RFID. Thus, the first group was disbanded in the name of RFID standardisation.[55] In October 2005, the Department of Science and Technology of MII issued Document No. 52, which approved the establishment of an RFID working group; reportedly, there is also a "Leading Working Committee for RFID" operating in Shenzhen. In addition, work on RFID is occurring in the Article Numbering Centre of China's Electronic Product Code (EPC Global-China) Working Group and the China Electronic Standardisation Institute's RFID Working Group.[56] Thus, as with other standards cases considered, there may have been a degree of disarray in advancing the cause of a Chinese approach to RFID, perhaps necessitating stronger central direction and coordination (as illustrated by the initiation of the MOST-led policy paper). According to a spokesman for MII, "the main obstacles to a national standard have been disagreements among concerned parties within China and the ability of the country's national standard to operate with the three other international standards — ISO/IEC 18,000, EPCGlobal and Ubiquitous ID."[57]

The "Generation 2" standard developed by EPCGlobal has received preliminary endorsement by the ISO. Despite interest in working with ISO in other areas of standards, however, thus far China has apparently been reluctant to subscribe to the ISO process

---

[54] Stackelback, "New Markets for an Old Technology."
[55] See "RFID Working Group Suspended: Uncertain Factor of China's New Standard," *SouthCn.com*, October 27, 2004, http://www.southcn.com/tech/yjzx/200410280852. htm (May 30, 2006).
[56] Stackelback, "New Markets for an Old Technology."
[57] Ibid.

on this standard, perhaps putting a strain on China's WTO commitments to support international standards where they exist.[58] The confusion over responsibilities for RFID in China and apparent lack of consensus within the government may also be reflected in a July 2005 incident in which some members of a Chinese delegation (including those from MII) chose not to participate in a scheduled US–China workshop on RFID hosted by the US National Institute of Standards and Technology.

THE CASES COMPARED

The discussion above reveals similarities and differences among the cases (see Table 4.1). The diversity of these experiences is explored in greater detail below.

Motivations

Although the broad motivations for promoting a national standards strategy can be found in the development of a technology policy consistent with China's WTO commitments, a number of other more specific factors can also be identified from these cases. In the first instance, as exemplified by the WAPI case, national information security — in combination with commercial opportunities — has played an important role. WAPI was developed in institutions with close ties to China's security apparatus, and WAPI's staying power may be explained in part by the influence of the security bureaucracy on Chinese policy. Information security, mixed with commercial considerations, also seems to be an important consideration in the RFID case as well (though the mix is apparently richer in commercial considerations in RFID).

In other cases, such as AVS and EVD, motivation for initiating a new standard is closely linked to the fact that the "relative gains" from becoming the "workshop of the world" are not to China's liking.

---

[58] Harmon and Downey, "Will China Throw in a Monkey Wrench?."

Table 4.1: Comparison of Chinese Standard Initiatives

Case	Motivation	Major international competitor	Domestic competitor	International cooperation	State's role in standardisation
EVD	Avoid royalty fees	Blu-ray HD DVD FVD (Taiwan)	HDV HVD	Yes? (Contact with LSI Logic and On2, controversial deal with NME for VMD technology)	State initiated the effort but state's role decreased dramatically when it evolved into commercial activities
AVS	Avoid royalty fees	MPEG4, H.264	No.	Yes	Initiated by the state but there are conflicts of interest in the AVS case. For example, CCTV preferred MPEG-4 for IPTV standard
TD-SCDMA	Avoid royalty fees; improve Chinese competitiveness in telecommunication industry	WCDMA CDMA2000	No (Major telecom operators also use WCDMA and CDMA2000)	Yes	Srong state support. State established special projects for development of SCDMA technology. Currently state's support lies in decisions about 3G licensing

(*Continued*)

Table 4.1: (*Continued*)

Case	Motivation	Major international competitor	Domestic competitor	International cooperation	State's role in standardisation
WAPI	Security	IEEE 802.11	No	No	Strong state support
RFID	Establish Chinese competitive status in RFID industry; security	EPC (Gen2)	No	Yes	State initiated, but confusing roles of different state agencies
IGRS	Establish Chinese competitive status in home networking field	DLNA	ITopHome	Yes. IGRS formed a consortium with Japanese and Koreans. Also, IGRS cooperated with DLNA.	State initiated but most efforts were from the industry, where differences between IGRS and Itop-Home emerge

Although benefiting in absolute terms from participation in international production networks, Chinese firms often feel that they are not getting a fair return because of excessive royalties on licensed technologies. Because the intellectual property that is incorporated into technical standards lies in the hands of foreign companies, license fees are thought to cut unacceptably deeply into the profits of Chinese firms. Hence, the strong emphasis placed upon developing products with Chinese intellectual property, and Chinese standards, in the *zizhu chuangxin* formulation.

Though questions of relative gains also figure into other cases, these questions get mixed with motivations relating to technology innovation objectives. In these cases, such as TD-SCDMA and RFID, growing Chinese technological capabilities in relation to the scale of the Chinese market argue for the development of Chinese standards. In this view, China is thought to have the technical capability to set standards, and given the size and importance of the Chinese market, should do so. For instance, as the largest and fastest-growing market in the world for cellular phones, China believes that there is no reason the Chinese should not be setting their own standards. In the case of RFID, the feeling again is that since China now supplies so much of the world's consumer goods, it should be setting its own standards for technologies pertaining to the shipping and inventories of such goods.

There may also be a growing influence of cultural preferences in standard-setting activities. Technologies, after all, do experience social and cultural "shaping". Unsurprising, therefore, is that certain standards developed in non-Chinese settings may not be as suitable for Chinese conditions. Thus, in addition to commercial considerations, the development of standards for next-generation telephony and the "digital home" may be motivated by cultural preferences — as would the active Chinese interest in the development of standards for the next-generation Internet (IP V6).[59]

---

[59] Although Internet standards are not covered in this report, there is an active interest in next generation Internet standards in China, in part to produce standards that are more accommodating to the need to express Internet addresses in Chinese characters.

Foreign Participation

Another issue pertaining to the current state of China's efforts to promote a national standards strategy is the role to be played by MNCs. Generally speaking, foreign companies have been dissatisfied with the access they have been given to Chinese standard-setting forums and continue to lobby for greater participation and transparency from the Chinese.[60] Nonetheless, MNCs have been active players in helping to provide technology for Chinese standards development (the role of Siemans in the development of TD-SCDMA is one such example) and many of the standards working groups now have foreign members. In most of the more prominent cases of Chinese standards initiatives, foreign know-how has been an important component in the development of the Chinese standard. Indeed, despite suggestions of techno-nationalist motivations (which are evident in some cases), Chinese standard-setting initiatives provide further evidence that technological development is increasingly an international (if not global) exercise and that a narrow techno-nationalism is likely to be self-defeating.

Implementation and Institutional Models

Another series of interesting questions concern Chinese strategies for implementing standards. Among these is the extent to which China will embrace market-driven approaches to standard-setting as opposed to the setting of standards by government or by formal standards bodies. This question is closely related to the important issue of whether European approaches to standards, more closely associated with the latter approaches, will have greater influence with the Chinese than US approaches which favour market forces and action through voluntary associations. Both Europe and the US have been actively working with China to promote their visions of a standards regime. Implementation issues also extend to whether

---

[60] Ann Weeks and Dennis Chan, "Navigating Chinese Standards Régime," *China Business Review*, May–June 2003, http://www.chinabusinessreview.com/0305/weeks.html (May 30, 2006).

China's regulatory capacity and ability to enforce standards are sufficiently developed. Such questions all suggest that China's standards strategy faces many uncertainties and is not necessarily guaranteed success.

THE ROLE OF THE STATE AND THE POLITICS OF STANDARDS

Understanding the consistency, or inconsistency, of Chinese motivations for China's standardisation projects requires attention to the variety of actors involved in the standards strategy, their formal roles in the emerging standards regime, and the diverse sources of initiatives for standard-setting. It is useful, therefore, to differentiate among those actors having formal institutional responsibilities for the overall standards system (centred in the SAC), those having policy responsibilities for the development of industrial technologies (MII, NDRC, MOST and research institutes), and Chinese companies and industrial associations (the players in the market who face global competition). Though each of these has strong interests in standards, the interests are not necessarily identical. The primary interests of the former lie in the establishment of a modern standards regime and the maintenance of credible relations with international standards bodies and the formal standards institutions of other countries. In pursuit of these interests, SAC will seek to build technical capabilities and professionalism upon which its legitimacy will rest, and will be open to cooperative activities in support of these goals.

Those in the second category, having policy responsibilities for advancing Chinese technological development, see their mission as one of protecting Chinese national interests in the face of powerful global forces shaping both the directions of technological change and the distributive consequences of that change. They can be expected to aggressively devise strategies that will enhance national technical competence. Some of these strategies will conflict with the interests of international companies and foreign governments and will at times test the limits of international regimes and agreements. At the same time, these players acknowledge the limits of Chinese technological capabilities and appreciate the importance of international cooperation.

Finally, those Chinese companies that are becoming increasingly important in standardisation are generally evincing a more pragmatic approach to standards, one that reflects their business interests. Though unable to dismiss the state-driven standardisation aspirations as found in national technology policy, Chinese companies and industrial associations can take comfort in the national industrial policy that is designed to insulate them from the full force of MNC competition. Yet, these firms also understand that their success will ultimately be determined in the marketplace and that a standards strategy that is not flexible and accommodating is likely to undermine that success. For some, financial success has been achieved by working within an architecture of standards and IPR that has already been established internationally; new government-supported initiatives for distinctive Chinese standards may not be welcomed by such firms.

In light of the diversity of actors and their interests, it is not surprising that the role of the state appears ambiguous and contingent upon the political dynamics of standard setting. As with other areas of public life in China, the role of the state is changing, and opinions regarding its proper role are often divided. In the WAPI case, for instance, there has been strong sponsorship of the WAPI standard from at least parts of the state, but as Scott Kennedy has argued, there are reasons to think that Chinese state support was by no means unified. Because of the important implications of WAPI for information security, WAPI's strongest support seemingly came from authorities in the state's security system. Other parts of the state, notably those associated with economic and trade functions, may have been much less enthusiastic after witnessing the intense negative reaction to WAPI from important foreign trade and investment partners.[61]

---

[61] Kennedy, "Political Economy of Standards Coalitions."

A somewhat different pattern of state behaviour is evident in the TD-SCDMA case. Though having played a role in supporting the development of the technology going into the standard, the state has until recently been somewhat more tentative in endorsing and accepting TD-SCDMA as a national standard, even as the standard is being recognised internationally by the ITU. By virtue of a regulatory role *vis-à-vis* the telecommunications industry, however, the state — in this case, the Ministry of the Information Industry — will play a critical role in the standard's ultimate use. Yet as Tan has demonstrated, multiple interests are involved in 3G standards, with major Chinese companies having already sunk costs in technologies more consistent with alternative standards.[62] As a result, MII is in the ambiguous position of wanting to promote an indigenous Chinese standard involving at least some Chinese technology — in keeping with MII's role as an agent of the "developmental state" — while simultaneously serving as a more neutral regulator in the face of market forces and competing interests from other Chinese players.[63]

A third pattern is seen in the digital home network case, where the state has approved the formation of two competing alliances of Chinese companies — one led by Lenovo, the other by Haier. In this case, the state seems to be retreating from an active role in standard-setting by letting market forces operate in standards development more in the regulatory state mode. On the other hand, the state's R&D support represents an active intervention to foster technological development in this area.

The AVS case represents another pattern. As in other cases, the state intervened in order to facilitate the organisation of the AVS working group (thus overcoming market failures in meeting

---

[62] Tan, "3-D Wireless Standards in China."

[63] A classic formulation of the differences between the "developmental state" and the "regulatory state" is that of Chalmers Johnson. As Peter Evans has argued, however, developmental states also have multiple repertoires in their efforts to enhance national economic and technological well-being. See Peter Evans, *Embedded Autonomy: States and Industrial Transformation* (Princeton, NJ: Princeton University Press, 1995). The authors are grateful for Scott Kennedy's reminder of Evan's perspective.

organisational costs) and has also provided R&D support. The work of the AVS group has, however, apparently proceeded largely independently of the state. As was the case with TD-SCDMA and the digital home cases, foreign companies have also been involved in the development of the standard. But, in the first critical commercial test of the standard — the procurement decision by SARFT — the state actually backed away from the indigenously developed Chinese standard and opted for the more familiar, but arguably technically inferior, MPEG international standard.

Thus, contrary to the impression first created in the WAPI case, defining the interest of the Chinese state in standards is by no means straightforward. Though the state is clearly committed to the development of Chinese standards — a commitment seen in the development of the standards strategy and in the inclusion of research on standards in major national R&D projects — there remains both a diversity of interests within the state regarding particular standards and a diversity of policy tools (such as regulation, procurement and R&D support) that can be employed (or, in the case of SARFT, not employed) in the implementation of standards policy.

Thus, the politics of standards in China cannot be understood simply as a matter of state direction. Kennedy has suggested that the political dynamics of contemporary high-tech standard-setting should be understood in terms of the relative strength of competing coalitions of interests.[64] The apparent failure of WAPI, thus, can be understood in terms of the standard's rather narrow constituency of interest, but in other cases, broader coalitions are emerging that involve both Chinese and foreign companies. Tan's work has also shown how various "interest groups" composed of Chinese and foreign companies — from both the service delivery and equipment manufacturing sectors — embrace competing standards. Though still the ultimate regulator, MII is one that can now only ignore market forces at great peril to the delivery of Chinese telecommunications services.

It is still too early to draw any firm conclusions regarding the general role of the Chinese state in standards development. On the

---

[64] Kennedy, "Political Economy of Standards Coalitions."

one hand, the diversity of patterns that this chapter has attempted to document might be interpreted as a reflection of a trend toward greater marketisation in which the state retreats to a more neutral regulatory role — as one might expect in a more laissez-faire economy. That same diversity, however, might also be a reflection of well-known problems within the Chinese government — the "stove-piping" and "fragmented authoritarianism" phenomena many observers have noted — in achieving effective coordination across multiple bureaucratic systems. According to this interpretation, greater state capacity would result in a more active and coherent state direction of the standards development efforts. In this context, the new long-term science and technology plan, which emphasises *zizhu chuangxin* and carries techno-nationalist overtones, would seem to be a prod to the state to achieve a more effective standard-setting process in the interest of enhancing Chinese technological capabilities. The growing importance of Chinese firms in the national innovation system, however, may limit an expansion of the state's role and be a force for greater techno-globalism. Though clearly seeking support and favours from the state, Chinese firms are also increasingly aware of global market realities and are involved with complex international commercial interactions. While Chinese companies certainly cannot ignore the wishes of the state, the idea that these enterprises march lockstep in implementation of the state's technology policies seems increasingly to be unfounded.

CONCLUSION

A national standards agenda is, conceptually, a complex phenomenon, one that is also made behaviourally complicated by the existence of competing interests and preferences with regard to standards, standard-setting mechanisms and the ways in which national standards activities fit within a global economy. The more prominent cases of standard-setting reviewed here suggest that the achievement of a consistency of preferences among the actors participating in China's standards strategy is by no means a simple matter. Preferences regarding standards vary among industry, government and the research community — and within each of these sectors as well. In light of these problems, it is not surprising that the overall record of success of the standards strategy is not compelling, as Kennedy has recently argued.[65]

Drafts of the standards strategy paper reveal the difficulties of reconciling the conceptual and behavioural complexities. China appears to appreciate some of the aspects of the US market oriented standard setting tradition, in which informal or consortium-like organisations play key roles in setting standards at fast moving technological frontiers. On the other hand, China seems to show a preference for working through established, institutionalised standards organisations, more in keeping with European and Japanese practices. Though much is made of the importance of harmonising domestic standards with international standards (in keeping with the terms of the TBT agreement), Beijing has also issued clear statements asserting that Chinese national interests should be served by China's standards system. When these two objectives seem to conflict, as in the WAPI case, the true intentions of China's standards strategy seem to be blurred.

The relationships among China's technical capabilities for standard-setting, the relative importance of the domestic market in China's standards strategy, and the role of multinational corporations in standard-setting activities are also important issues on the agenda. As suggested above, China's large market clearly shapes its thinking regarding the development of Chinese standards, but it is not entirely clear whether standards development should focus mainly on products for the Chinese market or for the international market. In the case of TD-SCDMA, for instance, the size of the Chinese market could sustain a Chinese standard. Conversely, the promotion of the Chinese standard for the domestic market may not serve the interests of Chinese handset producers who are seeking to penetrate and capture market share abroad, where different standards are in use.

Market power can be substituted for technological accomplishment, and some observers have argued that the technical quality of

---

[65] Ibid.

some prominent Chinese standards is behind international levels — despite China's plans to strengthen these standards. If true, this disparity would then suggest that China must either appeal to market power to advance Chinese standards or partner with multinational corporations to develop technologies and advancing standards; foreign participation of one sort or another is evident in most of the cases reviewed above.

In an earlier work, we argued that China's standards strategy is rooted in a deep-seated techno-nationalism, albeit one accommodated to the realities of techno-globalism.[66] In many ways, this "neo-techno-nationalism" continues to characterise China's technology policy and standards strategy. The cases presented above, however, provide new insights into the characteristics of Chinese techno-nationalism, in particular the ways in which this nationalism is intermingled with techno-globalism. Indeed, in reviewing individual cases of standards initiatives, the relative importance of techno-nationalism and techno-globalism seems to vary considerably across a spectrum, with WAPI exemplifying the former and AVS and perhaps IGRS the latter. The diversity of views regarding techno-nationalism, as evident in the standards strategy, reflects the broader discourse on techno-nationalism in technology policy as seen, for instance, in the ambiguities surrounding the concept of *zizhu chuangxin*.

Reviews of China's technology policy demonstrate both that there is an intense aspiration for technological progress in China that is backed by strong political will and increasingly abundant resources, and that standards are seen as an important part of national technology policy. At the same time, this discussion has shown that, due to technological weaknesses, institutional fragmentation and competing interests, the full implementation of a coherent standards strategy is often elusive. These conditions pose both challenges and opportunities for the international community: though unable to ignore the seriousness of purpose that China brings to its standards initiatives, the international community also

---

[66] Suttmeier and Yao, "China's Post-WTO Technology Policy."

has multiple opportunities for cooperating with China to reach mutually beneficial outcomes.

As indicated at the outset, standards have become an increasingly important issue in facilitating global commerce and in supporting the inter-operability of the technologies upon which international economic progress depends. China's rise as a great trading nation and a global manufacturing centre, combined with the country's growing technological capabilities and expanding technological aspirations, make an expanding Chinese role in the world of technical standards inevitable. However, the world of standards will always be one of an essential tension between the employment of standards as an instrument of cooperation that facilitates mutually beneficial interactions on one hand, and the use of standards in struggles for self-interested advantage on the other. China's commitment to enter this world not only complicates the struggle but also expands the value of pay-offs from cooperation. How the Chinese state approaches the management of this tension will be an important factor in insuring that the conflict generated by the inevitability of struggle does not compromise the promise of expanding benefits through collaboration.

Chapter 5

The Impact of Financing the High-Tech Industry on the Chinese Banking Sector

Yue Ma

INTRODUCTION

Since China adopted its economic reform and open-door policy in 1979, economic growth has well exceeded international average growth rates (see Table 5.1). For a large economy to sustain such high growth in the new century under intense competition and globalisation, the Chinese Government recognises that China must develop its high-tech industry. High growth countries such as the United States typically have advanced high-tech industries (see Table 5.2). Relatively young American companies such as Microsoft, Intel and Netscape have grown very rapidly. Recent economic theories have been advanced to provide a microfoundation for the creation of the high-tech firms in the high-income countries

Table 5.1: China's GDP Growth Rates in Comparative Perspective (percent)

	1995	1999	2000	2001	2002	2003	2004	2005
China	10.9	7.6	8.4	8.3	9.1	10.0	10.1	10.2
World	2.8	3.7	4.9	2.6	3.1	4.1	5.3	4.9
Advanced economies	2.8	3.5	3.9	1.2	1.5	1.9	3.2	2.6
US	2.3	4.4	3.7	0.8	1.6	2.5	3.9	3.2
Eurozone	2.6	3.0	3.9	1.9	0.9	0.8	2.1	1.3
LDCs	5.1	4.1	6.1	4.4	5.1	6.7	7.7	7.4
Brazil	4.2	0.8	4.4	1.3	1.9	0.5	4.9	2.3
India	7.6	6.9	5.3	4.1	4.7	7.2	8.0	8.5
Transitional economies								
Czech	6.4	1.3	3.6	2.5	1.9	3.6	4.2	6.1
Poland	6.0	4.5	4.2	1.1	1.4	3.8	5.3	3.4
Russia	−4.1	6.4	10.0	5.1	4.7	7.3	7.2	6.4

Notes: Figures are based on constant prices. Growth rates for the world, advanced economies and LDCs are based on the US dollar. Individual countries and Eurozone are based on national currencies.

Source: China's data come from *China Statistical Yearbook*, 2006. Data for the other countries are from *The IMF World Economic Outlook*, September 2006, 189, 197–199. Data for 1995 are from the *IMF World Economic Outlook Database*: http://www.imf.org/external/pubs/ft/weo/2006/02/data/index.aspx

and analyses have been put forward for the management in the high-tech industry.[1]

Table 5.3 divides the Chinese GDP into four sectors — agriculture, industry, construction and services. It shows that the industrial sector in the Chinese economy has been dominant over the last decade with a stable share of about 40 percent. Table 5.4 reveals that the output share of the high-tech industry in China's total industrial sector has been increasing progressively from 7 percent in 1995

---

[1] J. Tong, "High-Tech and High Capability in a Growth Model," *International Economic Review* 46 (2005): 215–243; S. Pass and B. Ronen, "Management by the Market Constraint in the High-Tech Industry," *International Journal of Production Research* 41 (2003): 713–724.

Table 5.2: Value-added of High-Tech Industry as a Percentage of Manufacture in Selected Countries (percent)

	1999	2000	2001	2002	2003
China	8.7	9.3	9.5	9.9	10.5
United States	22.1	23.0	18.3	17.7	18.6
Japan	17.8	18.7	16.8	15.9	16.8
Germany	10.4	11.0	10.4	10.6	—
France	14.0	14.1	14.1	13.5	13.8
United Kingdom	16.3	17.0	16.9	16.1	15.6
Italy	8.9	9.8	10.0	9.6	9.2
Korea	22.6	24.4	22.2	23.0	23.6

Notes: Figures are based on current prices.
Source: China Science and Technology Statistics website: www.sts.org.cn/sjkl/index. htm; OECD, *STAN Database*, 2004.

Table 5.3: Composition of China's GDP (percent)

	1995	1999	2000	2001	2002	2003	2004	2005
GDP	100.0	100.0	100.0	100.0	100.0	100.0	100.0	100.0
Agriculture	19.8	16.2	14.8	14.1	13.5	12.6	13.1	12.6
Industry	41.1	40.0	40.3	39.8	39.4	40.5	40.8	42.0
Construction	6.1	5.8	5.6	5.4	5.4	5.5	5.4	5.5
Service	33.0	38.0	39.3	40.7	41.7	41.4	40.7	39.9

Notes: Figures are based on current prices.
Source: *China Statistical Yearbook*, 2006, 58, National Bureau of Statistics.

to 11.3 percent in 2005. Over the same period, foreign-invested high-tech industry has accounted for a larger share of output than Chinese domestic high-tech industry. The Government supported state-owned high-tech firms experienced a declining share among the domestic high-tech industry, although they had a dominant position in the early years.

Research on how to develop the high-tech industry in China is abundant. For example, a research book, *Development Report on China's New and High-Tech Industry*, was published by China's

Table 5.4: Share of High-Tech and Traditional Industries in China (percent)

	1995	1999	2000	2001	2002	2003	2004	2005
Share of High-Tech Industry								
Total high-tech/total industry	7.0	9.8	10.9	10.9	11.4	12.0	11.6	11.3
Foreign high-tech/total high-tech industry	44.3	52.3	52.1	53.9	54.6	57.5	62.9	64.0
SOE high-tech/domestic high-tech industry	65.3	100.0	92.7	82.9	72.2	68.0	57.7	55.0
Share of Traditional Industry								
Traditional industry/total industry	93.0	90.2	89.1	89.1	88.6	88.0	88.4	88.7
SOE traditional/domestic traditional industry	60.1	66.6	65.0	63.6	60.2	57.2	55.3	52.6

Notes: Figures are based on value-added, in current prices; Total industry: Value-added of all the state-owned enterprises and non-state-owned ones that are above the designated size of RMB5 million worth of sales; Total high-tech industry: Value-added of all the state-owned high-tech enterprises and non-state-owned ones that are above the designated size of RMB5 million worth of sales; Foreign high-tech: Value-added of the foreign and joint-ventures high-tech enterprises that are above the designated size of RMB5 million worth of sales; SOE high-tech: Value-added of all the state-owned high-tech enterprises; Domestic high-tech industry: The output difference between total high-tech and foreign high-tech industry; Traditional industry: The output difference between total and high-tech industry; SOE traditional industry: The output difference between state-owned industry and state-owned high-tech industry.

Source: *China Statistical Yearbook*, 2006, 57; *China Statistics Yearbook of High Technology Industry*, 2006, 6, 24, 30; CEIC database.

Science and Technology Ministry in 1999.[2] It analyses various strategies to develop the high-tech industry in China. The Chinese Government in fact also provided a long list of preferential policies, such as a value-added tax refund and reduction of the customs duty

---

[2] See Science and Technology Ministry (Kexue jishu bu), *Development Report on China's New and High-Tech Industry (Zhongguo gao xin jishu chanye fazhan baogao)* (Beijing: Science and Technology Press (Kexue chubanshe), 1999).

for IT-related products to zero, to encourage investment in the high-tech industries. In addition, the development of High-Tech Industrial Development Zones (*Gaoxin jishu kaifaqu*) has played an important role in speeding up the growth of the high-tech industry.[3] However, little of the research to date investigates the consequences of the high-tech industry on the economy, especially the financial consequences.

While high-tech industry is at the top of the technology spectrum, most economies also have a low-tech industrial sector. Formally, high-tech (or low-tech) industries are defined by the OECD as those where the sector as a whole invests more than 5 percent (or less than 0.9 percent) of turnover in R&D.[4] High-Tech industries such as aircraft and pharmaceuticals industries are R&D-intensive with complex technology. In this chapter, "high-tech industry" includes both "high-tech" and "medium-high-tech" industries (such as the automobile industry). "Traditional industry" consists of the "low-tech" and "medium-low-tech" industries with mature, traditional technology, such as rubber and plastics manufacturing and textile industries. Table 5.4 indicates that traditional industries in China still had nearly 90 percent of the industrial output share in 2005. State-owned traditional industries produced more than half of the domestic traditional industrial output.

As a result, there is no doubt that traditional industry will continue to dominate the Chinese economy for the foreseeable future. Thus, the questions addressed here are: (a) what are the implications of developing the high-tech industry, (b) what impact does development of the high-tech industry have on the traditional industries and (c) what is the impact of financing the high-tech industry on the banking sector. Specifically, this chapter analyses the impact on the

---

[3] Y. W. Guo, "China Gives Preference to High-Tech Industries," *International Tax Review* 13 (2002): 37–39; L. Li, P. Hu and L. Zhang, "Roles, Models and Development Trends of High-Tech Industrial Development Zones in China," *International Journal of Technology Management* 28 (2004): 633–645.
[4] OECD, *Frascati Manual 2002: Proposed Standard Practice for Surveys on Research and Experimental Development* (Paris: OECD).

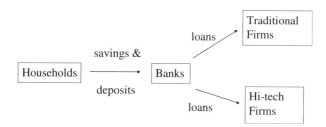

Figure 5.1: A Three-sector General Equilibrium Model

deposit and lending rates of bank loans, the total amount of loans borrowed by the traditional and high-tech sectors and the implications for household savings which are the primary source for the bank loans.

In order to carry out the dynamic comparative analysis, a prototype three-sector overlapping generations model is constructed (Figure 5.1). It consists of three sectors: household, banking and industrial. The household sector maximises its inter-temporary utility by allocating the income into saving and consumption. The banks accept savings in the form of deposits and then lend them to the firms.

The model solutions contrast two scenarios: (1) an industrial sector that is comprised of only traditional industries, and (2) an industrial sector to which a new high-tech industry is developed is introduced. The model is first solved under the assumption that there is only one traditional industry. Then it is solved again with the assumption that some new firms start to develop a high-tech industry along with the existing firms that continue to produce under the traditional technology.

MODEL WITHOUT HIGH-TECH INDUSTRY

Household Sector

Of the three sectors in the model, the household sector maximises its inter-temporary utility by allocating income into saving and consumption. The banks accept the savings in the form of deposits and in turn lend them to firms. Individuals in the household sector live for two periods such that at any point in time, τ, the economy is composed of two generations, the young and mature.[5] Households maximise an inter-temporal utility function with expected income, W_τ^e, which is the sum of expected profits of both the traditional industrial and banking sectors.[6] The income is transferable between consumption and production. Households decide how much to consume, $C_{y,\tau}$, and invest, S_τ, in the first period τ when they are young. When they mature in the second period, $\tau + 1$, households consume $(C_{o,\tau+1})$, all the savings, $(1 + r_\tau^s)S_\tau$, where r_τ^s is the deposit rate.

Specifically, the household sector maximises the following inter-temporal utility function:

$$U_{\tau,\tau+1}(C_{y,\tau},\, C_{o,\tau+1}) = (C_{y,\tau})^{1/2} + \beta_c(C_{o,\tau+1})^{1/2}, \qquad (5.1)$$

subject to the budget constraints in each period:

$$W_\tau^e = C_{y,\tau} + S_\tau \qquad (5.2)$$

$$C_{o,\tau+1} = (1 + r_\tau^s)S_\tau, \qquad (5.3)$$

where β_c is the time-discount factor of the consumer.

The first period budget constraint is division of the total income W_τ^e into period 1 consumption $C_{y,\tau}$ of the young and saving S_τ. The second period budget constraint is that the consumption $C_{o,\tau+1}$ of the mature is equal to the gross return from the period 1 savings

---

[5] B. T. McCallum, "The Role of Overlapping-Generations Models in Monetary Economics," *Carnegie Rochester Conference Series on Public Policy* 18 (1983): 9–44.

[6] That individuals maximise their utility function with *expected income* instead of maximising *expected utility* under uncertainty is a simplifying assumption. Strictly speaking, the two approaches are different due to Jensen's inequality. [See J. E. Ingersoll, *Theory of Financial Decision Making* (New Jersey: Rowman and Littlefield, 1987.)] Appendix B relaxes this assumption and derives a similar conclusion based on *expected utility* maximisation. However, it is found that the mathematics are more complicated and more tedious in Appendix B than in this simplified approach.

$(1 + r^s_\tau)S_\tau$. Therefore, the inter-temporal utility function can be rewritten as follows:

$$U_{\tau,\tau+1} = (W^e_\tau - S_\tau)^{1/2} + \beta_c [(1 + r^s_\tau)S_\tau]^{1/2}. \tag{5.4}$$

The first order condition to maximise this utility function is given by:

$$\partial U_{\tau,\tau+1}/\partial S_\tau = -1/2(W^e_\tau - S_\tau)^{-1/2} + 1/2\beta_c[(1 + r^s_\tau)S_\tau]^{-1/2}(1 + r^s_\tau) = 0. \tag{5.5}$$

Hence,

$$W^e_\tau - S_\tau = S_\tau/\beta_c^2(1 + r^s_\tau)$$

or:

$$S_\tau = W^e_\tau /\{1 + 1/[\beta_c^2(1 + r^s_\tau)]\}. \tag{5.6}$$

This solves the household problem given the savings rate, r^s_τ, and total income, W^e_τ.

Traditional Industrial Sector

Suppose the traditional firm employs a linear production function with quadratic variable costs to maximise its profits.[7] The input of production requires loans L^t_τ from the bank, and the production function at time period τ is[8]:

$$Y^t_\tau = A^t_\tau L^t_\tau, \tag{5.7}$$

where superscript t indicates the traditional sector, Y^t_τ is output and A^t_τ is productivity. Money in a production function can also be interpreted as an efficient financial system that is able to release capital, intermediate goods and labour from conducting transactions, all of

---

[7] See L. E. Jones and R. Manuelli, "A Convex Model of Equilibrium Growth: Theory and Policy Implications," *Journal of Political Economy* 98 (1990): 1008–1038; L. H. Roller, "Proper Quadratic Cost Functions with an Application to the Bell System," *Review of Economics and Statistics* 72 (1990): 202–210.

[8] For simplicity, it is assumed that the capital completely depreciates after one period.

which are devoted to production.[9] Assume that the production and management costs are quadratic functions of loans. This implies that the cost function is:

$$C^t(L_\tau^t) = B^t(L_\tau^t)^2, \qquad (5.8)$$

where B^t is a constant. The firm's profit function after deducting both $C^t(L_\tau^t)$ and total borrowing costs of the loan $(1 + r_\tau^t)L_\tau^t$ at any point of time, τ, is given by:

$$\begin{aligned} \pi_\tau^t &= Y_\tau^t - (1 + r_\tau^t)L_\tau^t - C^t(L_\tau^t) + \eta_\tau^t \\ &= A_\tau^t L_\tau^t - (1 + r_\tau^t)L_\tau^t - B^t(L_\tau^t)^2 + \eta_\tau^t, \end{aligned} \qquad (5.9)$$

where r_τ^t is the borrowing interest rate. The firm's profit is associated with uncertainty, η_τ^t. There is some probability that η_τ^t will take positive values, meaning that the business is successful. However, there are also some downside risks in which case η_τ^t will take negative values. It is assumed that these risks are symmetric so that $E(\eta_\tau^t) = 0$.

The decision problem of the firm is to choose a time path of borrowings in terms of bank loans that maximises the expected present discounted value of the profit flows π_τ^t:

$$v = \max E \sum_{\tau=0}^{\infty} \beta_t^\tau \pi_\tau^t \qquad (5.10)$$

subject to $\Delta L_\tau^t = \Delta(L_\tau^t)^s$, where β_t is the constant time-discount factor of the traditional firm, Δ is the first-difference operator and $\Delta(L_\tau^t)^s$ is the change of the supply of bank loans.

The current-value Hamiltonian is:

$$H_\tau^t = E(\pi_\tau^t) + \lambda_\tau^t \Delta(L_\tau^t)^s, \qquad (5.11)$$

where λ_τ^t is the co-state variable.

---

[9] S. Fischer, "Money and the Production Function," *Economic Inquiry* 12 (1974): 517–533; C. B. Mulligan, "Scale Economies, the Value of Time, and the Demand for Money: Longitudinal Evidence from Firms," *Journal of Political Economy* 105 (1997): 1061–1079.

The first order condition is given by:

$$\partial H^t_\tau/\partial L^t_\tau = \partial E(\pi^t_\tau)/\partial L^t_\tau = A^t_\tau - (1 + r^t_\tau) - 2B^t L^t_\tau = 0. \qquad (5.12)$$

Hence, the traditional firm's demand for loans at any time period, τ, can be solved:

$$(L^t_\tau)^d = (A^t_\tau - 1 - r^t_\tau)/2B^t, \qquad (5.13)$$

given the bank's lending interest rate r^t_τ.

Banking Sector

Banks maximise profits by offering banking services to their customers (depositors and borrowers).[10] In this model, banks take deposits from households and lend loans to firms. The banking sector has at least two advantages to channel the financial flows to the firms from the households. Firstly, the banks can reduce transaction costs due to economies of scale and their expertise. Secondly, banks can assess the bankruptcy risk of firms by establishing long-term customer relationships and efficient monitoring practices.[11]

Suppose the profit function of the bank at time period τ is:

$$\pi_{\text{bank},\tau} = (r^t_\tau - r^s_\tau)L^t_\tau - C_{\text{bank}}(L^t_\tau) + \varepsilon^t_{\text{bank},\tau}, \qquad (5.14)$$

where superscript t indicates parameters and variables related to the bank's service to the traditional sector, r^t_τ and r^s_τ are the interest rates of lending and savings deposits, respectively, L^t_τ is lending to firms, $C_{\text{bank}}(L^t_\tau)$ are the monitoring and management costs of the bank and $\varepsilon^t_{\text{bank},\tau}$ is a stochastic process with $E(\varepsilon^t_{\text{bank},\tau}) = 0$ which is

---

[10] This is the standard industrial organisation approach to modelling bank behaviour. For alternative approaches, see E. Fama, "Banking in the Theory of Finance," *Journal of Monetary Economics* 6 (1980): 39–57.

[11] See M. Gertler, "Financial Structure and Aggregate Economic Activity: An Overview," *Journal of Money, Credit and Banking* 20 (1988): 559–588; L. J. Mester, "Efficiency in the Savings and Loan Industry," *Journal of Banking and Finance* 17 (1993): 267–286.

related to the risks of both the loan repayment of the traditional firms and the credit market.[12]

It is assumed that banks are risk-averse in the sense that (a) the higher the risks associated with lending, the more resources they will spend on monitoring the project and (b) the larger the loan size, the more resources are devoted to assessing the risk of the project. Suppose the total risk indicator of lending to traditional firms is $\text{var}(\varepsilon^t_{\text{bank},\tau}) + \text{var}(\eta^t_\tau) = (\sigma^t_\tau)^2$ and that the bank has a quadratic cost function:

$$C_{\text{bank}}(L^t_\tau) = b^t\, \sigma^t_\tau (L^t_\tau)^2, \tag{5.15}$$

where b^t is the degree of risk-aversion of the bank.[13] A larger b^t indicates the bank is more risk-averse. As a result, the bank's profit function (14) can be rewritten as:

$$\pi_{\text{bank},\tau} = (r^t_\tau - r^s_\tau)L^t_\tau - b^t\sigma^t_\tau (L^t_\tau)^2 + \varepsilon^t_{\text{bank},\tau}. \tag{5.16}$$

The decision problem of the bank is to choose the lending time path to the traditional firm that maximises the expected present discounted value of the profit flows, $\pi_{\text{bank},\tau}$:

$$\max E\sum_{\tau=0}^{\infty} \beta^\tau_b\, \pi_{\text{bank},\,\tau} \tag{5.17}$$

subject to: $\Delta L^t_\tau = S_\tau - S_{\tau-1} + S_{\tau-1}(1 + r^s_{\tau-1}) - C_{o,\tau}$, where β_b is the time-discount factor of the bank; S_τ and $S_{\tau-1}$ are savings at time periods τ and $\tau - 1$, respectively; and $C_{o,\tau}$ is the withdrawal of savings by the mature for consumption.

The current-value Hamiltonian is:

$$H_{\text{bank},\tau} = E(\pi_{\text{bank},\tau}) + q_{\text{bank},\tau}\,[S_\tau + S_{\tau-1}(1 + r^t_{\tau-1}) - C_{o,\tau} - L^t_{\tau-1}], \tag{5.18}$$

where $q_{\text{bank},\tau}$ is the co-state variable.

---

[12] J. Dermine, "Deposit Rates, Credit Rates and Bank Capital: The Klein–Monti Model Revisited," *Journal of Banking and Finance* 10 (1986): 99–114.

[13] M. Kim, "Banking Technology and the Existence of a Consistent Output Aggregate," *Journal of Monetary Economics* 18 (1986): 181–195.

The first order condition is given by:

$$\partial H_{\text{bank},\tau} / \partial L^t_\tau = \partial E(\pi_{\text{bank},\tau}) / \partial L^t_\tau = r^t_\tau - r^s_\tau - 2b^t\sigma^t_\tau L^t_\tau = 0. \qquad (5.19)$$

Hence, the supply of loans by the banks to the traditional industrial sector at any time period, τ, can be solved:

$$(L^t_\tau)^s = (r^t_\tau - r^s_\tau)/(2b^t\sigma^t_\tau), \qquad (5.20)$$

given the lending rate r^t_τ and the deposit interest rate r^s_τ. This is in fact also the demand for deposits of the banks. It was found that the more risk-averse the bank is (with a larger b^t), or the higher the risk associated with the investment (with a bigger value of σ^t_τ), the less the lending from the bank.

Market Equilibrium Conditions

To close the model, the expected income, W^e_τ, of the young in the household sector is set to equate the sum of expected profits from both the traditional industrial and banking sectors, $E(\pi^t_\tau + \pi_{\text{bank},\tau})$, at time period τ:

$$W^e_\tau = E(\pi^t_\tau + \pi_{\text{bank},\tau}). \qquad (5.21)$$

The equilibrium conditions in the financial market, at any time period τ, are that:

(a) the supply of deposits (i.e., savings) must be equal to the demand of deposits (i.e., loans): $S_\tau = L^t_\tau$ and
(b) the supply of loans from the bank must be equal to the demand for the loans by firms: $(L^t_\tau)^s = (L^t_\tau)^d$.

These two equilibrium conditions therefore determine the market deposit rates, r^s_τ, and the lending rate, r^t_τ, at any time period, τ. However, the focus of this chapter is the impact of the high-tech industry on the banking sector. This is investigated below.

MODEL WITH BOTH TRADITIONAL AND HIGH-TECH INDUSTRIES

Suppose a new high-tech industry is introduced into the economy. The households, at any time period τ, continue to maximise their two-period inter-temporary utility function under the new deposit interest rate, r^s_τ. It is up to the banks to decide how many deposits are lent to the new high-tech industry and how many upward or downward adjustments are required for the loans to the traditional industry, at any time period, τ. The bank will continue to pay a single deposit rate, r^s_τ, to the depositors, but it may charge two different lending rates to the two different industries, r^t_τ and r^b_τ, respectively, due to (a) the monitoring costs, (b) the risks and (c) the fact that the returns of the investment associated with the two industries are quite different. Productivity is substantially higher in the high-tech industry than in the traditional industry. Yet, the risks associated with the high-tech industry are also significantly higher. There are at least three additional risks involved with the high-tech industry: (1) technology risk associated with both technical and quality uncertainty, (2) market risk related to the uncertainty of market acceptance, the time span necessary for the market to accept the new technology and competitiveness of the high-tech products in the market and (3) management risk which characterises the possibility of the lack of management expertise in the high-tech industry, especially in a less-developed economy such as China.[14] In such a situation, the advantages of the banking sectors (discussed above) become even more important in terms of reducing the transaction

---

[14] See J. L. Fu, Y. F. Jiang and J. J. Lei (ed.), *Technology Innovation: The Future of Chinese Enterprises (Jishu chuangxin: zhongguo qiye fazhan zh lu)* (Beijing: Enterprise Management Press (qiye guan li chubanshe), 1992) (in Chinese); C. Steindel, "Manufacturing Productivity and High-tech Investment," *Quarterly Review of Federal Reserve Bank of New York* 17 (1992): 39–47; M. W. Cardullo, *Technological Entrepreneurism: Enterprise Formation, Financing and Growth* (Philadelphia: Research Studies Press, 1999); L. M. Branscomb and P. E. Auerswald, *Taking Technical Risks: How Innovators, Managers and Investors Manage Risk in High-Tech Innovations* (Cambridge, MA: MIT Press, 2001).

costs and improving the quality of risk assessment. The details of the model's structure are outlined below.

Industrial Sectors

The demand for loans can be derived by maximising the expected present discounted value of the profit flows of the traditional industry and the high-tech industry, respectively

For the traditional industrial sector, the results are similar to (5.13):

$$(L^t_\tau)^d = (A^t_\tau - 1 - r^t_\tau)/2B^t. \tag{5.22}$$

For the high-tech industrial sector, suppose the firm has a profit function at time period, τ:

$$\pi^b_\tau = A^b_\tau L^b_\tau - (1 + r^b_\tau)L^b_\tau - B^b(L^b_\tau)^2 + \eta^b_\tau, \tag{5.23}$$

where superscript b indicates the high-tech industrial sector; $Y^b_\tau = A^b_\tau L^b_\tau$ is output; A^b_τ is productivity; L^b_τ is the bank loan; $(1 + r^b_\tau)L^b_\tau$ is the gross borrowing costs of the loan; r^b_τ is the interest rate of the loan; $C^b(L^b_\tau) = B^b(L^b_\tau)^2$ is production and management costs and B^b is a constant. The high-tech firm's profit is associated with uncertainty, η^b_τ. There is some probability that η^b_τ will take positive values, indicating that the business is successful. However, there are also some downside risks in which case η^b_τ will take negative values. It is assumed that $E(\eta^b_\tau) = 0$.

The decision problem of the firm is to choose a time path of borrowings in terms of bank loans which maximises the expected present discounted value of the profit flows π^b_τ:

$$\max E\sum_{\tau=0}^{\infty} \beta^\tau_b \pi^b_\tau \tag{5.24}$$

subject to $\Delta L^b_\tau = \Delta(L^b_\tau)^s$, where β_b is the time-discount factor of the high-tech firm, Δ is the first-difference operator and $\Delta(L^b_\tau)^s$ is the change of the supply of bank loans.

The current-value Hamiltonian is:

$$H^b_\tau = E(\pi^b_\tau) + \lambda^b_\tau \Delta(L^b_\tau)^s, \tag{5.25}$$

where λ^b_τ is the co-state variable.

The first order condition is given as follows:

$$\partial H^b_\tau / \partial L^b_\tau = \partial E(\pi^b_\tau)/ \partial L^b_\tau = A^b_\tau - (1 + r^b_\tau) - 2B^b L^b_\tau = 0. \tag{5.26}$$

Hence,

$$(L^b_\tau)^d = (A^b_\tau - 1 - r^b_\tau)/2B^b. \tag{5.27}$$

This solves the demand for loans by the firms in the high-tech industrial sector given the lending rate r^b_τ.

Banking Sector

Assume that the profit structure of the banking sector associated with industry i [$i = t$ (traditional) and b (high-tech) industries] is similar to (5.16) above. The profits of the bank consist of the joint profits from lending to both the traditional and new high-tech industries:

$$
\begin{aligned}
\pi_{\text{bank},\tau} &= \pi^t_{\text{bank},\tau} + \pi^b_{\text{bank},\tau} \\
&= [(r^t_\tau - r^s_\tau)L^t_\tau - C_{\text{bank},t}(L^t_\tau)] + \varepsilon^t_{\text{bank},\tau} \\
&\quad + [(r^b_\tau - r^s_\tau)L^b_\tau - C_{\text{bank},b}(L^b_\tau)] + \varepsilon^b_{\text{bank},\tau} \\
&= [(r^t_\tau - r^s_\tau)L^t_\tau - b^t\sigma^t_\tau(L^t_\tau)^2] \\
&\quad + [(r^b_\tau - r^s_\tau)L^b_\tau - b^b\sigma^b_\tau(L^b_\tau)^2] \\
&\quad + \varepsilon^t_{\text{bank},\tau} + \varepsilon^b_{\text{bank},\tau},
\end{aligned}
\tag{5.28}
$$

where r^t_τ and r^b_τ are the interest rates of lending (L^t_τ and L^b_τ) to the traditional and high-tech firms, respectively; r^s_τ is the interest rates on savings deposits; $C_{\text{bank},t}(L^t_\tau)$ and $C_{\text{bank},b}(L^b_\tau)$ are the monitoring and management costs of the bank related to the loans issued to the traditional and high-tech firms, respectively; and $\varepsilon^t_{\text{bank},\tau}$ and $\varepsilon^b_{\text{bank},\tau}$ are two stochastic processes with $E(\varepsilon^t_{\text{bank},\tau}) = E(\varepsilon^b_{\text{bank},\tau}) = 0$ which are related to the risk of the loan repayment associated with the traditional and high-tech firms, respectively. The total risk indicator of lending to the high-tech firms is $var(\varepsilon^b_{bank,\tau}) + var(\eta^b_\tau) = (\sigma^b_\tau)^2$, and b^b is the degree of risk-aversion of the bank lending to the high-tech industry.

The decision problem of the bank is to choose the time paths of the lending to both the traditional and new high-tech firms which maximises the present discounted value of the profit flows $\pi_{bank,\tau}$:

$$\max E\sum_{\tau=0}^{\infty} \beta_b^\tau \pi_{bank,\tau} \qquad (5.29)$$

subject to:

$$\Delta L^t_\tau = \phi_\tau[S_\tau - S_{\tau-1} + S_{\tau-1}(1 + r^t_{\tau-1}) - C_{o,\tau}], \qquad (5.30)$$

$$\Delta L^b_\tau = (1 - \phi_\tau)[S_\tau - S_{\tau-1} + S_{\tau-1}(1 + r^t_{\tau-1}) - C_{o,\tau}], \qquad (5.31)$$

where β_b is the time-discount factor of the banks and ϕ_τ is the proportion of the savings allocated to the lending to the traditional sector.

The current-value Hamiltonian is:

$$H_{bank,\tau} = E(\pi_{bank,\tau}) + q^t_\tau\phi_\tau[S_\tau - S_{\tau-1} + S_{\tau-1}(1 + r^t_{\tau-1}) - C_{o,\tau}] \\ + q^b_\tau(1 - \phi_\tau)[S_\tau - S_{\tau-1} + S_{\tau-1}(1 + r^t_{\tau-1}) - C_{o,\tau}], \qquad (5.32)$$

where q^t_τ and q^b_τ are the co-state variables.

The first order conditions are given as follows:

$$\partial H_{bank,\tau}/\partial L^t_\tau = \partial E(\pi^t_{bank,\tau})/\partial L^t_\tau = r^t_\tau - 2b^t\sigma^t_\tau L^t_\tau - r^s_\tau = 0, \qquad (5.33)$$

and

$$\partial H_{bank,\tau}/\partial L^b_\tau = \partial E(\pi^b_{bank,\tau})/\partial L^b_\tau = r^b_\tau - 2b^b\sigma^b_\tau L^b_\tau - r^s_\tau = 0. \qquad (5.34)$$

Hence, the supply of loans by the banks is:

$$(L^t_\tau)^s = (r^t_\tau - r^s_\tau)/(2b^t\sigma^t_\tau), \qquad (5.35)$$

and

$$(L^b_\tau)^s = (r^b_\tau - r^s_\tau)/(2b^b\sigma^b_\tau), \qquad (5.36)$$

given the lending rates r^t_τ and r^b_τ, and the deposits interest rate r^s_τ. The sum of these, $(L^t_\tau)^s + (L^b_\tau)^s$, are in fact also the aggregate demand for deposits.

IMPACT OF THE HIGH-TECH INDUSTRY ON THE ECONOMY

Similar to above, the model is closed by setting the expected income, W^e_τ, of the young households equal to the sum of the expected profits of the traditional and high-tech sectors and the banking sector, $E(\pi^t_\tau + \pi^b_\tau + \pi_{\text{bank},\tau})$:

$$W^e_\tau = E(\pi^t_\tau + \pi^b_\tau + \pi_{\text{bank},\tau}). \tag{5.37}$$

To evaluate the impact of the high-tech industry, the equilibrium conditions for the loans market are first laid out:

(a) $$(L^t_\tau)^s = (L^t_\tau)^d. \tag{5.38}$$

This states that demand for and supply of loans to the traditional sector must be equal, i.e.,

$$(r^t_\tau - r^s_\tau)/(2b^t\sigma^t_\tau) = (A^t_\tau - 1 - r^t_\tau)/2B^t. \tag{5.39}$$

Hence,

$$r^t_\tau = \theta^t_0 + \theta^t_1 r^s_\tau, \tag{5.40}$$

where

$$\theta^t_0 = b^t\sigma^t_\tau (A^t_\tau - 1)/(b^t\sigma^t_\tau + B^t)$$

and

$$\theta^t_1 = B^t/(b_t\sigma^t_\tau + B^t) > 0.$$

(b) $$(L^b_\tau)^s = (L^b_\tau)^d \tag{5.41}$$

This states that the demand for and supply of loans for the high-tech sector must also be the same. Parallel to (40):

$$r^b_\tau = \theta^b_0 + \theta^b_1 r^s_\tau,$$ (5.42)

where

$$\theta^b_0 = b^b \sigma^b_\tau (A^b_\tau - 1)/(b^b \sigma^b_\tau + B^b)$$

and

$$\theta^b_1 = B^b/(b^b \sigma^b_\tau + B^b) > 0.$$

(c) $$S_\tau = (L^t_\tau)^d + \delta (L^b_\tau)^d$$ (5.43)

This states that the total demand and supply of deposits of the economy must also be in equilibrium, where $\delta = 0$ is the case of Section 2 without high-tech industry and $\delta = 1$ is the case with high-tech industry.[15] The change of δ reflects the impact on the economy from a traditional economy to a mixed economy with high-tech industry. The deposit market equilibrium condition (c) above is rewritten as:

$$S_\tau = (A^t_\tau - 1 - r^t_\tau)/2B^t + \delta (A^b_\tau - 1 - r^b_\tau)/(2B^b)$$

or,

$$S_\tau = (A^t_\tau - 1 - \theta^t_0 - \theta^t_1 r^s_\tau)/(2B^t) + \delta (A^b_\tau - 1 - \theta^b_0 - \theta^b_1 r^s_\tau)/(2B^b).$$ (5.44)

Taking total differentiation on both sides of the above equation:

$$[(\partial S_\tau/\partial r^s_\tau) + (\partial S_\tau/\partial W^e_\tau)(dW^e_\tau/dr^s_\tau)]dr^s_\tau$$
$$= -(\theta^t_1/2B^t)dr^s_\tau - \delta(\theta^b_1/2B^b)dr^s_\tau + (L^b_\tau)^d d\delta.$$ (5.45)

---

[15] For $\delta \in (0,1)$, it may be considered as (artificially imposed) the case of credit-rationing, i.e., both the supply of and demand for loans are cut back by a factor of δ and (5.41) becomes $\delta(L^b_\tau)^s = \delta(L^b_\tau)^d$ (similar mathematical technique has been widely used in labour economics). See for example, D. Acemoglu, "Training and Innovation in an Imperfect Labour Market," *Review of Economic Studies* 64 (1997): 445–464.

From Appendix A:

$$dW^e_\tau/dr^s_\tau = 0. \tag{5.46}$$

Hence,

$$dr^s_\tau/d\delta = (L^h_\tau)^d/[(\partial S_\tau/\partial r^s_\tau) + (\theta^t_1/2B^t) + \delta(\theta^h_1/2B^h)] > 0, \tag{5.47}$$

where $(\partial S_\tau/\partial r^s_\tau) = W^e_\tau/[\beta_c(1 + r^s_\tau) + (1/\beta_c)]^2 > 0$.

The main findings of this chapter are that there are substitution and expansion effects on the bank loans. The substitution effect tends to substitute the loans borrowed by traditional industry by that of the high-tech industry. The expansion effect tends to increase the total bank loans due to the new activities in the high-tech industry. It dominates the substitution effect rendering an increase in total bank loans. To finance the increased economic activity the deposit rates must rise to attract more savings from the household sector. As a result, banks must charge a higher lending rate to the traditional industrial sector in order to cover the increased finance costs. However, the lending rate to the high-tech industry is not necessarily higher than that to the traditional industry, though the former has a higher return than the latter.

These findings fit the current economic and financial situation in China quite well. Table 5.5 shows that both the output and export shares of the high-tech industry have been increasing since the 1990s. Bank loans for tech-development in large and medium-sized enterprises have been increased steadily over the same period. Interestingly, consistent with the findings derived from our theoretical model, the balances of both savings deposits and loans as shares of GDP are rising.

CONCLUSION

This chapter has discussed the development of high-tech industries in post-reform China. Foreign-invested high-tech industries are found to have taken more than half of the output share in China.

Table 5.5: High-Tech Industry and Financial Development in China (percent)

	1995	1999	2000	2001	2002	2003	2004	2005
Output of high-tech industry/ total industry	4.3	5.9	6.9	7.1	7.9	9.2	9.7	10.6
Exports of high-tech products	7.9	14.1	16.6	19.4	22.8	27.3	29.9	28.6
Exports of primary goods	16.9	11.4	11.4	11.0	9.6	8.6	7.3	6.4
Bank loans for tech-development (billion RMB)	7.3	8.4	9.7	9.5	9.9	15.6	15.5	16.9
Residents savings deposit/GDP	51.4	72.7	71.9	75.8	82.5	94.2	92.2	80.6
Total loan balance of financial institutions/GDP	79.6	114.2	111.1	115.4	124.8	135.4	129.6	113.4

Notes: All figures are based on current prices; High-Tech industry/products are defined by the OECD as: (1) computers and telecommunications, (2) life sciences, (3) aerospace and aeronautics, (4) electronics, (5) opto-electronics, (6) computer integrated manufacturing, (7) biotechnology, (8) material design, (9) nuclear technology and (10) armaments. See T. Hatzichronoglou, "Revision of the High-Technology Sector and Product Classification", *OECD STI Working Paper* (Paris: OECD, 1997/2). Output of high-tech industry/total industry: Value-added of all state-owned high-tech enterprises and non-state-owned ones that are above the designated size of RMB5 million worth of sales as a percent of total industrial GDP. *China Statistical Yearbook of Science and Technology*, 2005, 6. *China Statistical Yearbook*, 2006, 57; "Exports of High-Tech Products" and "Exports of Primary Goods": The Percentages of these two categories as the exports of manufactured goods. *China Statistical Yearbook of Science and Technology*, 1999, 220–221; 2005, 104–105. *China Statistical Yearbook*, 2005, 625. Exports of high-tech products and primary goods in 2005 come from the Ministry of Commerce website, respectively: http://gcs.mofcom.gov.cn/aarticle/Nocategory/200602/20060201484767.html and http://kjs.mofcom.gov.cn/aarticle/bn/cbw/200601/20060101434776.html; Bank loans for tech-development: loans for large and medium-sized enterprises (billion RMB), *China Statistical Yearbook of Science and Technology*, 2005, 104–105; *China Statistical Yearbook*, 2005, 716; 2006, 827; "Residents Savings Deposit/GDP" and "Total Loan Balance of State Banks/GDP." *China Statistical Abstract*, 2000, 4 and 73; 2003, 84; 2005, 83; *Statistical Communiqué*, 1995, 2005, National Bureau of Statistics.

The state-owned high-tech industries initially dominated the domestic high-tech firms but have undergone rapid decline in recent years (see Table 5.4). A prototype three-sector overlapping generations model for a developing country was constructed consisting of household, banking and industrial sectors. Dynamic comparative analysis of the model solutions was conducted for two cases: (1) an industrial sector that has only traditional industry, and (2) a traditional industrial sector to which a new high-tech industry is introduced. It is found that the expansion effect of the high-tech industry dominates its substitution effect rendering an increase in the total bank credits. However, the implication is that the interest rates have to go up in order to attract more savings from the household sector.

The findings have several policy implications. If interest rates rise too high, due perhaps, to the fact that income is low in China, the Government may need to offer some interest subsidies to both the high-tech and traditional firms. It is necessary to subsidise the high-tech firms to give them extra incentive to develop R&D and sustain the long-term growth of the Chinese economy. It may be also necessary to subsidise the traditional firms during the transition process if the number of traditional firms that are affected by the high-tech industry is large. This will ensure social stability and a smooth transition for the unskilled workers in the traditional sector to the high-tech sector. However, it must be stressed that the Government may only consider the interest rate subsidies, not the deficit subsidies. This is to minimise the moral hazard problem and the detrimental consequences of the "soft-budget" constraint.[16] An even better policy perhaps would be to subsidise R&D activities by providing open-bid grants to both high-tech and traditional industries, a practice that has been implemented successfully by the US Government for some time. This provides incentive for the two industries to innovate and at the same time share the risk of R&D. Also, market interest rates may not rise too high to function properly.

---

[16] See B. Holmstrom and J. Tirole, "Financial Intermediation, Loanable Funds and the Real Sector," *Quarterly Journal of Economics* 112 (1997): 663–691; E. Berglof and G. Roland, "Soft Budget Constraints and Banking in Transition Economies," *Journal of Comparative Economics* 26, no. 1 (1998): 18–40.

ACKNOWLEDGEMENTS

This research was supported by a Competitive Earmarked Research Grant (No. LU3110/03H) from the RGC of the Hong Kong SAR Government. The author is grateful to the editor Elspeth Thomson, Ken Chan, Yak-yeow Kueh, Sung Ko Li, Shucheng Liu, Shu-ki Tsang, Zhijun Zhao and participants of the Economics Department Seminar held at Hong Kong Baptist University. Their helpful comments substantially improved both the quality and presentation of the chapter. However, the author is responsible for any remaining errors.

APPENDIX A

This appendix shows that $dW^e_\tau/dr^s_\tau = dW_\tau/dr^s_\tau = 0$ for the model with both traditional and high-tech industries. The four stochastic processes η^t_τ, η^b_τ, $\varepsilon^t_{\text{bank},\tau}$ and $\varepsilon^b_{\text{bank},\tau}$ approximate the risks associated with the profits of the traditional industry, the high-tech industry and the banking sector (which lends to both the traditional and high-tech industries), respectively. From the model closure rule:

$$
\begin{aligned}
W_\tau &= \pi^t_\tau + \pi^b_\tau + \pi_{\text{bank},\tau} \\
&= \pi^t_\tau + \pi^b_\tau + \pi^t_{\text{bank},\tau} + \pi^b_{\text{bank},\tau} \\
&= E(\pi^t_\tau + \pi^b_\tau + \pi^t_{\text{bank},\tau} + \pi^b_{\text{bank},\tau}) \\
&\quad + \eta^t_\tau + \eta^b_\tau + \varepsilon^t_{\text{bank},\tau} + \varepsilon^b_{\text{bank},\tau}.
\end{aligned}
\tag{A.1}
$$

Since the risk terms are additive to the profit functions:

$$
\begin{aligned}
dW_\tau/dr^s_\tau &= dE\pi^t_\tau/dr^s_\tau + dE\pi^b_\tau/dr^s_\tau \\
&\quad + dE\pi^t_{\text{bank},\tau}/dr^s_\tau + dE\pi^b_{\text{bank},\tau}/dr^s_\tau \\
&= (\partial E\pi^t_\tau/\partial L^t_\tau)(dL^t_\tau/dr^s_\tau) + (\partial E\pi^b_\tau/\partial L^b_\tau)(dL^b_\tau/dr^s_\tau) \\
&\quad + (\partial E\pi^t_{\text{bank},\tau}/\partial L^t_\tau)(dL^t_\tau/dr^s_\tau) + (\partial E\pi^b_{\text{bank},\tau}/\partial L^b_\tau)(dL^b_\tau/dr^s_\tau) \\
&= (\partial H^t_\tau/\partial L^t_\tau)(dL^t_\tau/dr^s_\tau) + (\partial H^b_\tau/\partial L^b_\tau)(dL^b_\tau/dr^s_\tau) \\
&\quad + (\partial H_{\text{bank},\tau}/\partial L^t_\tau)(dL^t_\tau/dr^s_\tau) + (\partial H_{\text{bank},\tau}/\partial L^b_\tau)(dL^b_\tau/dr^s_\tau) \\
&= 0.
\end{aligned}
\tag{A.2}
$$

$\partial H^t_\tau/\partial L^t_\tau = \partial H^b_\tau/\partial L^b_\tau = \partial H_{bank,\tau}/\partial L^t_\tau = \partial H_{bank,\tau}/\partial L^b_\tau = 0$ are all first order conditions for the respective Hamiltonians in Eqs. (5.12), (5.26), (5.33) and (5.34) in the main text.

This implies:

$$dW^e_\tau/dr^s_\tau = dE(W_\tau)/dr^s_\tau = E(dW_\tau/dr^s_\tau) = 0. \tag{A.3}$$

APPENDIX B

In the main text a simplifying assumption is made, namely, that individuals maximise their utility function with *expected income* instead of maximising *expected utility* under uncertainty. This appendix relaxes this assumption and derives a similar conclusion based on the *expected utility* maximisation approach.

Suppose the household maximises the following expected inter-temporal utility function:

$$\max EU_{\tau,\tau+1} = E[(C_{y,\tau})^{1/2} + \beta_c(C_{o,\tau+1})^{1/2}], \tag{B.1}$$

subject to the budget constraints in each period:

$$W_\tau = C_{y,\tau} + S_\tau \tag{B.2}$$

$$C_{o,\tau+1} = (1 + r^s_\tau)S_\tau, \tag{B.3}$$

where β_c is the time-discount factor of the consumer.

The inter-temporal utility function (B.1) is rewritten as follows:

$$\max E(U_{\tau,\tau+1}) = E\{(W_\tau - S_\tau)^{1/2} + \beta_c [(1 + r^s_\tau)S_\tau]^{1/2}\}. \tag{B.4}$$

The first order condition to maximise this utility function is given by:

$$\partial E(U_{\tau,\tau+1})/\partial S_\tau = E\{-1/2(W_\tau - S_\tau)^{-1/2} + 1/2\beta_c[(1 + r^s_\tau)S_\tau]^{-1/2}(1 + r^s_\tau)\} = 0. \tag{B.5}$$

Hence,

$$E(W_\tau - S_\tau)^{-1/2} = \beta_c(1 + r^s_\tau)^{1/2} S_\tau^{-1/2}. \tag{B.6}$$

Conditional on W_τ, totally differentiating both sides of the above equation:

$$-1/2\, E(W_\tau - S_\tau)^{-3/2}(-dS_\tau) = 1/2\beta_c[(1 + r_\tau^s)S_\tau]^{-1/2}\,dr^s$$
$$- 1/2\beta_c(1 + r_\tau^s)^{1/2}S_\tau^{-3/2}dS_\tau. \quad (\text{B.7})$$

Hence:

$$\partial S_\tau/\partial r_\tau^s = 1/2\beta_c[(1 + r_\tau^s)S_\tau]^{-1/2}/[\beta_c(1 + r_\tau^s)^{1/2}S_\tau^{-3/2}$$
$$+ E(W_\tau - S_\tau)^{-3/2}] > 0. \quad (\text{B.8})$$

Recalling Eq. (5.44):

$$S_\tau = 1/2\,(A_\tau^t - 1 - \theta_0^t - \theta_1^t\, r_\tau^s)/B^t$$
$$+ 1/2\delta(A_\tau^h - 1 - \theta_0^h - \theta_1^h\, r_\tau^s)/B^h. \quad (\text{B.9})$$

Taking total differentiation on both sides of the above equation:

$$[(\partial S_\tau/\partial r_\tau^s) + (\partial S_\tau/\partial W_\tau)(dW_\tau/dr_\tau^s)]dr_\tau^s$$
$$= -1/2(\theta_1^t/B^t)dr_\tau^s - \delta(\theta_1^h/2B^h)dr_\tau^s + (L_\tau^h)^d d\delta. \quad (\text{B.10})$$

From Appendix A:

$$dW_\tau/dr_\tau^s = 0. \quad (\text{B.11})$$

Hence,

$$dr_\tau^s/d\delta = (L_\tau^h)^d/[(\partial S_\tau/\partial r_\tau^s) + (\theta_1^t/2B^t) + \delta(\theta_1^h/2B^h)] > 0 \quad (\text{B.12})$$

since $(\partial S_\tau/\partial r_\tau^s) > 0$ according to (B.8).

This replicates the key finding of the chapter in (5.47): when δ increases from 0 to 1, the deposit interest rate r_s will rise. That is, the introduction of a high-tech industry into the economy will induce higher saving and consequently create an expansion effect on the total balance of loans. As a result, all other findings of the chapter carry through under the *expected utility* maximisation approach.

Chapter 6

Ningbo and Dalian: Patterns of Science and Technology Development

Jon Sigurdson

INTRODUCTION

The world's emerging knowledge society is not evenly distributed among or within countries. Relatively small territories — cities and their close surroundings — are becoming the key production areas. This also means that there is a shift away from a national perspective to a regional one in understanding the welfare of a nation. It is possible to identify three types of regional agglomerations:

- those where there already exists a strong industrial base which naturally provides good conditions;
- those where high-tech activities have started to agglomerate initially without government intent, and the government subsequently tries to encourage more of such activities to help them gain critical mass;
- those which have a weak industrial and technological base and the government deliberately tries to create a growth pole.

In China, the second category prevails. China's science and technology industrial parks are not evenly distributed and do not represent the actual distribution of population or economic activity. There is an inherent conflict between regional or localised development on one hand and the rapid concentration of industrial and technological activities on the other. In the second category, industrial and technological stimulation from the various levels of government is necessary because the local companies alone cannot attract more industries. To continue their development, it is imperative that they are allocated capital, engineers, scientists and land which are attractive for foreign multinational companies. Also critical are physical infrastructure such as water and power supplies, physical transportation, including easy access to ports and airports, and telecommunications. Institutional development must facilitate investment measures and offer transparent tax rules.

In this chapter, Ningbo and Dalian are used to illustrate the changes that are taking place in China today.[1] The process of learning lies not only in acquiring technologies, but also in promoting technological progress by releasing market forces. The gaining and accumulation of market experience — institutional settings, effective incentive mechanisms, developing marketable products, selling new products in the market, etc. — is more import than just acquiring particular technologies as such. However, this intensive learning process has primarily been limited to China's coastal areas, where institutional innovation and expansion of formal training and higher education may be the most significant contributing factors to China's progress in science and technology.

Ningbo and Dalian share a number of important and striking similarities. First, the Central Government has strongly supported them by providing both a framework and resources for various types of zones, industrial parks and science parks where national science and technology programmes can incubate. Second, the

---

[1] This chapter is based primarily on material collected during a field investigation in April 2005, with travel costs sponsored by the Asian Development Bank Institute in Tokyo.

regional governments have encouraged foreign direct investment (FDI) as well as the transfer of technology and management skills from all over the world to take place in these regions. Third, these regions have had the ideal combination of labour types: unskilled, skilled and professional (including researchers). Fourth, the directed but often spontaneous development of technological and industrial clusters has provided the basis for further development.

NINGBO

Situated south of Shanghai, Ningbo is one of the five cities under the direct jurisdiction of the State Council, enjoying the same rights as provincial governments in terms of economic planning and management. Its government has distinguished itself by providing strong support for private initiatives as well as institutional innovations, partly guided by the Central Authorities. Technological development has taken advantage of Ningbo's geographical and structural characteristics. A number of industries are port based, such as the petrochemical, iron and steel and paper industries. More port development will result in higher value-added and more downstream products. The petrochemical industry will expand into higher-valued products, and similar developments will take place within the iron and steel industry, i.e., the development of specialised stainless steel products. The Hangzhou Bay area provides favourable conditions for industries such as automobiles, home appliances and garments. The high-tech industries including electronics and information industries are slightly inland along the major highways.

The IT sector will become important and evolve from an earlier concentration of computer motherboard manufacturing. Ningbo has an agreement with the Chinese Academy of Sciences (CAS) to support Zhejiang University with a Network Technology Institute which will be located inside the High-Tech Park.

Ningbo has traditionally been a centre for car component industries, beginning with the early development of spark plugs and car wheels. This has occurred partly through a transfer of activities from Shanghai for plastic and die-metal moulding. Shanghai very soon affected Ningbo in a major way by forcing an industrial restructuring with private industry playing a pivotal role. Rapidly expanding demand from Japan, Germany and Taiwan also fostered development of the moulding industry. Machinery for plastics moulding developed at an early stage, with Haier buying many mould components from Ningbo.[2] The specialty of metal moulding has expanded and become very strong, attracting investment from Hong Kong, Korea and Japan.

Employment in the moulding industry in Ningbo now stands at about 100,000 workers, much expanded since 1978. Enterprises there are now able to deliver moulds for products ranging in weight from only a few milligrams to as large as 50 kilograms. Some have established subsidiaries in the US.

Ningbo's Development Zones

Ningbo has four national-scale development zones, one high-tech zone and 10 provincial and municipal-level development zones which cater to both shipping and trade sectors, as well as high-tech sectors. The state-level zones — Ningbo Economic and Technological Development Zone (NETD), Free Trade Zone, Export Processing Zone and Daxie — are all located in the Beilun District in east Ningbo near the coast.[3]

The Government established several state-level development zones beginning in 1979. Ningo was selected as the location for one such zone in 1984. The Ningbo Municipal Government in 2003 decided to merge the Beilun District with the Ningbo Economic and Technical Development Zone (NETDZ). Today, total employment stands at 380,000.

NETDZ is the largest state-level zone in Ningbo. By July 2002, 686 enterprises had settled there from nearly 30 countries and regions

---

[2] Haier manufactures household appliances such as freezers, refrigerators, washing machines, televisions, water heaters, air conditioners and microwave ovens, as well as laptop computers. The company's headquarters are in Qingdao, Shandong Province.

[3] Beilun is an international port in Zhejiang situated on the southern coast of Hangzhou Bay. Daxie Island is 40 kilometres east of Ningbo.

with total FDI amounting to US$2.1 billion.[4] The major industries include power generation, chemicals, stainless steel, shipbuilding, paper manufacturing, plastic and rubber, and high-tech industries.

Ningbo's High-Tech Park

The Ningbo High-Tech (NHT) Park opened in July 1999, jointly developed by the CAS and the Ningbo Municipal Government. The major products include computer motherboards, network terminals, IC components, photoelectric apparatus, light-reflecting materials, plasma display panels and simulators.

There were a number of attributes contributing to the creation of the NHT Park: its attractive location geographically and market-wise, the fact that the CAS did not have any major facilities in Zhejiang Province, and Ningbo's very good track record in private entrepreneurship. In some ways, it shares similarities with Hsinchu Industrial Science Park on Taiwan. Two other factors were also at work. The educational level had been rather low and needed to be raised through new initiatives. Second, more than 80 CAS staff members originate in Ningbo and constitute a tangible and very powerful lobby.

There is an expectation of rapid growth in software development. Zhejiang University established a Software Institute in October 2004, and it is hoped that Ningbo will have a large number of software companies employing more than 30,000. The Innovation Centre of the NHT Park was established in late 1999 and re-named the National High Tech Centre in October 2002 by Xu Guanha, the then Minister of Science and Technology. In March 2003, the CAS and Ningbo Municipal Government signed an agreement for the joint expansion of the High-Tech Industry Incubation

---

[4] Sixteen of the top 500 multinational companies (headquarters in parentheses) have set up ventures here, including Esso, Dow Chemical (Midland, MI, US), Mitsui (Tokyo), Mitsubishi Itochu (Tokyo), Marubeni (Tokyo), Asahi Chemical (Tokyo), Kanematsu (Tokyo), Sumitomo (Osaka), Iwai (Tokyo), Hoechst (Frankfurt), Mannesmann (Munich) and Samsung (Seoul).

Base of Ningbo's local CAS so as to integrate CAS talents and technology with Ningbo's advantages in terms of location and industrial policy. The Innovation Centre incorporates the following six major activities:[5]

1. Ningbo Software Park
2. Zhejiang Provincial Postdoctoral Innovation Base (Ningbo)
3. Ningbo Doctoral Innovation Park
4 Ningbo Overseas Scholars Innovation Park
5. Ningbo Undergraduate Innovation Park
6. Chinese Information and Science Computing Internship and Innovation Base

In addition, there are another two Pioneer Parks: University Pioneer Park and Ningbo Pioneer Park. Each county within Ningbo has its own municipal-level incubator, though together much smaller than the Innovation Centre within the NHT Park. More than 200 enterprises have been introduced to the Innovation Centre including what are referred to as research institutes, involving more than 3,600 staff, of which 150 are PhD holders and another 90 are overseas Chinese. The Innovation Centre presently has 270 member enterprises. Of these, 75 are physically present in the Centre building, while the rest are virtual members.

Creating and Using Brainpower: A Look at Ningbo's Institutions of Higher Learning

It is the university system, in particular, but also the education system, in general, which provides the foundation for China's future as a knowledge-based economy. Universities have undergone dramatic changes in recent years, and it is still too early to fully judge their performance. They have until recently not been involved in advanced research. Graduate studies were introduced only after major reforms started in the late 1970s.

---

[5] Ningbo High-Tech Innovation Centre, "Technology Global: Innovation Local" (brochure), Ningbo, 2003.

Enrolment in higher education increased rapidly after 1998. More than a third of all university students study engineering, and including science students the share is close to 40 percent, and increasing. Chinese universities will soon be graduating at least one million students each year in science and engineering. Many of them will specialise in electronics. Presently one out of every five Chinese postgraduate students is pursuing his/her studies abroad.

In 1997, China embarked on an ambitious reform plan — the National 211 Project — that should bring several of its universities into world leading positions during the coming century.[6] Selection of one hundred universities is expected to create a necessary focus on higher education to receive special attention and favourable funding. At the same time, many universities have been merged into more comprehensive entities. This was aimed at achieving a number of objectives, aside from giving the Ministry of Education full control of higher education, for example, upgrading the teaching and facilities at lower-tier colleges and reducing staff and administrative costs.

The Zhejiang University that came into being in 1998 was created from the former Zhejiang University, established in 1928, from the University of Medicine and Zhejiang University of Agriculture. In the early 1950s, the School of Liberal Arts and other parts were removed from Zhejiang University to be included in the Zhejiang Normal College that was merged with Hangzhou University in 1958. The present Zhejiang University is included in the 211 Project and is expected in 2017 to rank among the leading universities of the world. In 2003, there were 41,000 full-time students at Zhejiang University, including 30,000 undergraduates, 8,000 Master's degree students and 3,200 PhD candidates. There are also nearly 38,000 students enrolled in vocational education courses.

Project 211 is oriented mainly towards economic development in China, and emphasis will be given to support institutions and key disciplinary areas which are closely related to "pillar industries"

---

[6] "211" stands for the objective of bringing a number of Chinese universities into a Global One position in the 21st century.

where high-level professional manpower is needed. Priority will be given to some 25 universities which have a concentration of critical disciplines. These are expected to reach high international standards in both teaching and research and become models for other universities in China. The underlying objectives are to break away from the narrow disciplinary orientation that existed in the former university system, broaden the coverage of various disciplines and foster the emergence of cross-disciplinary teaching and research.

Zhejiang Wanli University (ZWU) was created from a former provincial institution of higher learning, the Zhejiang Junior College of Training Teachers for Agricultural Technology, which was established in the early 1950s. ZWU is supervised by the Zhejiang Education Department and operated by the Zhejiang Wanli Education Group (ZWEG). It has two campuses, Huilong and Qianhu. The Junior College and College of Commerce includes departments such as foreign languages, law, culture and media, artistic design, computer science, electronic information engineering and life sciences with altogether 38 specialties in junior college programmes. ZWU offers eight specialties in undergraduate programmes.

In 2003, there were more than 8,000 full-time students, and the Adult Education Programme had more than 1,000. ZWU has seven laboratory centres and three key municipal laboratories. The University pursues national science research as well as economics and management issues. There are three research institutes: Institute of Culture, Institute of Biological Technology and Ningbo Industrial and Economic Development Research Centre.

The university encourages its staff to look for new models applicable to China's economic development. It is so far the only market-economy university in China. It is a private university, but the land and buildings belong to the local government. Though it follows the university regulations set by the Ministry of Education, it receives no financial support for its teaching activities which have to be covered from much higher than average tuition fees compared to those levied at nationally supported universities. For perspective, the student fees at Fudan University in Shanghai are around RMB4,000 per year, while those at ZWU are RMB16,000.

When ZWU started, it had 1,200 students in a three-year programme. Total enrolment now stands at 16,000 of which 10,000 are studying for four-year university degrees while the rest are taking three-year diploma programmes. It is expected that total enrolment will stabilise around 20,000.

Creating a new-style university like ZWU reflects the reform policies of the Ministry of Education which has encouraged experimental models to meet the rising demand for higher education in Eastern China. In the past, private universities have offered only diploma training. ZWU is actively pursuing funds for its laboratories and research activities and is exploring ways to collaborate with firms. An important objective is to train students and staff, and it is involved in the Nottingham–Ningbo University for which premises have been built on a new campus. In March 2004, the Chinese Ministry of Education approved the establishment of Ningbo–Nottingham University as China's first Sino-foreign university.[7] It was founded jointly by the University of Nottingham of Britain and the ZWU in Ningbo with a reported investment of RMB600 million.

The Nottingham–Ningbo University will ultimately have about 4,000 students who will study business and the natural sciences. The Vice-Chancellor of the new university is Professor Yang Fujia, currently Dean of the University of Nottingham and a member of the CAS. Dr Ian Gow, current Deputy President of the University of Nottingham and Dean of its Business School, will be the Managing Deputy President. Professor Yang has been a guest of ZWU and has played an important role in the creation of the new university. Nottingham failed to establish desired partnerships with Fudan and Tongji universities in Shanghai, and with Tsinghua University in Beijing.

The new university is supported by both Ningbo City and the Zhejiang Provincial Government. The Ministry of Education will assess the results after three years and promote a number of similar universities if all is found to be going well. The annual tuition fee of

---

[7] "First Sino-foreign University Approved to Be Set Up in East China City," *People's Daily*, March 25, 2004 at http://english.people.com.cn/200403/25/eng20040325_138422.shtml.

RMB50,000 covers the cost of teaching which will initially be all done by staff from Nottingham University. Students will spend an extra initial year to acquaint themselves with English and the international character of the university. The final degree will be a BA that meets UK requirements. In September 2005, the first 900 students began the same courses as their counterparts in Nottingham in finance and business management, international communications and international studies.[8]

Another interesting university development originates in Ningbo, but is located in Beijing. Geely University is known mostly for its investor, the Geely Group. Managers felt a need to train their own workers, so it was decided in 1994 to invest RMB50 million to create a college. A deal to do the training through an existing college in Hangzhou came to naught. Its application to set up a school in another Zhejiang city was also rebuffed when the local authorities liked the idea so much that they decided to open their own school. Beijing Geely University (BGU) was finally opened in Beijing in 2000. In the first year it enrolled about 3,500 students, and in the second, 7,500. It is an international and new type of higher education institute qualified to issue certificates and diplomas. It is located in the Beijing Zhong Guancun Chang Ping Science and Technology Park, close to the Olympic Village, and meets national requirements in social economic development. It has established 14 colleges and schools, including a Business School, Information and Technology College, Journalism and Communication College, and Finance and Security College.

Ningbo's recent enrolment expansion has taken place in various types of professional colleges (see Table 6.1). An obsession with commercialising university research has apparently created a conflict of interest as many colleges have become cradles of entrepreneurship, and new technologies are being used as the basis of business ventures at an increasing rate. A number of incubators have taken the form of campus-based science parks. However, China's major universities have produced some of the best-known names in the technology sector.

---

[8] Jane Macartne, "University Establishes an English Outpost in China," *The Times*, September 16, 2005 at http://www.timesonline.co.uk/article/0,,3-1782356,00.html.

Table 6.1: Institutions of Higher Learning in Ningbo City

Institution	Supervisory body	Annual intake	Established
Ningbo University	Ministry, delegated to Ningbo City	6,500	1985
1. Ningbo Engineering College	Ningbo City	2,500	1983
2. Ningbo Professional Technology College	Ningbo City	2,500	1959
3. Ningbo Garment Professional College	Ningbo City	1,700	2002
4. Ningbo City Technology College	Ningbo City	2,500	2003
5. Ningbo City Light Textile Professional Technology College	Ningbo City	1,700	1979
6. Ningbo Tian Yi Professional Technology College	Ningbo City	1,500	2004
7. Zhejiang Industrial and Commerce Professional Technology College	Zhejiang Province	2,000	2001
8. Zhejiang University Ningbo Science and Engineering College	Zhejiang Province	3,000	2001
9. Zhejiang Wanli College	Ningbo City	5,500	1999
10. Zhejiang Medical Higher Training School	Zhejiang Province	1,800	1999
11. Ningbo Red Eagle Professional Technology College	Ningbo City	3,500	2001
12. Public Security Maritime Higher Training School	Public Security	500	1999
13. Ningbo Teachers' College	Ningbo City	2,500	1984
14. Ningbo Radio and TV University	Ningbo City	1,500	1979
Total		36,200	

Peking University Founder Group Corp, established in 1986, now has total assets of RMB6,000 million, with shares in 17 other companies and a controlling stake in four listed companies. Its core business has diversified from word processing software to hardware, Internet-related products and systems integration. A non-profit school system and its highly specialised teaching and research may not always resist the temptation of the business world. Research-obsessed scholars and market-oriented managers usually have very different perspectives.

Assuming that the expansion of higher education will continue, China could have more than 120 million citizens with university or college education by 2020. Simultaneously, it could be expected that 25–30 percent would have received degrees/diplomas in engineering or science disciplines (see Figure 6.1). However, there can be little doubt that this expansion will require not only substantial financial resources but also daunting improvements in the quality of teaching staff.

Ningbo's Outstanding Enterprises

Geely Group

Starting in 1986, the Geely Group began by making parts for refrigerators. Three years later, it entered into the advanced decoration materials industry and manufactured the first magnalium bent board in China. In April 1992, the company started manufacturing motorcycles, and in 1996 various activities were organised into the Geely Group Co Ltd, and the first scooter in China came out in 1997. It decided to enter the automobile industry in the same year. The first Geely car was manufactured in the company plant in Linhai City, Zhejiang on August 8, 1998. Geely produced 150,000 cars in 2004 in plants with an annual capacity of 200,000. Over time, annual capacity is expected to reach 600,000.

The Geely Group is comprised of a number of enterprises, mainly in auto and motorcycle manufacturing. It operates two nongovernmental universities, one in Linhai and the other in Zhongguanzun in Beijing with enrolments of 3,500 and 20,000, respectively. The Group also includes hotels and resort inns, as well as factories producing decorative materials. The Group has invested in the Shanghai Metop International Trade Co Ltd, which serves primarily as the export marketing instrument for Geely cars.

Ningbo Bird

The present "Bird" came into being in October 1992 when five engineers, newly graduated from various universities (three of them from Xinan Jiaotong University) embarked on the manufacture of pagers. They were discussing with various investors their need for funds when Fenghua County Government in Ningbo decided to support them. Subsequently, the five engineers all moved to Fenghua County and spent several months developing samples of pagers that proved to be functional but not durable. The development of marketable products took another three years by which time employment had grown to 200.

In 1997, the company experienced a breakthrough and sold 350,000 pagers which generated revenues of RMB180 million. The following year one million pagers were sold, bringing in RMB500 million. However, it was realised that pagers were being rapidly replaced by mobile phones; so the company decided to expand in another related direction.

By then, the local government through its SOEs had invested 45 percent of the company's capital with another 44 percent from the accumulated capital of the five founders, and the remainder from other companies. The decision to move into handset manufacturing was taken in 1998. The company managers realised that the success of the company depended on access to capital and technology, thus listed it on the Shanghai Stock Exchange in July 2000. This brought in RMB600 million in new capital.

In the meantime the company had been holding discussions with various potential partners and in early 1999 reached an agreement with Sagem in France. That year 100,000 units were produced with revenues of RMB1,100 million. The official government licence to manufacture handsets was granted in 1999. In the following year Bird quit the production of pagers to concentrate on handsets. Before long, production was expected to reach 20 million, and Bird was destined to become the top domestic producer in China, followed by TCL Mobile, but still trailing Nokia.[9]

Handsets account for 99 percent of the company's production, with system products (repeaters) making up the remaining one percent. Handsets will remain important, but the company is looking for new possibilities, as the high growth rates cannot continue forever. When

---

[9] TCL Mobile was founded in Huizhou, Guangdong Province, in 1999.

the growth rate levels out, it will be necessary to find new products. However, almost all R&D is still concentrated on handsets.

Bird employs some 9,000 sales people, including 5,000 who work in Bird sales units and after-sales services, and another 4,000 who are indirectly employed by retailers. TCL relies more on retailers, while Bird has many more sales outlets that are directly controlled. Bird has greatly benefited from its relationship with Sagem, especially in terms of technological development. This relationship has also been very beneficial to the French company, as it is not only receiving royalties but is also selling components to Bird. In 2001, the company started to develop its own models. By now, most of the more than 30 models per year are developed inside Bird.

There is no doubt that the profit margin for handsets will come down, forcing foreign manufacturers to withdraw as their costs are much higher. With lower costs, many handset manufacturers in China will go abroad. In 2002, Bird exported 200,000 handsets to Southeast Asia and Sagem for separate distribution.

Ningbo Haitian Machinery

Founded in 1966, the present Haitian Machinery Co Ltd was originally a village and township enterprise. It became a leading manufacturer of plastic moulding equipment in China after starting as a nameless small village mill. It has grown to become the largest plastic machinery supplier in China with a total staff now of more than 1,800 and revenues of more than RMB1,500. There is a large customer base not only in China, but also in more than 50 countries, including the US, the UK and Australia.

Haitian became a shareholding company in 1997, with some shares held by the Government. Demag in Germany provided advanced technology for Haitian's development of machines. Eventually they formed a joint venture in which Haitian has been able to acquire the most advanced production technology, including management, while Demag through Haitian has been able to enter into Haitian's marketing network both in China and abroad. This has made it possible to introduce "Enterprise Resource Planning" management software and office automation systems which increase operational efficiency and save costs. Haitian today has a complete national sales network and maintains service centres in Hong Kong, Indonesia and Turkey.

Haitian is today a world leader in plastic moulding equipment, including a number of specialised varieties. Haitian has an R&D Centre for plastic machinery that was established in 2000, and now has 15 staff. It complements a technology department (100 staff) that had been set up earlier to handle technology development.

The projected production is expected to reach 13,000. In earlier years, moulding machines were extensively used for producing parts for TV sets and other household products. The demand today has shifted to the automobile sector and IT industry where plastics and multimaterial components are used extensively.

DALIAN'S EMERGING SOFTWARE INDUSTRY

Dalian is located in northeast China at the southern tip of the Liaoning peninsula and serves as a major international port. It has a population of 6.4 million and has developed a comprehensive business environment which has attracted some 10,000 companies, constituting one-third of all foreign direct investment (FDI) in northeast China (defined as Liaoning, Heilongjiang and Jilin provinces). The main local industries are machinery manufacturing, shipbuilding, fishery, chemical engineering and electronics. The latter industrial segment has become increasingly important, and Dalian is today an internationally recognised centre for software development. The software industry is a fledgling sector in a highly competitive environment nurtured by software parks, software institutes and software companies. In 2004, its sales there reached US$30 billion, or 3.3 percent of the global software industry.[10] A variety of factors,

---

[10] China's software industry has experienced an average annual growth rate of 30–40 percent though exports account for only about 10 percent of China's software industry. This means that approximately 90 percent of the IT services are directed towards the domestic market, while the corresponding figure for India is 30 percent. These figures are extracted from a presentation, prepared by Marin T. Tinschev for the China International Software and Information Service Outsourcing Summit (CSIO), held in Dalian, June 24, 2005.

such as its geographical location in northeast Asia, convenient transportation, good basic infrastructure and a highly qualified labour force, have in a major way contributed to this development.

To help develop the software industry, Dalian plans to register a business income of RMB50 billion (US$6.02 billion) in the next 10 years by developing business processing outsourcing (BPO) services, creating 150,000 job opportunities.[11] It also intends to devote more effort towards developing the computer software industry to help boost the local economy and manufacturing industries across northeastern China. Specifically, software companies will focus on areas such as digital control of high-performance machine tools, automobile navigation positioning systems and integrated circuit design. Urgent upgrading of the IT of companies in the northeast along with steps to revitalise the old industries in the northeast is required.

The Software Industry

China's software market has been increasing at an annual average rate of 38 percent. In 2004, the industry employed 700,000 people, and sales reached RMB220 billion (about US$27 billion). However, this accounts for only 3 percent of the global market.[12] The country's export volume in the same year, estimated at US$2.8 billion, was only one-tenth that of India's.[13]

China's software outsourcing depends heavily on the Japanese and South Korean markets, and demand is dominated by lower-end services such as testing and coding. To improve China's software

---

[11] Dai Yulin, "Global Software Markets in Dalian's Sights," *China Daily*, February 28, 2005.

[12] Although China may within the next few years produce some 25 percent of global information technology products, its contribution to software and integrated circuit (IC or chip) production is still limited. It has become the world's largest IC market, but domestic chip production remains modest. However, China represented 21 percent of the world's IC consumption in 2005 when America's IC market was more than five times the size of China's IC market (Mark Lapedus, *EE Times*, January 8, 2006).

[13] "Software Fair Opens in Dalian," *China Daily*, June 23, 2005.

industry from volume-oriented to more quality-oriented development, the Ministry of Information Industry plans to provide strong support in three different areas.[14] First, it will help domestic companies build their own brands in both domestic and overseas markets. Second, software multinationals will be encouraged to set up R&D centres in China. Third, domestic companies will be encouraged to acquire internationally adopted professional certifications to enhance their processing management skills.

Dalian Software Park

A number of software bases, since the 1990s, have been established in various locations in China, primarily in the coastal regions. There are presently 11 nationally designated software bases. Dalian Software Park (DSP) was the first to be given this title in 2001 by the Ministry of Information Industry (MII) and the then State Development Planning Commission. The other 10 national software bases are located in Beijing (Zhongguancun), Shanghai (Pudong), Chengdu, Xian, Jinan, Hangzhou, Guangzhou, Changsha, Nanjing and Zhuhai.

The already existing IT industry and closeness to Korean and Japanese companies looking for possibilities to outsource software development prompted the Dalian Municipal Government in 1998 to build a software park to nurture the city's IT industry. The Government at the time offered substantial financial support. A private businessman, Mr. Sun Yinhuan, chairman of the Dalian-based Yida Group, became the Park's developer, and he founded the Dalian Software Park Co Ltd, which became the major investor for the Park.

Dalian is promoting its software industry in the global market.[15] The city's software industry began in the 1980s with general software development followed by outsourcing in the early 1990s. The dramatic growth of software outsourcing began in the late 1990s.

---

[14] Zhu Boru, "Software Sector Gears Up for Fast Development," *China Daily*, June 23, 2005.
[15] Dai Yulin, "Global Software Markets in Dalian's Sights," *China Daily*, February 28, 2005.

This is driven by three categories of companies. First, a substantial number of the multinational companies such as Nokia, Ericsson, GE, IBM, Intel, Microsoft, Accenture, Omron, Alpine, Panasonic Communications, Matsushita Electric, Sony, NEC, HP and SAP have offices in Dalian. Some have their own product R&D centres. Second, a number of successful software companies such as Neu-Soft, Huawei, SC&S and Sunyard are also present in Dalian. Furthermore, the city also has some 150 local software companies that are targeting markets in Japan, the US and Singapore.

Software contracting for export has become a major element in Dalian's information technology (IT) industry, especially export to Japanese enterprises, which account for 95 percent of the total. So far, Dalian is the only city in China that has been authorised to establish a series of state-level software zones, including the National Software Industry Base, Model City of Software Industry, International Software Training Base and the National Software Export Base. In 2004, the total sales volume of the software industry reached RMB7 billion (US$863.13 million), of which software exports amounted to US$200 million. Since 1999, the sector's sales volume has maintained a growth rate of 70 percent, and its annual export growth rate has stayed above 80 percent.[16]

Over the past five years, several of the city's 450-odd software companies have attracted investment from Microsoft, Intel, NEC and other foreign giants. To this end, concrete steps to develop IPR-based software products, train specialists and improve IT services so as to comprehensively upgrade its software industry have been taken. Furthermore, in the last five years, more than 10 subsidiary companies of the city's software industry have been established in Japan, Korea, the US and Malaysia.

To improve the software industry in Dalian, the city will invite well-known foreign and domestic companies to set up headquarters for technological development, support and service, covering the global market, especially the Asia-Pacific Region. To foster fledgling companies and research projects, Dalian established several high-tech

---

[16] Zhu Chengpei, "IT Power," *China Daily*, September 12, 2005.

incubators, including the Incubator at the DSP, the Incubator at the Dalian High-Tech Zone and the Dalian Private High-Tech Enterprises' Incubator. The local government decided to support a second phase of the Park to make the DSP a prominent software and information service centre in North Asia. This phase has been allocated about 10 square kilometres and will involve investment of RMB15 billion (US$1.8 billion).[17]

The sector is facing staff shortages at the top levels, i.e., people who have work experience in multinationals and/or possess management skills needed for complex software projects. Engineers who are good at developing certain applications in the traditional sectors are urgently needed. Foreign language deficiency, considered another obstacle for domestic software makers wanting to expand overseas, must be improved through bilingual training, and relevant departments in colleges and universities are being encouraged to promote such training. Presently, 35 tertiary institutions in China have established software institutes.

Dalian High-Tech Industrial Zone

The Dalian High-Tech Industrial Zone (DHTIZ) was one of the first state-level high-tech zones approved by the State Council in March 1991. Covering an area of 24.6 square kilometres, it is comprised of the No. 5 Highway Industrial Area, Qixianlin Industrial Base, Youjiacun Industrial Base, Huanghelu Science Plaza and some other sections. It has established close relations with more than 20 countries and regions in the world. There are about 1,700 enterprises, 380 of which involve foreign elements and 360 are recognised as high-tech.

The No. 5 Highway Industrial Area is situated in northeast Dalian's "economic artery" and covers an area of nine square kilometres adjacent to the Economic Zone, the Bonded Trade Zone and the Golden Pebble Tourist and Resort Zone. It is comprised of Industrial, Commercial and Residential Sections. According to the

---

[17] Xiao Yin, "Government and Firm Forge Partnership in Dalian," *China Daily*, November 6, 2003.

Dalian Municipal Overall Plan, the No. 5 Highway Industrial Area will be built into a "Double D Science Bay", based on digital and life (DNA) sciences.

The Qixianling Industrial Base is a key area for the development of high-tech industries. Comprised of Industrial, Incubator, Tourist and Convalescent and Residential Sections, this base covers an area of almost six square kilometres. The Industrial Section has Electronic Information, Biomedical, New Material and Energy-saving and Environmental Protection Sections. Nearly one hundred high-tech enterprises, such as China Hualu Electronic Information Group, Luming Technology Group, Kyoritsu Sieki (Dalian), etc., have already settled in the Industrial Section.

The Qixianling Industrial Base is an ideal location for newly graduated Chinese students from overseas universities to set up high-tech enterprises by themselves or with others. At present, there are already 22 enterprises established by overseas Chinese PhDs and holders of Master's degrees from North America and Europe. The state-level Dalian Incubator Service Centre has already incubated 120 enterprises, of which 18 are high-tech. A good number of medium- and small-sized successful high-tech enterprises such as Yinglian Technology Co Ltd, Yongxing Pharmaceutical Co Ltd, Bolong Dynamite Co Ltd and Optics Co Ltd. have developed very good market prospects. The Youjiachun Industrial Base of Dalian High-Tech Industrial Zone includes the "China Torch Plan Software Industrial Base" in the DSP with an area of three square kilometres.

Dalian Economic and Technological Development Zone

The Dalian Economic and Technological Development Zone (DETDZ) is the first national economic zone of this kind, approved by the State Council in 1985. Some 36 square kilometres of its area has been developed, housing 1,310 foreign investment enterprises. Thus far, there has been a total investment of US$10 billion, contracted foreign capital of US$6.7 billion and actually used foreign capital of US$3 billion. Japan has provided the largest amount of

FDI, followed by Hong Kong, the US and Korea. Annual industrial output is now about RMB30 billion. Accumulated investment of RMB8.4 billion in infrastructure and public service utilities provides strong support for further development. This zone will be a centre for manufacturing and export-oriented processing, as well as trade and service industries.

The DETDZ has a very important role to play in the further development of China's three northeastern provinces. It is one of the earliest areas that the Central Government opened up to the outside world. As it progressively upgrades to global industrial standards, it will be able to absorb more advanced technology and then diffuse it throughout the region.

Dalian Ascendas IT Park

The Dalian Ascendas IT Park was launched in June 2005. It will eventually cover an area of 35 hectares and be completed no later than 2012.[18] Ascendas first entered China in 1995 with its Suzhou Industrial Park in Jiangsu Province. It pioneered the ready-built facilities (RBF) concept which came to be seen as a model for other park developers. The activities of Ascendas now include parks in Shanghai, Beijing, Shenyang, Xian, Shenzhen and Chengdu. The success of the Singapore Science Park and India's International Tech Park has established Ascendas as a skilful developer of science and IT parks in Asia. The park in Bangalore houses some 100 companies and 16,000 IT professionals. It is the expectation of both Dalian and Ascendas that several high-ranking Indian IT companies will be attracted to locate among the international community of companies in Dalian.

Software Companies in Dalian — Examples

Neusoft Group Ltd

The Neusoft Group originates from the Computer Software and Network Engineering Research Laboratory that was established in 1988

---

[18] Zhu Chengpei, "Destination Dalian," *China Daily*, August 8, 2005.

within the computer department at Northeast University (NEU) in Shenyang. This laboratory in 1990 became the NEU Computer Software Research and Development Centre. Subsequently, in collaboration with Alpine Japan, Neu-Alpine Software Research Institute became the Neu-Alpine Software Co Ltd in 1993.

The foundation for the Neusoft Park was laid in 1995, and Neusoft incorporated Northeast University's Computer Imaging Centre. Subsequently, the company started its exploration in computerised tomography (CT) and other medical fields. In 1996 the NEU Software Group Ltd was founded and started to collaborate with Toshiba. Construction of Neusoft Park in Dalian began in 1998 and now includes the Neusoft Institute of Information Technology (more details given below). Other related activities include the Neusoft Chengdu Institute of Information Technology and Neusoft Nanhai Institute of Information Technology. A strategic consolidation was carried out in 2003 in which Alpine, Toshiba, Bao Steel and other strategic investors became shareholders of the Neusoft Group. Philips and Neusoft Medical Systems Co Ltd, a joint venture, was founded in 2004.

The core businesses of Neusoft include software and related services, digital medical products and e-Hospital solutions, and IT education and training. Software revenues dominate, accounting for 73 percent with another 22 percent for the second category and 5 percent from IT education and training. The company has more than 6,000 employees, and its sales revenue in 2004 reached RMB2.4 billion. Neusoft has 40 branches in different cities across China and overseas branches in the US, Japan and Hong Kong.

Dalian Lumei Optoelectronics Corporation

Dalian Lumei Optoelectronics Corporation (DLOC) is a joint venture of the US-based Lumei Optoelectronics Corporation, previously AXT Optoelectronics, and Dalian Luming Science and Technology Group. DLOC is the largest supplier of patented afterglow materials in the world.[19] It produces LED chips which are used widely in solid-state

---

[19] Zhu Chengpei, "Dalian Develops Semiconductor Lighting Venture," *China Daily*, March 19, 2004.

lighting and fibre-optic communications. It has attracted a core team of Chinese students who studied abroad and have filed more than 30 patents worldwide in the LED field. It exports more than 30 percent of its LED chips and is aiming to become a world-leading supplier of ultra-bright LEDs.[20]

The Dalian Luminlight Science and Technology Group was founded in 1992 and is recognised for its expertise in photo luminescent pigment and luminescent products.[21] The company has, as have many catalyst companies in Mainland China, undergone a quick transition towards leading edge technology-based products. It employs less than 500 people, of which more than 100 are engaged in R&D.

China has become the largest manufacturer and exporter of lighting products and has potential for a new lighting industry. The Dalian Luming Scientific and Technological Park will ultimately evolve into an international R&D and marketing centre for luminescent and nanotechnology materials. Construction of the Park that is now referred to as the Dalian Photonics Industry Park started in 2003. It is part of an effort to attract 300 high-tech enterprises to Dalian.[22]

Dalian High-Think Computer Technology Co Ltd

The Dalian High-Think Computer Technology Co Ltd (DHC), established in 1996, is today one of the leading software companies not only in Dalian but in China as a whole.[23] In February 2004, it was certified at Capability Maturity Model (CMM) Level 5 and is one of the few software companies in China having reached this level.[24]

---

[20] Ibid.

[21] "Welcome Dalian Luming to the Community," *CompoundSemi News*, August 22, 2003.

[22] Zhu Chengpei, "Dalian Develops Semiconductor Lighting Venture," *China Daily*, March 19, 2004.

[23] See the Dalian High-Think Computer Technology Co website at http://www.dhc.com.cn.

[24] For explanation, see http://sixsigmatutorial.com/CMM/CMM-Intoduction.aspx?ref=aw&gclid=COfy0vjTnIMCFShUDgodvAi5MQ.

The year after the founding of the company, it entered into a partnership with Anshan Iron and Steel Company and established Dalian Hua and Automotive System Co Ltd. In 1998, it started collaboration with the NEC public system in Dalian and with NTT Data System Integration in Beijing. One year later, it established a presence in Japan with DHC Japan Co. In 2001, it entered into cooperation with General Electric Japan and established branches in Jinan and Beijing. In 2002, NEC, NTT Data and Hitachi Soft became shareholders of DHC. This expanded company established the Hitachi Software Dalian Development Centre which focuses on software development and services and provides application system development, system integration, outsourcing, engineering and IT training. DHC has about 2,000 employees, of which 83 percent have Bachelor's Degrees, 7.4 percent have Master's Degrees and 20 percent have training or work experience abroad. Part of its success comes from its early entrance into the Japanese market, seeking development and established partnerships with several well-recognised Japanese enterprises.

The DHC has become China's largest software exporting firm, reaching more than 1,800 personnel in 2005. Following a memo with the National Development and Reform Commission, Microsoft agreed to support the development of China's software industry. It chose to invest in DHC in 2005.[25] IBM had already set up a software centre in Dalian in 2003 and announced it will have 20,000 engineers in China by 2010, a substantial increase over the 600 reported at the end of 2004.[26]

Foreign IT Companies in Dalian

Japanese companies are playing an important role in local development which is exemplified by Matsushita Electric Industrial Co Ltd,

---

[25] Zheng Yanyuan, "Microsoft Invests in Dalian Software Firm," *China Daily*, October 11, 2005.

[26] Liu Baijia, "Dalian on Global Software Talent Hunt," *China Daily*, August 17, 2005.

Oki Electric and D2E2.[27] Matsushita Electric decided in early 2005 that the company would gradually shift the development of software used in digital home appliances for the Chinese market to a unit located on the Mainland. It sought to reduce the time and costs of the development process and to make TVs and other appliances compatible with China's broadcasting format and the Chinese language. To that end, Matsushita is expanding its staff at its development centre in Dalian which was established in 2004. It decided to hire some 2,000 college-trained engineers in China over three years until April 2008. This will strengthen its R&D operations for home electronics appliances and its incorporate software.[28] It will also not only provide Matsushita in China with important manufacturing bases, but also turn its operations into an R&D centre that can serve the global market place. The company already has operations in Dalian, Shanghai, Guangzhou and Beijing.[29] An initial task was to devise software used for flat-screen TVs that Matsushita planned to release simultaneously worldwide.

Oki is located in Dalian Information Technology Park and will develop software for monochrome LED printers to be sold in China and elsewhere. The firm recruited 30 staff in the autumn of 2005 and will expand to 100 to develop software for colour printers and multifunction units to be sold in Asia and the Pacific region.[30]

The expanding role of Dalian in software development can also be illustrated with the business plans of D2E2 which is a systems

---

[27] D2E2, based in Tokyo, specialises in the translation of manuals, contracts, websites and databases in several sectors: automotive, computer (hardware and software), construction, energy, semiconductors, telecommunications, transportation, utilities, etc. Oki Electric, based in Tokyo, is involved in information systems, telecommunications systems and electronic devices. Matsushita Electric Industrial Co Ltd, based in Tokyo, is best known for its Panasonic brand consumer electronics.

[28] "M'shita to Bolster RD Ops in China via More Local Hires," *Nikkei Interactive*, February 15, 2005.

[29] "Ma'shita Elec to Localize Digital Appliance Software Ops in China," *Nikkei Interactive*, February 7, 2005.

[30] "Oki Data To Bolster Printer Business in China," *Nikkei Interactive*, October 19, 2005.

development firm whose services are designed to help companies move into Chinese markets.[31] With a new base in Germany, D2E2 will assist in employee education for German automakers in China. The main function will be translating employee manuals into Chinese and developing a Web-based system to distribute the translated material to all related employees. The translation will be outsourced, while the system will be built by a subsidiary of D2E2 in Dalian. This will allow the Dalian unit to build a new system in only three weeks to one month.

Talent Hunting and Nurturing in Dalian

Human resources are a critical bottleneck for the continued rapid development of the software industry in Dalian which is drawing on the rest of Liaoning and the other two provinces of northeast China (see Table 6.2).

Dalian expects to recruit a great number of high-level specialists from home and abroad. In 2005, the 22 universities, 40 colleges and 200 research institutes produced 4,000 computer majors and 10,000 engineers (if graduates from training institutes are included). However, the total demand is already around 30,000 and could triple over the 2006–2008 period.[32]

The most important universities are (1) Dalian University of Technology, (2) Liaoning Normal University, (3) Dalian Railway University, (4) Neusoft Institute of Information Technology, (5) Dalian

Table 6.2: Students in Northeast China Taking IT as Their Major

	Dalian	Liaoning	Jilin	Heilongjiang
Students — IT major	11,230	25,000	15,000	12,000
Graduates in 2004	3,800	7,500	3,500	2,500
Graduates in 2005	4,000	8,000	4,000	3,000

---

[31] "D2E2 To Expand Services for Firms Moving Into China Markets," *Nikkei Interactive*, February 23, 2005.
[32] Ibid.

Medical University, (6) Northeast University of Finance and Economics, (7) Dalian Aquaculture College, (8) Dalian Maritime University and (9) Dalian Foreign Language University. By 2010, it is estimated that the city's software industry will require 150,000 professionals.

The DSP currently has 200 software engineers from Japan, India, the US, Korea, Germany and Ireland. The city has 40 colleges and some 200 research institutes. The number of experienced software engineers in Dalian was 26,000 in early 2005.

In examining China's software industry, comparisons are always made with Bangalore in India. This is not surprising considering that Bangalore has more than 150,000 software engineers. However, China has made impressive progress in technology education and is producing between 250,000 and 350,000 software engineers every year. This equates to three times the number in India.[33] However, China must still work at increasing the size of its software companies which already exist in India with Infosys having 30,000 employees and Wipro hiring 2,000 during one quarter in 2005.[34]

China has only recently been able to capture marginal segments of the booming market for computerised financial services. It must meet the twin challenges of language capability and intellectual property security. Freeborders, a US company developing custom software for the financial services, retail and high-tech software industries, already sees large possibilities of having financial services developed in China. Presently, most of Freeborder's China operations are located in Shenzhen.[35]

The software industry in Dalian has in the past relied heavily on low-cost out-sourcing contracts. This is partly a reflection of skill levels within the local talent pool. To remedy the situation, Dalian started a worldwide hunt for software professionals in August of 2005.[36] The Mayor of Dalian announced that in order to solve the shortage of

---

[33] "China Takes a Chip off India Model," *China Daily*, August 26, 2005.
[34] These companies both originate in India. Ibid.
[35] Ibid.
[36] Liu Baijia, "Dalian on Global Software Talent Hunt," *China Daily*, August 17, 2005.

talent, the city would recruit people not only in a number of Chinese cities, but also in Canada, the US, Singapore, Korea, India and Japan. Dalian together with local companies from Korea and Japan set a goal to recruit some 10,000 engineers including at least 3,000 senior positions to meet the needs of more than 100 companies. This is obviously an attempt to compete with Beijing to be the top IT outsourcing centre in China.[37] A German consultancy company, Roland Berger Strategy Consultants, reported that Dalian aims to employ 200,000 people in its software industry by 2012 and reach total revenues of about RMB80–100 billion, and exports worth US$4 billion.[38]

Dalian University of Technology started a Software School in 2001 and has entered into close collaboration with IBM which has an IBM Technology Education Centre. The Neusoft Institute of Information Technology (NIIT) was established in Dalian in 2001. Among institutions of higher learning directly under the Ministry of Education, it is the first independent institute geared to fostering IT manpower.[39] It provides trained manpower for the IT industry and urgently needed talent for the information technology community. It is an example of innovative IT education and will significantly contribute to broad-scale education of IT manpower at the undergraduate level.

The NIIT is a full-time institution of higher learning, offering regular undergraduate programmes. Being an independent school of Northeastern University and jointly established by Northeastern University and the Neusoft Group (see above), it has been able to integrate resources from both the renowned university and the leading enterprise. It has a separate campus from the university. Northeastern University is one of the prominent multidiscipline universities in China, and has been listed in the national "Project 211" and "Project 985".[40]

---

[37] Ibid.
[38] Ibid.
[39] "NEU and Neusoft Establish Information Institute," *China Daily*, May 29, 2004.
[40] For "Project 211," see the section on Ningbo. "Project 985" was announced by President Jiang Zemin on May 4, 1998. It was another call for more world-class universities in China.

The Ministry of Education requires that the curriculum of independent institutes be formulated primarily to meet the need for local development with a focus on specialisations that are urgently needed in the market.

The cooperation between Neusoft Group and Northeastern University started in 2000 when Neusoft invested several hundred million dollars to jointly establish an IT institute in the DSP. In the latest stage, the university and company plan to establish an independent institute offering regular undergraduate programmes.

The institute offers mainly engineering courses but will also offer business and arts courses with computer science and technology, information technology and business management, digital arts and foreign languages. NIIT accepted its first batch of 1,000 undergraduate students in September 2004.

CONCLUSION

Software companies in China are hindered by distance factors which include physical and cultural (including national, organisational and professional aspects) differences. In order to become international competitors, Chinese software companies must change strategy and organisational structures as well as their policy for human resource development and leadership. This will require changes within and between corporate organisations in China, and with customers/partners outside the country. In the past, most companies have either waited for overseas partners to approach them or entered into collaboration with foreign companies already present in the Chinese market. Success in the international marketplace will require an overseas presence, moving engineers to overseas sites and starting to develop applications inside the premises of their clients — and taking over particular product development. The case of Dalian reflects China's overall development of its software industry.

Development of China's Semiconductor Industry: Prospects and Problems

Michael Heng Siam-Heng

GROWTH POTENTIAL FOR THE SEMICONDUCTOR INDUSTRY IN CHINA

The front page of the *International Herald Tribune* on December 12, 2005 carried the catchy headline "China Overtakes US as High-technology Supplier".[1] A month later, *China Daily* reported that China's integrated circuit (IC) market in 2005 ranked number one for the first time, surpassing the United States' and Japan's.[2] The report added that China's IC market had grown 32 percent to US$40.8 billion in 2005, much greater than the 8 percent growth rate for the IC industry worldwide.

---

[1] "China Overtakes US as High-technology Supplier," *International Herald Tribune*, December 12, 2005, 1.
[2] "China's IC Market Leaps to Top for 1st Time," *China Daily*, January 11, 2006 at http://www.chinadaily.com.cn/english/doc/2006-01/11/content_511243.htm (December 14, 2005).

The IHT news report was based on statistics compiled by the Organisation for Economic Co-operation and Development, according to which China exported US$180 billion worth of information and communications technology (ICT) products in 2004, surpassing for the first time, US exports of these worth US$149 billion.[3] China's ICT exports grew 55 percent in 2003 and 46 percent in 2004.

This steady growth reflects the fact that China has become the production centre for many global manufacturers of IT hardware and consumer electronics. In 2004, China-based production accounted for 85 percent of the total US$62.7 billion worth of ICT goods produced by Taiwanese manufacturers in 2004 (an increase of 21.8 percent over 2003).[4] The ICT and electronics goods industry accounted for 44 percent of China's total exports in 2003 and employed 4 million people.[5] Most of the current ICT products exported from China were previously produced in Taiwan, South Korea and elsewhere in the Asia Pacific region. The ICT manufacturing industry in China is an illustration of the modus operandi of transnational companies which organise their R&D, design and production, sales and services on a global basis.

As the key component of ICT products is semiconductor devices (popularly known as chips), China's production of ICT goods has created a huge demand for chips. Moreover, the IC content of electronics goods has been increasing over the last few decades. *IC Insights* reported that the value of semiconductors in electronics systems increased from 4 percent in 1965 to 19 percent in 2003, and forecast that it would rise further to reach 25 percent by 2008.[6]

Foreign, Taiwanese and Hong Kong-Macau companies operating in China have an ever-increasing demand for chips. They accounted

---

[3] "OECD Finds that China is Biggest Exporter of Information Technology Goods in 2004, Surpassing US and EU" on OECD website at http://www.oecd.org/document/8/0,2340,en_2649_201185_35833096_1_1_1_1,00.html (March 2, 2007).

[4] See DigiTimes.com, March 3, 2005 (April 2005).

[5] Figures given by Zhang Qi of the Chinese Ministry of Information Industry in her keynote address to *SEMICON China 2004 Electronics News*, March 17, 2004 at www.news.com/ (October 18, 2005).

[6] PriceWaterhouseCoopers, "China's Impact on the Semiconductor Industry," 2004.

for 75 percent of China's chip consumption in 2004.[7] Domestic sales values have shown a healthy growth. Even in the recession year of 2001, sales value reached US$15 billion, an increase of 29 percent. (The increase in 2000 was 78 percent).[8] The Chinese ICT market is expected to reach US$124 billion by 2010.[9]

China is currently producing only a small fraction of the chips required to satisfy the demand of its electronics industry. According to Zhang Qi, Director-General of the Chinese Ministry of Information Industry, China imported more than 80 percent of its semiconductors in 2003.[10] The gap is likely to increase steadily in the years ahead.[11]

The top producers of semiconductor devices are the United States, Japan, South Korea and Taiwan. American and Japanese companies are the main suppliers of chip production equipment. China had a US$50.5 billion deficit in integrated circuits, and a US$7 billion deficit in other semiconductor devices in 2004.[12] China's demand for chips has driven semiconductor firms to invest there. As manufacturers of commodity products, including ICT goods, are particularly cost conscious, they have a strong preference for local supply chains which reduce transportation and insurance costs.

---

[7] "Kuaguo dianzi gongsi zaihua touzi yu xinpian caigou zhuangkuang yanjiu bao-gao, 2005 Nian" (2005 Study Report on Electronic MNCs' Investments in China and the State of Semiconductor Chips Purchasing) at http://market.ccidnet.com/pub/report/show_4525.html (November 15, 2005).

[8] Xianmin Xi, *Semiconductor Manufacturing Equipment STAT-USA Market Research Reports*, 2003.

[9] "China IC Market Leaps to Top for 1st Time," *China Daily*, January 11, 2006 at http://english.people.com.cn/200403/08/eng20040308_136890.shtml (February 2006).

[10] "Chinese Chipmaker Gains World's Largest Market Share," *People's Daily*, March 8, 2004 at http://english.people.com.cn/200403/08/eng20040308_136890. shtml (April 2004).

[11] George Koo, "Semiconductor's Imperfect Virtuous Triangle," *Taiwan and China Semiconductor Industry Outlook Conference*, February 7, 2007, Santa Clara, CA. See http://www.taiwan-china-outlook.com/presentations/deloitte.pdf (March 9, 2007).

[12] "OECD Finds that China is Biggest Exporter of Information Technology Goods in 2004, Surpassing US and EU," http://www.oecd.org/document/8/0,2340,en_2649_201185_35833096_1_1_1_1,00.html (December 2005).

SIGNIFICANCE OF THE CHIP INDUSTRY
AND ITS BUSINESS MODELS

The electronics industry generates transformative technologies which are used in a broad range of economic activities. Thus, its development is central to the competitive position of most industries.[13] This sector now accounts for the largest share of industrial output and employment, and it continues to grow rapidly. It has come to symbolise the foundation of high-tech industry.[14] As semiconductors are the most high-tech component of electronics hardware, the Japanese call them the "rice of industry".[15] The economic and political implications of the chip industry as the core in this booming sector are obvious.

Chips are also a vital ingredient in national defence in that they form an indispensable component of modern weapon systems. In recent years, China has been developing very large-scale ICs which, for example, can be used in phased-array radars.[16] From March 1986 to August 1988, the Government launched three programmes to develop its high-tech capabilities, namely the 863 Programme,[17] the

---

[13] Stephen Cohen and John Zysman, *Manufacturing Matters: The Myth of the Post-Industrial Economy* (New York, NY: Basic Books, 1987).

[14] John Zysman and Michael S. Borrus, "From Failure to Fortune? European Electronics in the Changing World Economy," BRIE Working Paper, no. 62 (1994).

[15] John A. Mathews and Dong-Sung Cho, *Tiger Technology: The Creation of a Semiconductor Industry in East Asia* (Cambridge: Cambridge University Press, 2000).

[16] John J. Tkacik, Jr, "Strategic Risks for East Asia in Economic Integration with China," *The Heritage Foundation* (2002) at http://www.heritage.org/Research/AsiaandthePacific/WM171.cfm (March 2, 2007).

[17] In March 1986, four senior Chinese scientists wrote to Deng Xiaoping proposing that China should follow the global high-tech trends. The Chinese leader immediately approved the plan which was known as the National High Technology and Development Programme, or 863 Programme. Ten billion RMB were allocated over a period of 15 years and the focus was on biotechnology, space technology, information, lasers, automation, energy and new materials. The plan was extended in 2000. See the Chinese Government website at http://english.gov.cn/2005-08/12/content_21701.htm (January 7, 2006).

973 Programme[18] and the Torch Programme.[19] In mid-2000, it issued another document "Policies to Encourage the Development of the Software and IC Industries" which promised to simplify the process of approving joint venture or wholly foreign-owned IC enterprises and give the IC industry appropriate intellectual protection and various incentives. The 10th Five-Year Plan (2001–2005) also gave details about Government support given to the sector.

Over the 11th Five-Year Plan (2006–2010), China will concentrate on a national innovation system with a view to eventually becoming a first- class innovator with strong science and technological capabilities by 2050.[20] A fundamental component of this plan is technical standards. Chinese standard-setting is designed to decrease dependence on foreign know-how by developing domestically-controlled intellectual property (IP). Development of indigenous IP is a point of national pride, giving the country technological independence and reducing the burdensome royalty payments paid by domestic producers of high-tech goods.[21]

---

[18] Complementing the 863 Programme, the 973 Programme or National Basic Research Programme concentrates on basic research. Approved by the Government in June 1997 and launched in 1998, it is organised and implemented by the Ministry of Science and Technology. It involves mainly multi-disciplinary, comprehensive research on important scientific issues in such fields as agriculture, energy, information, resources, population, health and materials, providing theoretical bases and scientific foundations for solving problems. See the Chinese Government websites at http://www.973.gov.cn/English/Index.aspx (March 2, 2007); http://english.gov .cn/2006-02/09/content_184156.htm (March 2, 2007).

[19] Launched in August 1988, the Torch Programme is China's most important high-tech industry programme and a national guideline programme. As such it includes: organising and putting into action a series of development projects for high-tech products with advanced technology levels and good economic benefits in domestic and foreign markets; establishing high-tech industrial development zones throughout the country and exploring management systems and operation mechanisms suitable for high-tech industrial development. See the Chinese Government websites at http://english.gov.cn/2006-02/09/content_184156.htm (March 2, 2007) and http://www.china.org.cn/english/scitech/141584.htm (March 2, 2007).

[20] Cao Cong, "China Planning to Become a Technological Superpower," *East Asian Institute Background Brief*, no. 244, May 26, 2005.

[21] Greg Linden, "China Standard Time: A Study of Strategic Industrial Policy," *Business and Politics* 6, no. 3, art. 4 (2004).

As a result of technological advance, standardisation, growing market and intense global competition, the chip industry has undergone restructuring so that there are now two business models.[22] In the traditional model, an integrated device manufacturer (IDM) performs every step of the chip-making process within the firm including design, manufacture, testing and packaging. These companies see fabrication capability as a core competence, especially when it comes to production of their most advanced chips. Examples of IDMs are Intel, Advanced Micro Devices, Motorola, IBM, Texas Instruments and Lucent. These companies continue to account for the majority share of the global chip market (more than 85 percent in 2003.)[23]

In the new model, different firms specialise in separate activities, namely, design, fabrication, testing and packaging. There are several attractive features: each member firm in the supply chain operates with more flexibility than in the traditional model and is able to respond more quickly to external events.[24] Operational times are shorter and more efficient. As a result, business risk can be reduced by as much as a third of that of IDM companies while financial leverage can be increased.

The designing of chips is a highly skilled job, usually carried out by university-trained IC design engineers. A complex chip such as Pentium 4 requires the services of hundreds of designers over five years.[25] Fabrication is done in "pure play foundries" called "fabs" for short.

Before the advent of pure play foundries, IC firms had to rely on IDMs to produce for them. The arrangement was unsatisfactory for

---

[22] Jeffrey T. Macher, David C. Mowery and Timothy S. Simcoe, "E-Business and Disintegration of the Semiconductor Industry Value Chain," *Industry and Innovation* 9, no. 3 (2004): 155–181.

[23] *IC Insights*, quoted in PriceWaterhouseCoopers, 2004.

[24] Chun-Yen Chang and Po-Lung Yu, "The Development of Taiwan's IC Industry," in *Made in Taiwan — Booming in the Information Technology Era*, ed. Chun-Yen Chang and Po-Lung Yu (London: World Scientific, 2001).

[25] Clair Brown and Greg Linden, *Offshoring in the Semiconductor Industry: A Historical Perspective* (University of California, Berkeley: Institute of Industrial Relations, 2005).

two reasons: firstly the risk that the IDMs would copy their designs, and secondly that the IDMs would give priority to fabrication of their own chips and contract out any extra work. It is therefore easy to understand why the new business model was particularly welcome.

The most advanced fab produces 12-inch wafers with 90-nanometer process technology. Highly automated, and requiring reliable water and power supplies and treatment plants to purify highly toxic waste products, they cost at least US$3 billion to build while an 8-inch fab costs about US$1 billion.[26] They must operate at a certain level to break even. Insufficient orders mean a loss of several hundred million dollars a year. Clients producing high-end sophisticated chips generally want to take advantage of size miniaturisation in their latest products and to be kept informed about the upgrading plans of all the fabs they are working with. However, it is usually only the top-tier fabs that can afford continuous miniaturisation.

CURRENT CHIP PRODUCTION IN CHINA

Most chip production in China is restricted to specific-application chips (personalised digital products), commodity memory chips and other low-end products. While the demand for high-end chips is set to grow, most of the market demand (80 percent) is for low-end chips. This is why Huajing Shanghua's six-inch production lines could make a profit of US$9 million while running at 80 percent capacity during the recession year of 2001.[27]

Many foreign firms are relocating some of their chip production activities to China in order to gain a foothold in this lucrative market. The market downturn from 2000 to 2003 speeded up the process when large numbers of marginally profitable production facilities in the West incurred losses.

---

[26] Muh-Cheng Wu, "IC Foundaries: A Booming Industry," in *Made in Taiwan — Booming in the Information Technology Era*, ed. Chun-Yen Chang and Po-Lung Yu (London: World Scientific, 2001).

[27] Xianmin Xi, *Semiconductor Manufacturing Equipment STAT-USA Market Research Reports*, 2003.

Major players like Intel, AMD and Micron Technology have thus far limited their investment in China to low-end test and assembly facilities (See Appendix for full names and origins of major international semiconductor companies). While they would very much like to become more deeply involved, they fear that China may develop a competitive IC industry.[28]

The Chinese chip industry is distributed over four regions: the Yangtze River Delta (YRD), Beijing–Tianjin, Pearl River Delta (PRD), and Chengdu–Xian. YRD has industrial clusters served by good infrastructure, Beijing–Tianjin has the advantage of being near the political capital and Qinghua University, PRD is the workshop of major IT hardware producers, while Chengdu–Xian has ample supply of labour, power and water, and is the traditional home of the Chinese electronics industry.

All four regions have testing and packaging plants. The Chengdu–Xian region is the only one without a chip fabrication facility. However, given the growth of the electronics industry, it is just a matter of time before it too will be able to attract chip fabrication investment.

China had 57 fabs: 17 three-inch fabs, 15 four-inch fabs, six five-inch fabs, seven six-inch fabs, 10 eight-inch fabs and two 12-inch fabs as of July 2004.[29] The older generation fabs, some of which have been relocated from overseas, produce lower-duty chips used in household appliances such as refrigerators. The newer ones use the most advanced production facilities and aspire to be global players. Two prominent names in this category are Grace Semiconductor Manufacturing Corporation (GSMC) and Semiconductor Manufacturing International Corporation (SMIC), both legally domiciled in the Cayman Islands.

GSMC has two fabs in Shanghai, one producing 12-inch wafers, the other, eight-inch (reaching a monthly capacity of 27,000 wafers

---

[28] Report to Congress of the US–China Economic and Security Review Commission, November 2005.

[29] "SMIC: An Introduction," June 2005, SMIC website at http://www.smics.com/website/enVersion/fileCenter/SMIC_General_Presentation.pdf (March 2, 2007).

in the second half of 2004). Run by Taiwanese businessman Winston Wong, the company has attracted much media attention. One of its founders is Jiang Mianheng, son of former Chinese President Jiang Zemin and one of its directors is Neil Bush, brother of US President Bush.[30]

SMIC has fabs in Shanghai and Beijing. It acquired its production technology from non-US firms, e.g., the 12-inch fab in Beijing bought its technology from German partner Infineon. Other technological sources have been Chartered Semiconductor, Toshiba and Fujitsu. SMIC is very much a global chip company. Financing comes from Goldman Sachs, Motorola, H & Q Asia Pacific and the Shanghai City Government. Its customers are international: Infineon, Samsung, Fujitsu, Texas Instruments, Broadcom (United States), and STMicroelectronics of Europe. In October 2003, Motorola announced that it would transfer its eight-inch wafer fabrication facility in Tianjin to SMIC, in exchange for SMIC's shares.[31]

China had 479 chip design houses at the end of 2005, according to the Chinese Semiconductor Industry Association. There were about 380 domestic firms and the rest were design units of international MNCs operating in China. Two domestic IC design firms, Action Semiconductor (revenue of US$155 million in 2005) and Vimicro (revenue of US$95 million), were successfully listed on the NASDAQ stock exchange.[32] However, most of the Chinese design houses are much smaller, with only 11 of them earning more than US$25 million in 2005 and only 30 of them had revenue of more than US$5 million.[33]

The design sector has shown very robust growth from US$129 million in 2000 to an estimated US$1,590 million in 2005 — a 12-fold increase in six years. The potential for healthy growth is excellent,

---

[30] "Neil Bush: No Saving Grace," *Businessweek Online* website at http://yahoo. businessweek.com/technology/content/dec2003/tc2003128_9007_tc058.htm (March 2, 2007).

[31] Motorola Press Release at http://www.motorola.com/mediacenter/news (March 2, 2007).

[32] PriceWaterhouseCooper, "China's Impact on the Semiconductor Industry," 2007.

[33] Ibid.

based on: (a) very great demand, (b) strong support of local foundries, (c) return of experienced designers from abroad and (d) support from downstream electronics companies.[34]

The central processing unit (CPU) is regarded as the jewel in the crown of the chip industry. With the support of the Chinese Academy of Sciences (CAS) and the 863 Programme, the Computer Institute of the CAS initiated an ambitious project in 2001 to design and produce China's own CPU, called "Dragon Chip". Reducing the country's dependence on foreign suppliers, this is a major step forward from both economic and national defence viewpoints.[35]

On April 22, 2005, "Dragon Mark 2" was introduced to the public. A consortium consisting of the Computer Institute of CAS, SMIC, the Haier Group[36] and four others was established to manage the production of personal computers and laptops based on the new CPU.[37] The aim is to produce computers costing no more than RMB1,000 to serve the vast rural population.

FAVOURABLE FACTORS

The key factor in China's favour is its large population. The huge, low-cost labour pool, combined with reasonably good infrastructure, has turned China into the "factory of the world". The presently booming economy also represents a potentially lucrative market for

---

[34] "SMIC: An Introduction," June 2005.

[35] 2004 Gao Keji Fazhan Baogao (High Technology Development Report 2004), Zhongguo kexueyuan (Chinese Academy of Sciences) (Beijing: Science Publications Press, 2004).

[36] Haier is the world's fourth largest white goods manufacturer and one of China's top electronics and IT companies. It has 240 subsidiary companies and 30 design centres, plants and trade companies and more than 50,000 employees throughout the world. Haier specialises in technology research, manufacture, trading and financial services. Global revenue was RMB103.9 billion (US$12.8 billion) in 2005. See the Haier website at http://www.haier.com (February 10, 2006).

[37] "Muqian longxin erhao mianlin de shouyao wenti shi ruhe kuaisu tuiguang yingyong" (The Main Problem Faced by the Dragon Chip Mark 2 is the Need to Speed Up its Widespread Use). See Veryol website at http://www.veryol.com/product/cpu/news/2005-04-22-15057.htm (March 2, 2007).

consumer goods and is expected to grow yet further. For example, China is now perceived to be the most important market for mobile telephones.

Having identified the lack of chip production capacity as a critical bottleneck in the information industry, the Government has taken several steps to rectify the problem.[38] Before China's accession to the WTO, it imposed a 17 percent value-added tax on imported semiconductors compared to a 3 percent value-added tax on those made locally. This 14 percentage point difference represented an enormous pricing advantage geared to persuade chip producers to abandon potential investment plans in Taiwan in favour of the Mainland. Other measures included granting tax exemptions for the first 10 years and not taxing skilled workers with any capital gains tax when they sell the stocks given to them by their company.[39]

Using the science-tech model of *zhengfu yindao, qiye canyu, shichang yunzuo* (government initiative, corporate participation and market orientation), the Government is aiming to upgrade the chip industry from "made in China" to "innovated by China".

By virtue of its size, China can afford to follow a dual industrial structure, i.e., to nurture both large and small firms. The large flagship companies are encouraged to develop profitable global brands and become globally competitive. This is essentially the Korean model. At the same time, small, ambitious firms are given space in science park incubators. These firms are designed to be nimble and dynamic, able to play complementary and supplementary roles to the huge conglomerates by exploiting small, but profitable, niches. This is the Taiwanese model.[40]

The Government has been able to demand and entice technology transfers from investors attracted by the opportunity to market

---

[38] Xianmin Xi, *Semiconductor Manufacturing Equipment STAT-USA Market Research Reports*, 2003.

[39] "How China is Quickly Capturing the World's Semiconductor Industry," *Manufacturing and Technology News* 10, no. 15 (August 4, 2003) at http://www.manufacturingnews.com/news/03/0804/art1.html (March 2, 2007).

[40] Greg Linden, "China Standard Time: A Study of Strategic Industrial Policy," *Business and Politics* 6, no. 3, art. 4 (2004).

and manufacture their goods in China. More than a hundred laboratories are conducting research and development, some of them for the global market.[41] In the electronics sector, foreign companies have been prepared to compromise, especially when they are vying for positions in the government-controlled market. In 1990, Alcatel, NEC and Siemens were given exclusive rights to sell telecoms switches in China in exchange for transferring IC technology to Chinese IC manufacturers.[42] SMIC has managed to import the most advanced fabrication technology from European equipment firms, effectively bypassing the Wassenaar Agreement which blocks the export of dual use technologies to China.[43] Without such US restrictions, China's IC industry would no doubt have grown much faster.[44]

The current trend is for foreign companies to outsource to East Asia, with China being the fastest growth area in this industry. One result is that many overseas Chinese in the IC industry are returning to work in China. Some have chosen to work in the top Chinese universities, playing a crucial role in narrowing the knowledge gap between China and the rest of the world. For example, the School of Microelectronics of Fudan University, which has a focus on advanced IC technology, recruited Professor Dian Zhou of the University of Texas at Dallas. He in turn went on to attract four faculty members from the United States and two from Europe.[45] Similarly, Taiwanese professionals who gained experience in the American IC industry are now heading fabs based in the Mainland, e.g., Richard Chang (SMIC), Tong Liu (ASMC), Pong Fan (Hua NEC) and Nan-Hsiung Tsai (GSMC) after spending some time working in the Taiwanese ICT sector.[46]

---

[41] UNCTAD, *World Investment Report 2001: Promoting Linkages* (New York: United Nations, 2001).

[42] "Peking Using Digital Switching Market," *Business China*, December 24, 1990.

[43] The Wassenaar Arrangement, named after the Dutch town where the pact was signed in 1996, requires equipment vendors and their prospective Chinese customers to obtain government approval for sales of advanced technologies.

[44] *International Herald Tribune*, December 12, 2005, 10.

[45] Jon Sigurdon, *Technological Superpower China* (Northampton, MA: Edward Elgar, 2005), Chapter 9.

[46] Hsing-Hsiung Chen and Jian-Hung Chen, 2005.

Engineering companies in China and Korea have produced some low cost manufacturing equipment able to capture some market share from US and Japanese equipment firms. An example of one such Asian equipment company is Jusung Engineering from South Korea. The emergence of such Asia-made wafer fab equipment is lowering the entry barrier for those Chinese companies which have limited financial resources.[47]

PROBLEMS

The problem most cited in business and research literature is the technology embargo (export restrictions) imposed by the United States under the terms of the Wassenaar Agreement.[48] However, most countries have not let this deter them from exporting advanced chip manufacturing equipment to China.[49]

Chip makers are forming global alliances to lower the cost of developing new technologies and to share the risks of building new plants. For example, IBM partnered with Sony, Toshiba, Samsung, Infineon, AMD and Chartered Semiconductor to build a new 12-inch fab in East Fishkill, New York in the second half of 2005.[50] This strategy makes them more cost effective and their factories better utilised. Chinese companies by themselves cannot compete against such big alliances in terms of financial and human resources, and the large alliances may not want to include a Chinese company for fear of losing their IP rights.

After the initial euphoria about Chinese Government support for the chip industry, there is a creeping doubt about its commitment. Many investors are disappointed by the stock performance of SMIC

---

[47] Interview in October 2005 with an industrial expert based in Singapore. The expert wished to remain anonymous.

[48] See for example, Xianmin Xi, *Semiconductor Manufacturing Equipment STAT-USA Market Research Reports*, 2003.

[49] Clair Brown and Greg Linden. *Offshoring in the Semiconductor Industry: A Historical Perspective* (University of California, Berkeley: Institute of Industrial Relations, 2005).

[50] See http://informationweek.desktoppipeline.com/business/56900805 (February 10, 2006).

which has made it more difficult for this company and other chip makers in China to raise capital to embark on expansion schemes. A senior figure within SMIC said it was forced to raise capital overseas, which is much more expensive. Though the Chinese Government has provided many incentives to "kick start" the industry in the past several years, some foreign observers are not sure whether the Government will continue to identify the semiconductor industry (wafer production, in particular) as a key target industry.

In the long term, China must develop its own semiconductor production equipment industry. It has been pointed out that "equipment development and manufacturing prowess are tightly linked, representing a capability embodied in people and organised in firms, but not tradable across national boundaries. A failure to capture the benefits of such linkages domestically will not be compensated by the purchase of advanced production equipment from abroad."[51] This point is very relevant in light of the experience of TSMC and UMC of Taiwan, which never purchase manufacturing equipment from foreign companies because they believe that their IC development programme would be restricted if foreign companies controlled all the needed technologies.[52] TSMC and UMC have always tried to contribute new technologies to the process, and this spirit of self-reliance and hard work has contributed to the success of Taiwan's IC industry. Moreover, with such expertise as an asset, they can collaborate in R&D and form strategic alliances with global players. China has some way to go in emulating TSMC and UMC. Government assistance in this direction is much needed.

THE REAL CHALLENGE

The gap between China and the West is closing quickly. Two years ago, China's technology was said to be 15 years behind international

---

[51] Jay Stowsky, "The Weakest Link: Semiconductor Production Equipment, Linkages and the Limits to International Trade," BRIE Working Paper, no. 27 (1987).

[52] Chun-Yen Chang and Po-Lung Yu, "The Development of Taiwan's IC Industry," in *Made in Taiwan — Booming in the Information Technology Era*, ed. Chun-Yen Chang and Po-Lung Yu (London: World Scientific, 2001).

levels in terms of products, and 10 years behind in terms of R&D.[53] The most pessimistic assessment is that the current gap is five years.[54]

The weak link in the chain is the design. It is here that the most creative work is done, where the most value is added and where the pay is highest. The research firm iSuppli forecast that by 2006 China would require 20,000 new design engineering graduates per year, but the country was producing only 400 each year, based on the figure available in 2003.[55] The good news is that China has formed a preliminary talent training base and plans to train 40,000 IC designers over a six- to eight-year period.[56]

Developing a full-fledged IC industry requires engineering talents, management and organisational skills, exploitation of market potential and financial resources. The best organisation format for doing this seems to be a tightly knit cluster of firms as in the software industries of India, Israel, Ireland, Brazil and China.[57]

CONCLUDING REMARKS

There are sound reasons for China to develop its semiconductor industry. It is the most important sector within the hardware component of the IT and consumer electronics industry as well as defence weapon systems. Producing more chips within China will reduce the country's chip trade deficit. It will provide an opportunity to develop China's own technological capability. Though remarkable progress has been made in the chip industry, there are still weak

---

[53] Xianmin Xi, *Semiconductor Manufacturing Equipment STAT-USA Market Research Reports*, 2003.

[54] Interviews with two industrial experts, one based in Singapore and the other based in Shanghai in October 2005, who wanted to remain anonymous. Both gave a figure of three to five years, which is consistent with that given by Wu and Chua (2004).

[55] PriceWaterhouseCoopers, 2004.

[56] Ibid.

[57] Ashish Arora and Alfonso Gambarddla. *From Underdogs to Tigers: The Rise and Growth of the Software Industry in Brazil, China, India, Ireland and Israel* (Oxford: Oxford University Press, 2005).

links. In terms of an integrated production infrastructure, domestic suppliers of chip equipment are required. In terms of value creation, there is need for a strong domestic IC design industry. In the short term, the Government would do well to encourage and support Chinese technologically savvy firms in buying such technological and managerial capability. Given the country's huge trade surpluses, the Government should be in a comfortable position to do so. Beyond the short term, however, what is needed are entrepreneurs who take a long-term view, a robust financial system and high-quality research universities.

ACKNOWLEDGEMENTS

Most of the research for this chapter was done when the author was a Visiting Senior Research Fellow at the East Asian Institute, National University of Singapore. He would like to thank Professor John Wong of EAI for his thoughtful comments and supply of some research materials.

APPENDIX

Major International Semiconductor Companies		
Commonly known name	Name in full (if applicable)	Home base
Alcatel		France
AMD	Advanced Micro Devices	United States
AT&T		United States
Chartered Semiconductor		Singapore
Fujitsu		Japan
GSMC	Grace Semiconductor Manufacturing Corporation	Cayman Islands
Haier Group		China
Huajing Shanghua		China
IBM	International Business Machine	United States
Infineon		Germany
Intel		United States
Lucent		United States
Micron Technology		United States
Motorola		United States
NEC		Japan
Philips		Netherlands
Samsung		South Korea
Siemens		Germany
SMIC	Semiconductor Manufacturing International Corporation	Cayman Islands
Sony		Japan
STMicroelectronics		Switzerland
Texas Instruments		United States
Toshiba		Japan
TSMC	Taiwan Semiconductor Manufacturing Company	Taiwan
UMC	United Microelectronics Corporation	Taiwan

China's Online News Industry: Control Giving Way to Confucian Virtue

Johan Lagerkvist

China's political leaders today try, by subtler and softer means than in previous decades, to control the state-controlled news industry and especially its newest offspring, the online news industry. The core dilemma in this dynamic is not at all novel. Ever since Deng Xiaoping decided on a new economic reform programme in 1978, the main problem has been letting go of Maoist oppressive control of society and individuals while keeping the country stable and orderly. The harsh and systematic level of repression against intellectuals, many working in the mass media, during the anti-rightist campaign of 1957 and Cultural Revolution initiated in 1966 have not returned. Tragic mass jailings of dissenting reporters and prisoners of conscience also followed the decision to close down the "democracy wall" of debating posters in West Beijing in 1979 and the remarkable chain of tragic events that followed the crushing of the students' democracy movement 1989.

Nevertheless, a recurring theme of "medium-sized repression" during the 1980s and 1990s was the campaigns attacking so-called

spiritual pollution coming to China from the outside world.[1] The perceived remedy and bulwark against this creeping "peaceful transformation" of Chinese souls was to advocate socialist virtues. In the
beginning of the 21st century it seemed that the admonishing of
Chinese people to cultivate their personal selves according to the
scripted protocol of socialist virtues gave way to a pre-revolutionary
concept of cultivating one's virtuous spirit. As a result, classical
Confucian ideas and notions of proper behaviour seemed to crawl
back into the picture. It is increasingly obvious today that China is
contributing to the processes that go under the name globalisation.
But it is less clear to what extent Chinese value orientations are
becoming globalised with the opening-up of their country. It is also
unclear what ideological means or resources of resistance are used in
China to resist cultural globalisation, both on the popular-citizen
level and at the party-state level. One wonders if there perhaps is a
cultural reservoir waiting to be tapped at both levels, consciously as
well as subconsciously, in order to gain a secure identity as this large
and proud nation opens up to the world at an astonishing speed.

STRIVING FOR A SELF-SANITISING INTERNET INDUSTRY

The above question concerning the turn towards tradition was one
of a series of questions that prompted this study of online news
organisations in China.[2] Adjectives like "healthy", "cultivating", "rule
according to morals" turn up in policy documents, newspaper edito-
rials and in intellectual writings so often that an investigation into
the deeper meaning of their usage is necessary. This study focuses
on how staff of the Qianlong Municipal Online News portal in
Beijing and Shanghai's Dongfang Network in 2003 and 2004 perceived the different demands from more than 100 million Chinese
surfers and an unknown number of propaganda officials in charge

---

[1] Jonathan D. Spence, *The Search for Modern China* (New York: W.W. Norton,
1999), 699.
[2] The analysis in this chapter is based on in-depth interviews conducted with editors
and journalists working in the online news industry in Beijing and Shanghai in 2003.

of monitoring Internet content. At the end of the 1990s, the Internet was not as regulated as it is today. At that time, private web portals like Sina and Sohu were able to write political news stories on their own accord quite unconstrained but they are no longer allowed to do so. In this very commercialised yet authoritarian media system, they are obliged by law to copy political news items only from authorised state news sources like *Xinhua* News Agency.

How does this wish for moral guidance play out in the dynamics between entrepreneurs in the online news industry and the local propaganda departments in Bejing and Shanghai? The public news portals are extremely important instruments for the Communist Party of China (CPC). They are part of the effort not to lose the agenda-setting function in the globalised age of the Internet. Intuitively, one would assume that online news, blogs and bulletin board systems in China allow more space for critical discussion than does the traditional news media. This is definitely true. The inherent logic is that external forces of globalised communications technology, global popular culture and World Trade Organisation protocols are together exerting pressure on China. Several scholars who argue that globalising influences are progressive in their effects on China have raised this topic.[3] While the author believes this line of argumentation is basically right, the foreign impact is less than most analysts think. It will be primarily domestic factors of an economic and organisational kind that contribute to liberalisation of the Chinese online media sector. My interviews with online news editors and journalists in Beijing and Shanghai show there are now more demands on newsroom staff to be efficient, well educated and profit-oriented. Sensitive political news is often reported first in Chinese chat forums. This trend was long unnoticed by Western observers. Now, the subdued but still important role in Chinese society played by bulletin board systems, blogging and podcasting

---

[3] See for example Tony Saich. *Governance and Politics of China* (New York: Palgrave, 2001), 310; Supachai Panitchpakdi and Mark L. Clifford. *China and the WTO. Changing China, Changing World Trade* (Singapore: Wiley, 2002), 35; Thomas L. Friedman, *The Lexus and the Olive Tree* (New York: Anchor Books, 2000).

are part of the conventional wisdom. Thus, the pressures often associated with media globalisation are in fact originating from market change within the domestic media system.

The interests of ordinary citizens are becoming economically important. Under the impact of media commercialisation, all media organisations (be they state-owned or private) must compete for people's interest. This gives online news editors a strong argument for negotiating the boundaries of online news and info-tainment with Party officials. What is interesting is that when private web portals were no longer allowed to produce news, the new official news organisations seem to have created room for a sort of "strategic negotiation." Why? The reason is that because municipal news portals are administered, financed and supervised under the auspices of the municipal governments in Beijing and Shanghai, officials there may entertain a false notion of security. According to one informant in Shanghai, this may be why the municipal online news organisations appear to have greater room for social reportage than one might expect.[4] That is one reason why the public portals have been able to negotiate the boundaries of online space with the Party officials who decide what is harmful media content. As a result, officials in charge of propaganda and news control in the State's General Administration of Press and Publication and the CPC's Central Propaganda Department have had to lower their guard and play a more subtle game than before.

Having to accommodate market demand, and at the same time, assume the traditional role of mouthpiece in the global information age poses a dilemma for the online journalist who must adjust to a situation where he/she is caught in the crossfire of demands between Government propaganda officials and the Chinese public. Two news editors acknowledged how the diverging views between the Party's ideologues and news reporters cause them a constant headache.[5]

---

[4] Interview conducted with a news editor of *Dongfang wang* in Shanghai, October 2003.

[5] Two separate interviews conducted in October 2003 with the manager of Qianlong News Academy and the managing editor of *Qianlong wang* revealed the continued existence of this phenomenon in Chinese mass media organizations.

Nevertheless, reporters today seem to show less readiness than before to heed the commands of the propaganda apparatus, since its orders increasingly conflict with the professionalism of reporters and the interest of the public, tired of viewing, reading and listening to old-fashioned propaganda.

Thus, the interviews conducted in Beijing and Shanghai show how the special relationship between online reporters and censors in China is undergoing change. One *Qianlong* news editor outlined what it means to be routinely scrutinised by propaganda officials:

> Foremost, online media organisations run by the Government have a responsibility, and that is to spread the voice of the Party and Government. At the same time, we must offer netizens news of a fresh kind, including information on entertainment. One must say that there are some contradictions in all of this, but that does not mean you have only one thing and not the other, or that there is a sharp dichotomy between them. While spreading the message of the Party and Government we can also make good on offering netizens the things they like. It is not as inseparable as fire and water. On the issue of handling reporting we are learning from each other. We are saying that reporting is an art form where you must avoid mechanical copying and the simple and crude "I-decide-what's-right" way of reporting.[6]

This statement is very interesting as it indicates that as the relative importance of hard news versus propaganda changes, the relationship between newsmakers and the propagandists of the CPC is also bound to change. This was clearly reflected by China's Vice-President, Zeng Qinghong in a *People's Daily* article written on October 8, 2004. In it he spoke of the need:

> To uphold the principle of the Party controlling the media, guide the media in combining the embodiment of what the Party advocates and the reflection of public sentiment.

Zeng's exhortation well illustrates the perceived need for continued CPC control of the mass media but also a confirmation that the

---

[6] Interview conducted with the managing editor of *Qianlong wang* in Beijing, October 2003.

learning process mentioned by the *Qianlong* news manager is indeed occurring. Without taking into account what the public wants to read, or reflecting their sentiments, the online public will vote with a click of the mouse. The propagandists defending the monopoly on power held by the CPC are becoming aware of the need to deliver their political content in a new way. Otherwise, no one will ever surf official news sites and be persuaded of the Party's perspective on an issue.

This ongoing learning process involving news managers and propaganda officials is no longer a simple one-way process. But is it a result of globalisation? It can be argued that the globalisation of the world's media industries and the universal market logic, according to which most of them operate, are bringing challenges to the Chinese media system. But the impacts of media globalisation are only indirectly influencing China. It is true that new information and communications technology are pluralising the Chinese media system, but the driving forces are coming from inside China. The crucial task for the CPC and the Chinese Government is naturally to steer these largely internal/domestic pressures in favourable directions. The Government is determined to keep the online news industry within limits set by the CPC. In 2006, it seemed like the vigilance concerning so-called unhealthy flows of information reached an all-time-high. Arrests of cyber-dissidents and sentences against investigative journalists, new regulations forcing individual bloggers to register with the Government and propaganda officials secretly guiding public discourse in Internet chat forums are clear testimony to that. The evolution of delegated self-censorship to online media organisations is reinforced by conveying notions of "healthy content", "harmful information", and burdening journalists and editors with the responsibility to contribute to the construction of what China's president Hu Jintao has called "harmonious society."

Following the limitations on what kinds of media organisations are allowed to publish original news items, breaking political taboos has become rare among China's non-official media outlets. News stories that discuss sensitive topics like political independence for Chinese minorities, the spread of unofficial religions, workers' rights or rural health problems are now definitely off limits. Instead of political pluralisation, increasing social pluralisation has made it safe to break social taboos. It is even revenue-generating. In the Chinese Internet landscape of today, breaking social taboos has become a profit-making strategy for the Chinese-run Nasdaq-listed web portals in China. In turn, showing more nudity in order to generate profits is used by state-controlled media organisations to boost their own seriousness in news reporting and claims of moral superiority. Sensationalism is ridiculed when they boast how reliable they are in reporting the truth. Persuasion of this sort is proving quite success-ful. However, it is truly a paradox that when more than 111 million information-seeking Chinese Internet users in 2006 rushed online to access less censored political news, state-controlled online media continued to score very high in terms of trustworthiness. Chinese citizens, so long accustomed to the language and style of official news propaganda, should perhaps think more critically of the offi-cial media outlets, especially after the cover-up of the SARS out-break in 2003.[7]

NEW CONFUCIANISM FOR A POST-COMMUNIST PARTY

What reasons lie behind this counterintuitive media logic? In order to understand the underlying reasons there is a need to look back to the final years of former President Jiang Zemin's regime. Anne-Marie Brady has argued that Jiang differed from Mao Zedong and Deng Xiaoping in his stress on "traditional" Chinese values, in addition to the CPC's own "traditional" Marxist–Leninist values.[8] She also con-tends that the goals of Jiang Zemin's "spiritual civilisation campaign"

---

[7] SARS is the abbreviation for "Severe Acute Respiratory Syndrome." "It is a respiratory disease in humans which is caused by the SARS coronavirus. It's first major epidemic outbreak occurred in China, between November 2002 and July 2003, with 8,096 known cases of the disease, and 774 deaths." See the World Health Organization's summary at http://www.who.int/csr/sars/country/table2004_04_21/en/index.html (March 28, 2007).

[8] Anne-Marie Brady, "Regimenting the Public Mind: The Modernisation of Propaganda in the PRC," *International Journal* 57, no. 4 (Autumn 2002).

followed a familiar pattern harking back to late-Imperial China stressing the superiority of Chinese culture and a cautious approach to foreign ideologies. During the 1990s it became increasingly clear that market friendly policies cohabited ideologically within still authoritarian political structures that put ever more emphasis on moral guidance. In January 2001, Jiang Zemin spoke to the leading propaganda cadres of the CPC saying, "We must strengthen the socialist judicial system, rule in accordance with the law while at the same time strengthen consciousness about socialist virtues and rule by moral guidance." Following the speech a number of political tracts conveying the President's message on the need for a new sense of morals in a rapidly changing China were published. Two of the most important books reflecting this trend were Lu Shizhen's *Ruling the Country in Accordance with the Law*, and Ding Ximan's *Lawful and Moral Rule.*[9] Jiang's new moral politics also shaped his ideological legacy, as manifested in his theory of the "Three Represents", now part of the CPC's ideological canon. It may seem odd that a ruling communist party long bent on eradicating everything reminiscent of feudal state philosophy and popular Confucian thinking would turn 180 degrees to a point where parts of this cultural heritage again are deemed both useful and viable. And as history shows, the communists were never the only partisan grouping to argue that Confucianism was an outdated *ism* without a future. In the early 20th century, liberal thinkers like Yan Fu and Hu Shi and socialist reformers like Chen Duxiu all condemned "the shop of Confucius" during the New Culture Movement. All the same, after classical neo-Confucianism was proclaimed to be completely out of date with the modernising demands of the news age, heralding democracy, industrialisation and equality between classes, Confucian thinking was difficult to erase even from the minds of leading communist cadres like Liu Shaoqi. In 1951 Liu wrote the little pamphlet *How to Be a Good Communist*, which echoed sentiments

---

[9] Lu Shizhen (ed.), *Ruling the Country in Accordance with Law (Yi de zhi guo)* (Beijing: Xinhua chubanshe, 2001); Ding Ximan (ed.), *Rule by Law and Rule by Virtue (Fazhi yu dezhi)* (Baoding: Zhongguo jiancha chubanshe, 2001).

and morals transferred through the millennia to generations of Chinese political leaders.[10] The rationale behind this creeping comeback of Confucian ideas may have been a maturing insight about the positive function of traditional morality to demand service to a higher cause, through the bettering of one's moral character. Liu Shaoqi and other leaders of the People's Republic of China in the 1950s no doubt realised, on an unconscious level, how successful Confucianism had been as a practical statecraft in ancient China. Through its long history, in order to control a large country with a huge population split among various religious belief systems, local cultural practices and ethnicities, Confucianism became the working formula for keeping an enormous society at least at times reasonably stable.[11] Naturally, the communist leadership, whilst atop an extremely hierarchical Leninist political system could not advocate anything else than their professed egalitarianism. But what they could propagate, as Liu's little pamphlet so clearly evokes is the study of exemplary role models, i.e., the model worker or model soldier, to look up to and emulate. The end result of this cultivation of socialist virtues, or socialist *xiuyang*, would be a happy person in a harmonious society — that is the good communist.

In 1978, Deng Xiaoping's economic reform policies opened China to the world. Following the opening came an expected loss of legitimacy for the CPC. People's belief in and loyalty towards Leninist ideology and Maoist thinking became impossible to maintain in the decades following the successful conversion from a planned economy to a market-oriented national economy. Now, in the wake of China's staggering economic growth rates and increasing income disparities in contemporary Chinese society, there thus seems to be a turn to Confucianism, or the values associated with it.

---

[10] Liu Shao-Chi, *How to Be a Good Communist* (Beijing: Foreign Languages Press, 1951).

[11] Peasant uprisings in ancient and modern China occurred, but in comparison with the statecrafts and ideologies of other empires of the ancient world which did not outlast the fall of their imperial regimes like Mogul India, Zoroastrian Persia or the Hellenistic empires following the death of Alexander the Great, China's Confucianism has showed remarkable resilience over the centuries.

Herein, an appropriate term describing this new turn to old reliable sources for holding society's relations together is "new Confucianism." The intellectual and philosophical tasks of new Confucianism are well described and discussed in three informative volumes.[12] These must be separated from its use as a political-strategic and ideological tool in the current political climate of the People's Republic.[13] Still, since the thought currents of new Confucianism and statecraft's ideological use of Confucianism, old and new, are blurred at the edges, significant overlaps between the cultural and political realms exist — not least in Mainland China.[14] The overlaps originate from the continued inter-dependence between the so-called establishment intellectuals, the CPC and the bureaucracy in today's China. Like Theodore DeBary, this author is concerned with how the pragmatic, technocratic elite in Beijing is involved in financing and supporting the cultural turn for utilitarian ends of statecraft.[15] What does the New Confucianism mean to China's political leaders, and how does it show itself in current political rhetoric? For the political leadership, this ideological shift consists of two components: the challenge against political stability coming from abroad and domestic risks to the current status quo. The first component is a way to combat the influx of alternative political and social ideas from outside China as a result of increasing

---

[12] Umberto Bresciani, *Reinventing Confucianism: The New Confucian Movement* (Taipei: Taipei Ricci Institute for Chinese Studies, 2001); John Makeham (ed.), *New Confucianism: A Critical Examination* (New York: Palgrave Macmillan, 2003); Cheng Chung-ying and Nicholas Bunnin (eds.), *Contemporary Chinese Philosophy* (Malden: Blackwell Publishers, 2002).

[13] Contemporary intellectuals within the academic field of national studies (*guo xue*) or philosophy are to be found within this discourse on new confucianism. They and others have termed this turn to national tradition *post-confucianism* (*hou ruxue*).

[14] On the closeness between the CPC, state bureaucracy and so-called Establishment Intellectuals during China's communist era, see Carol Lee Hamrin and Timothy Cheek (eds.), *China's Establishment Intellectuals* (Armonk M.E. Sharpe, 1986).

[15] DeBary, Theodore, "The New Confucianism in Beijing," *Cross Currents* (Winter, 1995).

economic and cultural globalisation. With outside ideas may come renewed demands for political liberalisation, the possibility to create areas of freer speech where environmental and human rights issues can be discussed, and the acceptance of provocative lifestyles associated with pop culture. Since these challenges cannot be met with brute force or censorship, the threat from a greater pluralism of ideas against social and political stability must also be met by "soft power", i.e., ideological or value-based arguments. Herein lies the value of the Confucian turn. This turn is evident not only in the CPC and among parts of the state bureaucracy, but also in society itself. Especially noteworthy and remarkable is the trend among private entrepreneurs to profess Confucian values. One obvious reason is of course that to follow the Party's ideological line on being a moral businessman not shirking responsibilities *vis-à-vis* the state and people may entail rewards in the form of large contracts from the state. Another reason has to do with ideas of public relations or cultivating an image as a responsible business leader. This imagery corresponds to the second domestic component that threatens political stability from within China's borders. As the income gaps within urban areas and between the cities and the countryside continue to widen, the tensions between those unable to cash in on the market economic reforms and the nouveau riche flaunting their wealth together with corrupt officials seems likely to spark social instability in Chinese society. Naturally this latter reason can also be viewed as a utilitarian strategy. If other industry leaders display criminal greediness and care only for maintaining corrupt practices, the goodwill coming from appearing as the moral Confucian businessman may prove safer and perhaps even lucrative in the end. The ideologues in the CPC hope that officials and entrepreneurs will feel bound by the new moral guidance provided by new Confucianism. Their wish is that with a joint focus on creating a harmonious and healthy society, loyalty towards the current political system and the revitalisation of the nation, social stability in China will be maintained in the end.

NEW CONFUCIANISM AND CHINESE MEDIA POLICY

There is no uniform state ideology on what constitutes the negative effects of the Internet. Nonetheless, the official position on building a harmonious and healthy Internet environment often singles out some specific dangers in the Chinese mass media. These dangers usually concern pornography, online gaming, religious superstition, negative discussions of the CPC and its leaders, encouraging succession from the state and sometimes issues of foreign policy.[16] A case in point is when one *Qianlong* editor went too far in the eyes of the local propaganda officials in Beijing concerning the sensitive issue of North Korea:

> He published a few things that can be debated in academic circles only. And afterwards he received a lot of criticism of a very severe and serious kind.[17]

The examples of how the leaders of privately owned web portals regularly demonstrate a willingness to bow to Party propaganda leaders in official statements are plenty. As for these web portals, they have no choice but to acquiesce to the ever changing maze of old and new laws, notices and regulations from various government bodies. There is really no alternative, for in order to operate an Internet business in China you must naturally obey the law. The key question for the future is if the managers of web portals are happy about the current situation. They are under pressure from shareholders and the Government while having to serve the rather unfaithful hordes of Internet surfers who easily shift to other web pages if the atmosphere in one web portal gets tougher on free speech. As Internet laws and the implementation of them are to a large extent

---

[16] In July 2001, former President Jiang Zemin called for reinforced legislation against what he called superstition, pornography, violence and pernicious information on the Internet. See Duncan Hewitt, "China Acts on Net 'Addicts', Chinese Police Want to Monitor Internet Activity," *BBC News Online*, July 20, 2001, http://news.bbc.co.uk/1/low/world/asia-pacific/1448423.stm, accessed March 28, 2007.

[17] Interview conducted with the managing editor of *Qianlong wang* in Beijing, October 2003.

delegated to companies themselves, this means they must devote energies and resources to spying on their business clients lower in the value chain (say, an Internet service provider policing the ways Internet café owners go about policing their customers) and on the public using their web portal services, chat rooms, bulletin board systems and instant messaging systems. On the surface and in official statements, the delegation of Internet law enforcement is loosely sketched out in the "joint statements between the industry and the Government to promote a healthy Internet." In an interview with the young managing director of web portal Sina's Shanghai branch, the manager argued for the casual nature in the relationship between his commercial entity and the publicity department, and his positive view on the joint statements.[18] In a sense, this manager is also a good example for the above-mentioned process of learning that is occurring between online media professionals and propaganda officials, i.e., from the other end of the spectrum. Notions of Confucian responsibility for society's cohesiveness and continued stability are conferred to a changing censorship hierarchy with the officials at the top, individual users at the bottom and media managers in between.

CONCLUDING REMARKS: A CONSTRAINING CONFUCIAN POLITICAL CULTURE

It is possible to sketch out the rise of public opinion as a result of online news, online political commentary and strategic negotiation in the online media sector in contemporary China.[19] But on the analytical level this knowledge must be balanced against the continued relevance of the authoritarian political culture, drawing on classic Confucian ideas of stability and social harmony when judged necessary. Herein, arguments about how many globalisation theorists

---

[18] Interview conducted in Shanghai, March 2005.

[19] Johan Lagerkvist, "The Rise of Online Public Opinion in China," *China: An International Journal* 3, no. 1 (March 2005); Johan Lagerkvist, "In the Crossfire of Demands: Chinese News Portals Between Propaganda and the Public," in *Chinese Cyberspaces*, (eds.), Jens Damm and Simona Thomas (Routledge, 2006).

ignore cultural communities are important. Some in the debate argue that the Western focus on economic interests has edged aspects of culture into the shade, dismissing them as unimportant in modern high-tech societies. Nation–states still continue to be the most important shaper of media systems. Apart from framing the activities of media organisations by laws and regulations, they have many informal ways of influencing the media. It is obvious that informal pressure is also felt by non-Chinese online media companies like Yahoo, Google and Microsoft, who fear being ostracised from the Chinese media market. Therefore, it is reasonable to argue that the challenges to China's state-controlled media system and the changes it is undergoing have more of a domestic than a global dynamic in the age of globalisation. Google announced its launch of a Chinese language search engine aimed at mainland Chinese users in January 2006. Google.cn filters out certain keywords deemed inappropriate by the Chinese authorities, something the Google.com engine cannot do. In response, Google has stated that having a search engine that openly acknowledges it censors searches is better than having only Chinese search engines on the scene. Nobody knows the long-term prospects of Google being able to change China, but it is obvious that China's leaders have already changed Google. The story of how Google is domesticised in China is indicative of how domestic media policy works today in the face of global challenges.

Much like in Singapore, policy-makers, legislators and CPC ideologues are turning to more nuanced forms of censorship. The similarities between censorship strategies in diverse Chinese societies and diaspora communities are not necessarily due to Confucian roots. On the other hand, one cannot overlook the fact that when Chinese leaders like Singapore's former prime minister Lee Kuan Yew and China's former president Jiang Zemin drew upon aspects of Confucianism in speeches, they contributed to the political project of re-constructing a symbolic universe of "statecraft Confucianism" for the modern Chinese world. Media organisations in China are still under heavy pressure from the Party-state to publish healthy content, while at the same time gradually learning from the market logic now at work in

China. With respect to this learning process, it seems that although the online news industry is in the inferior position, media company managers have much more leverage and bargaining power today in China than before the media market reforms. Although the Party-state and online media managers agree on the need to construct a healthy and harmonious Internet world within "the great firewall of China", the dialogue is not without conflicts of interest. Therefore, it is likely that the state's all-encompassing monopoly on what may constitute "the truth" and the influence of the CPC on public opinion are diminishing with the arrival of new Internet services. Nevertheless, in this era of an economically globalising China, this knowledge needs to be tempered by the fact that the power of the propaganda units in terms of controlling the online news flow continues to be felt by newsmakers — offline as well as online. Change is coming to the Chinese media scene, but it is due more to domestic change than to globalisation pressures. The authoritarian culture — sometimes draped in the traditional language of statecraft Confucianism, albeit for the late modern age — must continue to be factored into the equation.

List of Editors and Contributors

Cong CAO is a Senior Research Associate with the Neil D. Levin Graduate Institute of International Relations and Commerce at the State University of New York where he also coordinates Levin's Global Talent Index Project. He received his PhD in sociology from Columbia University and has worked at the University of Oregon and the East Asian Institute at the National University of Singapore. He is interested in the social studies of science and technology with a focus on China. He is the author of *China's Scientific Elite* (London and New York: RoutledgeCurzon, 2004), a study of Chinese scientists holding elite membership in the Chinese Academy of Sciences, and *Talent and China's Technological Edge* with Denis Fred Simon (Cambridge and New York: Cambridge University Press, forthcoming).

Michael HENG Siam-Heng is a Senior Research Fellow at the East Asian Institute, National University of Singapore. He has held academic appointments in Australia, China, Malaysia, The Netherlands and Singapore. He holds a BSc (Hons) in physics, Diploma in education, MSc in computer studies and PhD in information systems (Vrije Universiteit, Amsterdam). He was a winner of the Emerald Literati

Network Award for Excellence in 2006 for his paper on supply chain management. He is the Asia-Pacific Editor of the *International Journal of Electronic Customer Relationship Management,* an Associate Editor of the *Journal of Electronic Commerce Research* and an editor of the *International Journal of Value Chain Management.* He co-edited *Supply Chain Management: Issues in the New Era of Collaboration and Competition* (Hershey, PA: Idea Group Publishers, 2007). His research interests cover globalisation, electronic business, information systems strategy and organisational change.

Albert Guangzhou HU is Associate Professor of Economics at the National University of Singapore. He received his BA in international finance from Nankai University and PhD in international economics from Brandeis University. His research interests include the economics of technological change, international economics, industrial organisation, and in particular, the Chinese economy. His research has appeared in such journals as *China Economic Review, Economic Development and Cultural Change, International Journal of Industrial Organisation, Journal of Comparative Economics, Research Policy* and *Review of Economics and Statistics.* He has also been a short-term consultant for the World Bank.

Johan LAGERKVIST is a Senior Research Fellow with The Swedish Institute of International Affairs (SIIA). He received his PhD in Chinese from Lund University. His dissertation, *China and the Internet: Unlocking and Containing the Public Sphere,* was published by Lund University Press in 2006. He has published articles and book chapters in several international scientific journals and research anthologies, as well as served as guest editor for two theme issues of *Contemporary Chinese Thought.* He is a board member of the Nordic Association for China Studies. He is currently working on a research project financed by the Swedish Research Council on issues of law implementation in China. In another project supported by SIIA, he is researching the implications of Chinese nationalism on the peaceful development policy of China.

Ding LU is Professor of Economics at Sophia University, Tokyo. A graduate from China's Fudan University, he obtained his PhD from Northwestern University. Before joining Sophia University, he was at the National University of Singapore and University of Nebraska at Omaha. His research interests include international trade and investment, and regional economic development. He has published several books and dozens of papers in peer-reviewed journals and book chapters. Most of his publications pertain to development issues in Pacific Asia, particularly the Chinese economy. His books include *Entrepreneurship in Suppressed Markets: China's Private Sector Experience* (New York: Garland, 1994), *State Intervention and Business in China: The Role of Preferential Policies* (UK: Edward Elgar, 1997), and *China's Telecommunications Market: Entering a New Competitive Age* (UK: Edward Elgar, 2003).

Yue MA is Professor of Economics at Lingnan University, Hong Kong. He obtained his BSc in Mathematics from Xiamen University and PhD in Economics and Econometrics from Manchester University. He specialises in the economics of exchange rates and banking, with particular reference to the Mainland Chinese and Hong Kong economies, His publications have appeared in *Economic Journal, China Economic Review, European Economic Review, Singapore Economic Review* and *Journal of International Money and Finance.* He is a member of the editorial board of the *Journal of Chinese Economic and Business Studies*, UK, and *International Trade* (Guoji maoyi wenti), Beijing.

Ping LIN is Professor of Economics at Lingnan University, Hong Kong. He received his PhD from the University of Minnesota. His research interests include industrial economics, foreign direct investment and technology transfer, competition policy, and the theory of banking. His publications have appeared in the *Journal of Economic Theory, European Economic Review, Journal of International Economics, Journal of Industrial Economics, Oxford Economic Review and International Journal of Industrial Organization.* He has been a consultant to the Asian Development Bank, the Government of Hong Kong Special Administrative Region, the Organization for Economic Co-operation and Development and the State Council of the People's Republic of China.

Jon SIGURDSON is Professor in Research Policy, and Director of the East Asia Science and Technology and Culture Programme at the Stockholm School of Economics. He has degrees in engineering and economics (University of Technology and Gothenburg University, respectively). He has had visiting professorships in Japan and Australia and been a Senior Visiting Research Fellow at the East Asian Institute of the National University of Singapore. His most recent publication is *Technological Superpower China* (Northampton, MA: Edward Elgar, 2006). As a researcher in science policy he has developed special expertise in technology management at national and company level with a focus on areas such as: (1) global structures for research and development and their interaction with national systems for innovation; and (2) structural changes in the electronics and information technologies industries. His present research focus is regional changes and dynamic city developments in China.

Richard P. SUTTMEIER is Professor Emeritus of Political Science at the University of Oregon. He did his BA at Darmouth College in philosophy and his PhD in political science at Indiana University. His research interests include Chinese science and technology policies, the management of environmental and technological risks in China, high technology development in China, comparison of Chinese and Indian science and technology policies and international perspectives on the ethics of new technologies. He has served as a consultant to the International Development Research Center of Canada, Senior Analyst at the Congressional Office of Technology Assessment, consultant to the World Bank and the United Nations Development Programme, and as the Director of the Beijing Office of the Committee for Scholarly Communication with China.

Elspeth THOMSON is a Fellow at the Energy studies Institute, National University of Singapore. She received her PhD in Chinese Economic History from the School of Oriental and African Studies, University of London. Her main research interests are Asian energy and transport. She authored *The Chinese Coal Industry: An Economic History* (London and New York: RoutledgeCurzon, 2003). An edited volume, *Energy Conservation in East Asia: Towards Greater Energy Security*, will appear in 2008. She has published articles concerning various aspects of Asia's energy sector in *The China Quarterly, Pacific and Asian Journal of Energy, Journal of Applied Statistics, China Review, East Asia: An International Quarterly, and Perspectives*. She co-edits the East Asian Institute's journal, *China: An International Journal*. Through the 1990s she taught at Simon Fraser University in Vancouver and Lingnan University in Hong Kong.

YAO Xiangkui is currently a PhD candidate in Computer and Information Science at the University of Oregon. He received his BA in journalism from the Institute of International Relations in Beijing and his MA in Political Science from the University of Oregon. His research area is requirements engineering and wearable computing. He is a student member of the Association for Computing Machinery.

Jing A. ZHANG is Assistant Professor of Strategic Management at the Faculty of Commerce, Chuhai College of Higher Education, Hong Kong. She received her PhD from the University of Wollongong. Zhang's research interests focus on innovation and corporate strategies, firm resources/capabilities and innovation, and strategic management. She has published articles in international journals such as *International Journal of Business Studies* and *R&D Management*. She is also a keen supporter of the profession through the membership of several professional associations including Asia Academy of Management, and China Association of Science and Technology Indicators.

Index